Aycock Brown on the OUTER BANKS

John Railey &
Nancy Beach Gray

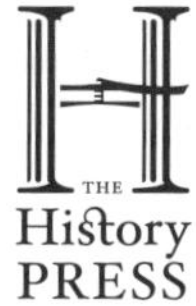

Published by The History Press
An imprint of Arcadia Publishing
Charleston, SC
www.historypress.com

Title page: Map of the Outer Banks. *Coastal Impressions.*

First published 2026

Manufactured in the United States

ISBN 9781467171397
Hardcover ISBN 9781540299406

Library of Congress Control Number: 2026935636

Notice: The information in this book is true and complete to the best of our knowledge. It is offered without guarantee on the part of the authors or The History Press. The authors and The History Press disclaim all liability in connection with the use of this book.

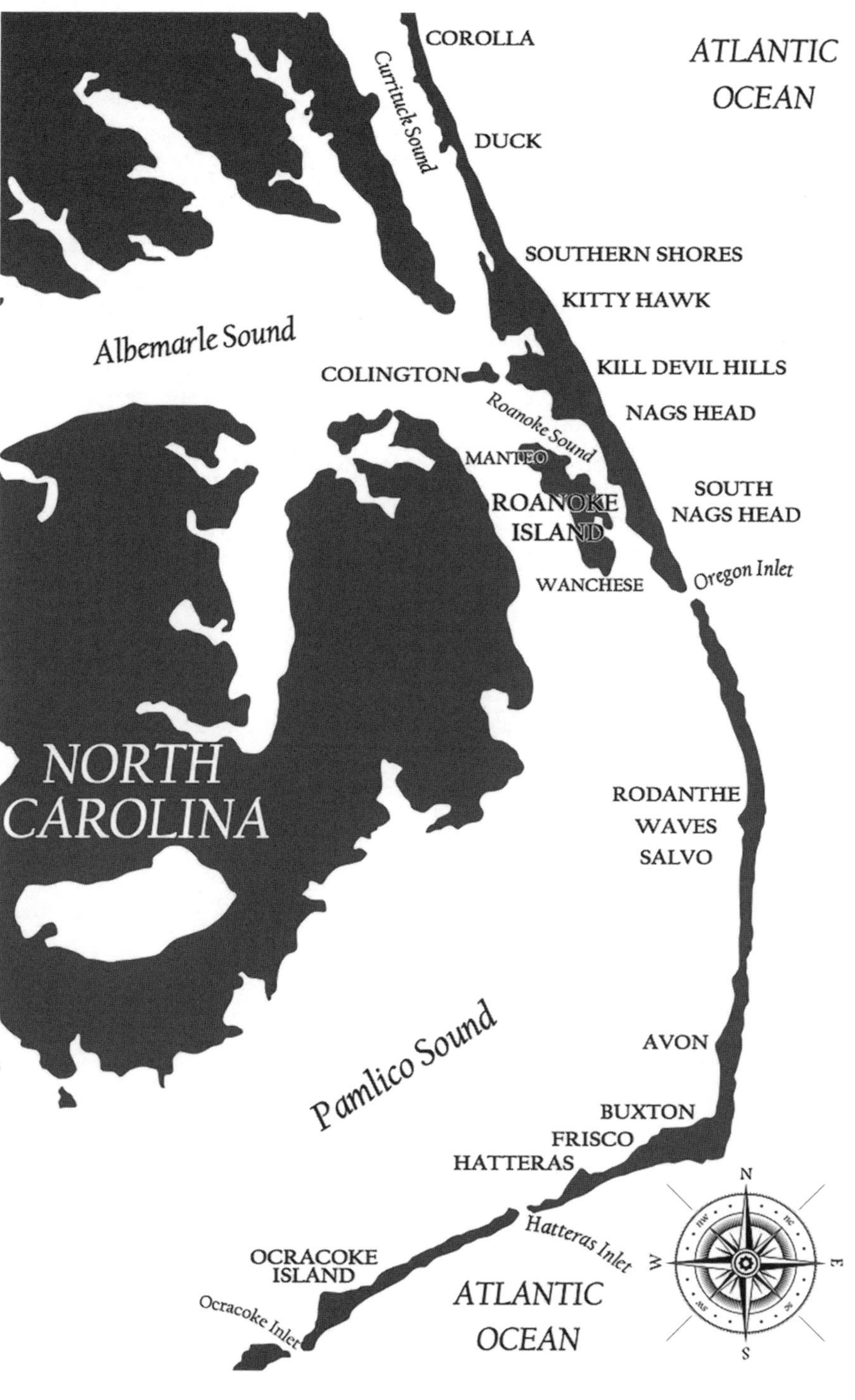
COROLLA
ATLANTIC
OCEAN
Currituck Sound
DUCK
SOUTHERN SHORES
KITTY HAWK
Albemarle Sound
COLINGTON
KILL DEVIL HILLS
Roanoke Sound
NAGS HEAD
MANTEO
ROANOKE
ISLAND
SOUTH
NAGS HEAD
WANCHESE
Oregon Inlet
NORTH
CAROLINA
RODANTHE
WAVES
SALVO
Pamlico Sound
AVON
BUXTON
FRISCO
HATTERAS
Hatteras Inlet
OCRACOKE
ISLAND
Ocracoke Inlet
ATLANTIC
OCEAN
N
E
S
W

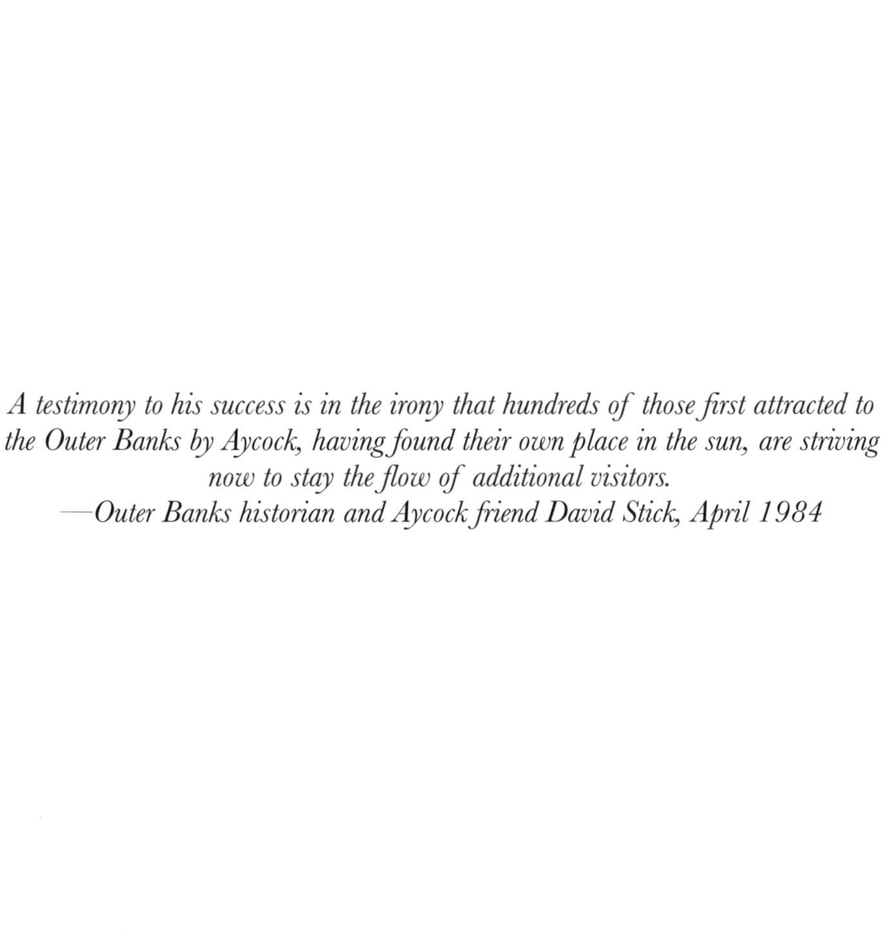

A testimony to his success is in the irony that hundreds of those first attracted to the Outer Banks by Aycock, having found their own place in the sun, are striving now to stay the flow of additional visitors.

—Outer Banks historian and Aycock friend David Stick, April 1984

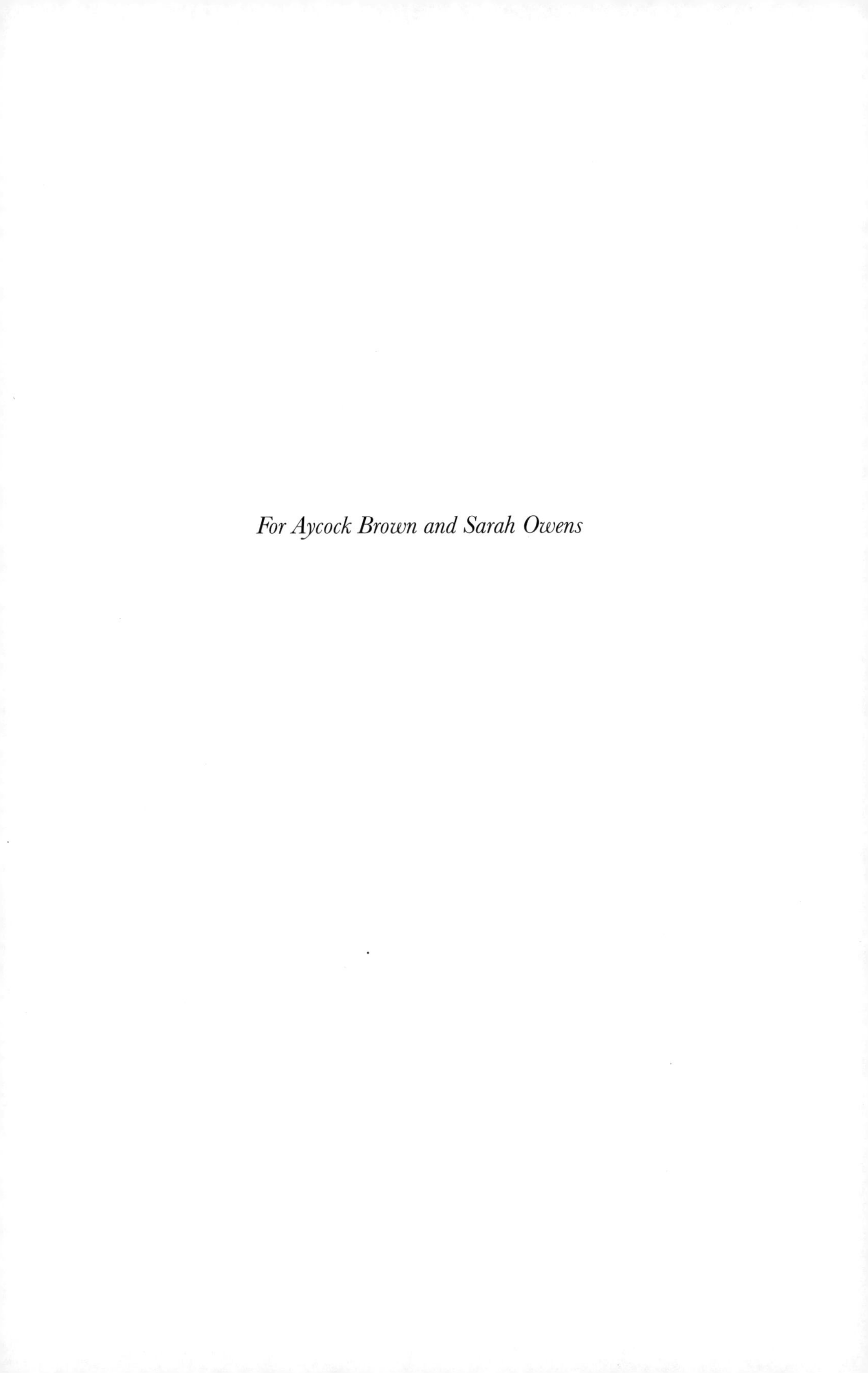

For Aycock Brown and Sarah Owens

CONTENTS

AUTHORS' NOTE

Imagine the Outer Banks with vast, beguiling barren stretches of beach running for miles. Cottages on stilts here and there along a two-lane road by the sea. No TVs, few phones save for pay phones in their glass boxes in random parking lots. A handful of local grocery stores, not supermarkets. Mom-and-pop motels and just a few majestic hotels, beach queens. And a few thousand visitors, mostly from the nearby coastal plain of North Carolina and the Tidewater region of Virginia, in a short summer season from Memorial Day to Labor Day, served by a few thousand locals along with summer help of high school and college kids. How did the Banks get from there to today, a coveted vacationland crowded with McMansions, upscale hotels and restaurants (one that even includes a spa), and endless entertainment for the more than five million visitors who spend more than $2 billion annually, coming in on the area's approximately thirty-seven thousand permanent residents? From cottages renting for less than $100 a week to ones commanding up to $65,000 weekly. One man, all but forgotten, small of stature but gigantic of heart, almost singlehandedly brought us here.

If you really want to know the Outer Banks, you might want to understand photographer Aycock Brown. He was the visionary, from his courageous work during World War II torpedo attacks off our coast until his death in 1984, who literally put the Banks on the map, as many have said. This book will, for the first time, explore exactly how and why Aycock did that. A native of the North Carolina mountains, he was, like so many Outer Bankers before him and so many to come, a transplant who found his true self on the Banks. After early misstarts, he essentially taught himself his photographic and public-relations skills, eventually playing a leading role—with his associate Sarah Alford Owens—in making the Outer Banks one of the most sought-after resort locations in the nation. Today, tourists daily take thousands of shots with their cell phones, many of them of decent quality, and post them on the Internet, going out to the world. But the relatively few tourists in Aycock's heyday shot photos with Kodaks and Polaroids, often blurred, their distribution usually limited to friends and family. Aycock stood alone in shooting high-quality images. From a darkroom in his Manteo home, his photos went far and wide, published in newspapers and magazines across the country.

Aycock met his bride-to-be, Esther Styron, on an Ocracoke Island dock in the late 1920s. He married his hopes to hers and, ultimately, to those of their beloved Banks. Their dream lives on. Sure, there's overdevelopment. But the water and beaches—the natural majesty that Aycock shot so well that their feeling crawls into your soul—live. "He was a man before his

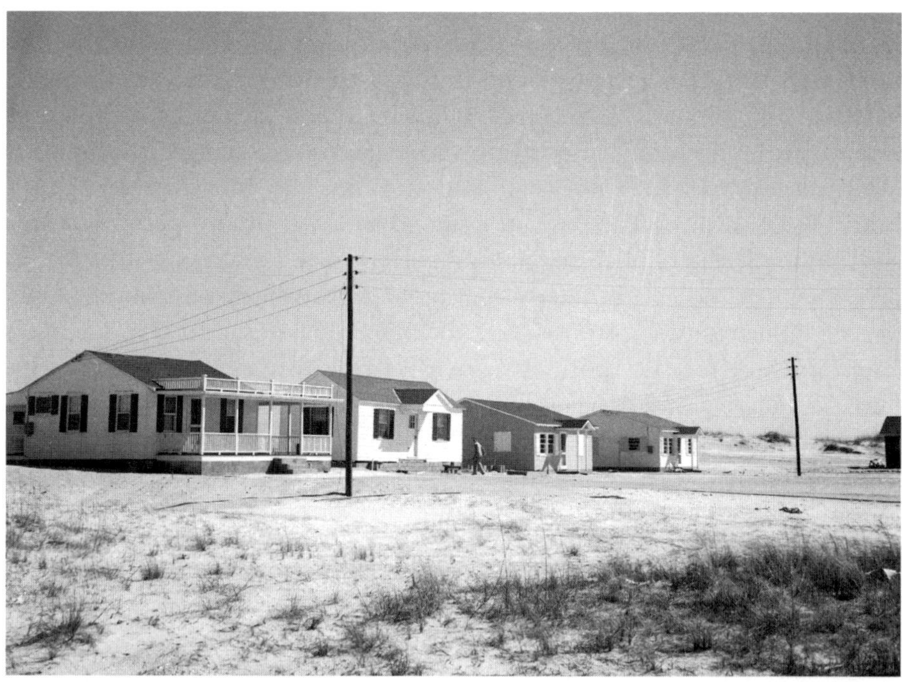

Visitors to the Outer Banks started to prefer oceanfront over Soundside accommodations in the 1930s. Quaint rental bungalows like the Seafoam Cottages in Nags Head began to dot the beach. *ABC, OBHC, SANC.*

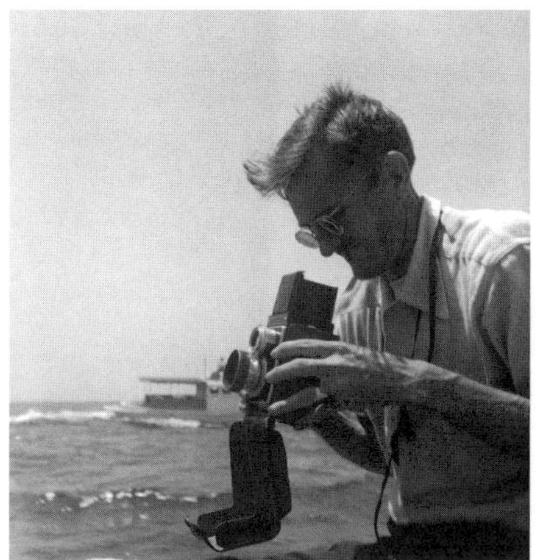

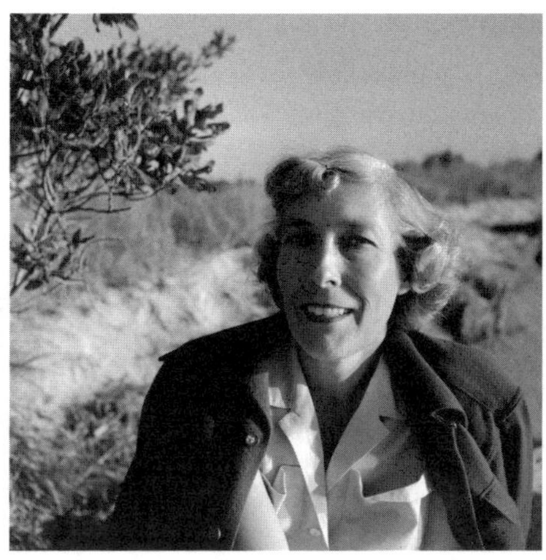

Left: By the 1940s, Aycock was already acquiring some of the components of his signature look: squinted eyes behind glasses, a pencil-thin mustache, and a camera strap around his neck. *ABC, OBHC, SANC.*

Right: Ocracoke native Esther Styron Brown, pictured here in the early 1950s at about age forty, was Aycock's devoted wife and a stay-at-home mother to their three children: Brantley, Billy, and Gale. *ABC, OBHC, SANC.*

time and he loved Dare County beyond anything," said family friend Kathy Spencer.

In the parallel time of the Banks, where some locals still speak in a wonderful brogue of Old England, Aycock is right there with us, a pied piper shooting and laughing. You're here because of him.

Many of Aycock's photos appear courtesy of the National Park Service, Cape Hatteras National Seashore (NPS, CHNS); the Aycock Brown Collection (ABC); and the Outer Banks History Center, State Archives of North Carolina (OBHC, SANC).

PROLOGUE

Imagine a sun-kissed early summer morning in the late 1970s. Aycock Brown, in his seventies but still a Peter Pan, leaves his modest frame house on Sir Walter Raleigh Street in Manteo and climbs into his Chevrolet landboat of a car with the license plate bearing his first name in all caps. He cruises through downtown Manteo, stopping at the Duchess of Dare restaurant for a quick cup of coffee. Then on to *The Coastland Times* newspaper office to shoot the breeze with owner/publisher Francis Meekins and courthouse reporter Gaylord Godwin. Finally, he swings by the courthouse to gossip with longtime Sheriff Frank Cahoon, he of the swept-back gray hair and lantern jaw. Aycock, aristocratically soft-spoken and garrulous and tending to end sentences with "Don't you see?" is gathering information.

The three—Aycock, Meekins, and Cahoon—go way back, symbiotic relationships, with Aycock's photos having greatly helped the paper's sales and the sheriff's repeated reelections and bringing Aycock nationwide cachet among his fellow journalists, through work such as that shot he'd done of the sheriff standing stern by a confiscated moonshine still many moons ago. This spot of sand named Roanoke, surrounded by the Sounds of Roanoke, Pamlico, Croatan, and Albemarle, with the ocean just across the Roanoke, is their island kingdom.

Leaving the courthouse, Aycock might have said hello to one of his former models, Dotty Fry, still beautiful. Getting in his car, Aycock may have also seen and greeted Dotty's mom, Cora Mae Basnight, walking down the street, whom he'd long shot as Agona, the Native American maiden in *The Lost Colony* outdoor drama.

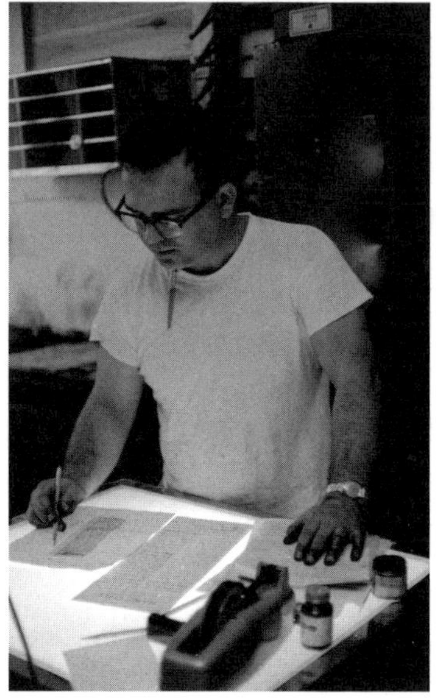

Newspaperman Francis Meekins works over a light box in *The Coastland Times* office in 1950. He inherited the paper from his father, newspaper founder Victor Meekins, and took it to a wider audience with the help of Aycock's photographs. *ABC, OBHC, SANC.*

Mist is rising off Shallowbag Bay, which elbows around Manteo, the county seat. At the docks, pelicans roost on pilings and seagulls sing. A soft breeze rolls through, laden with the wonderfully salty smell of the Roanoke, softly rattling the brass on the riggings of the docked boats. Men working around the docks raise their veiny, tattooed arms to wave at Aycock.

He returns their greetings. They are his friends. He has a big home library and loves newspapers such as *The Times* of London and the Paris edition of *The Herald Tribune* delivered to his house daily, but he's comfortable with all his fellow islanders. He knows things about them. He knows who will be led from the jail adjacent to the courthouse to stand trembling before humorless judges and face charges ranging from drunk driving to brawling and, these days, drug smuggling. He doesn't tout his knowledge. Boasting is not his game. But telling stories is in his skinny bones. He's done that about the emerging Outer Banks for more than forty years through his photos and words, chronicling a transformational shift.

Aycock is the only soul on the planet to have nurtured, with his photos and correspondence with a Hollywood producer, the start of Andy Griffith's rise to fame *and* to have photographed the last witness of the Wright brothers' 1903 flight on the Outer Banks *and*, more than a half century later, one of the most glorious beneficiaries of that first flight, astronaut John Glenn. He also photographed and lived through one of the worst storms on his coast—and named it, forever, the Ash Wednesday Storm.

He's old, but long before Jimmy Buffett began selling the dream of eternal beach youth to the country, Aycock was doing just that. He is skittery as a blue heron in his trademark Panama hat and Hawaiian shirt, a cigarette hanging from the perpetual grin beneath his pencil-thin mustache, three big cameras dangling from his neck. He's an islander to his core, never meant for the buttoned-down culture of his native mainland, having happily left it in his rearview mirror decades ago. Aycock on the job, shooting photos, is a man in his element, making the work look easy, almost effortless, even though he's constantly striving to be better, like Sinatra privately swimming endless underwater laps to make it look so easy when he took the stage and held those notes forever.

Aycock drives away from downtown, nodding at the Drafty Tavern squatted in the misty marsh on Manteo's outskirts, quiet now in the early morning but set to rowdily rock again in a few hours as office workers join commercial fishermen, shooting pool, eating pizza, and, most of all, chugging beer, some of the patrons devolving into fights that keep the local cops, lawyers, and judges in business. Customers drive to the bar, some in pickup trucks laden with fishing equipment and dents—"love bumps." Others, rich boys in shiny boats and commercial fishermen in

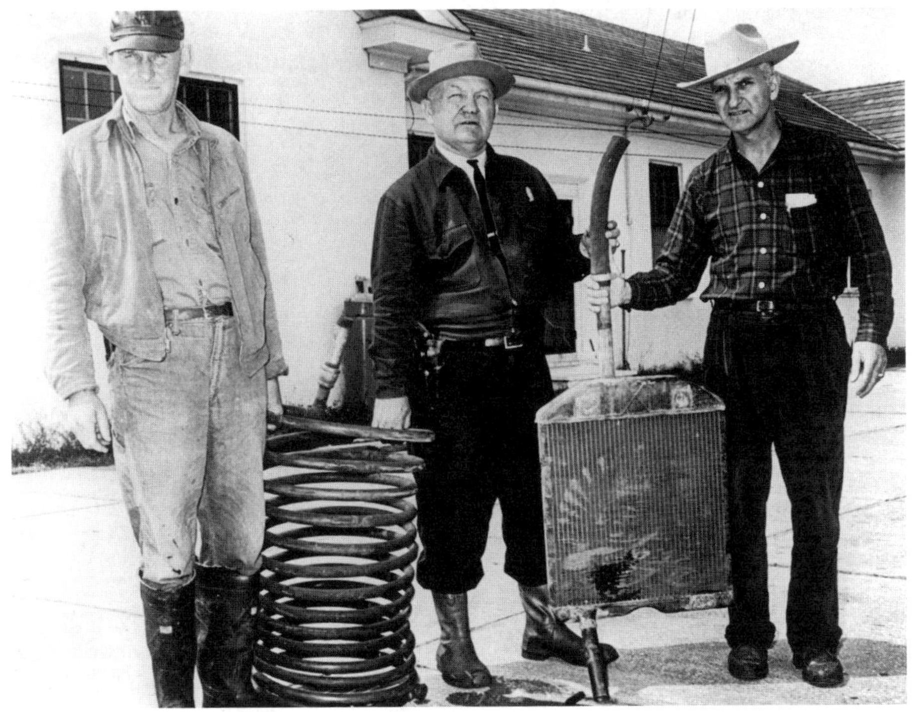

Moonshining in Dare County was declining when Sheriff Frank Cahoon (*right*) was elected in 1946, but a shot of Cahoon with two deputies and a confiscated still from East Lake made for an opportunistic photograph to circulate statewide for Aycock and Cahoon. *ABC, OBHC, SANC.*

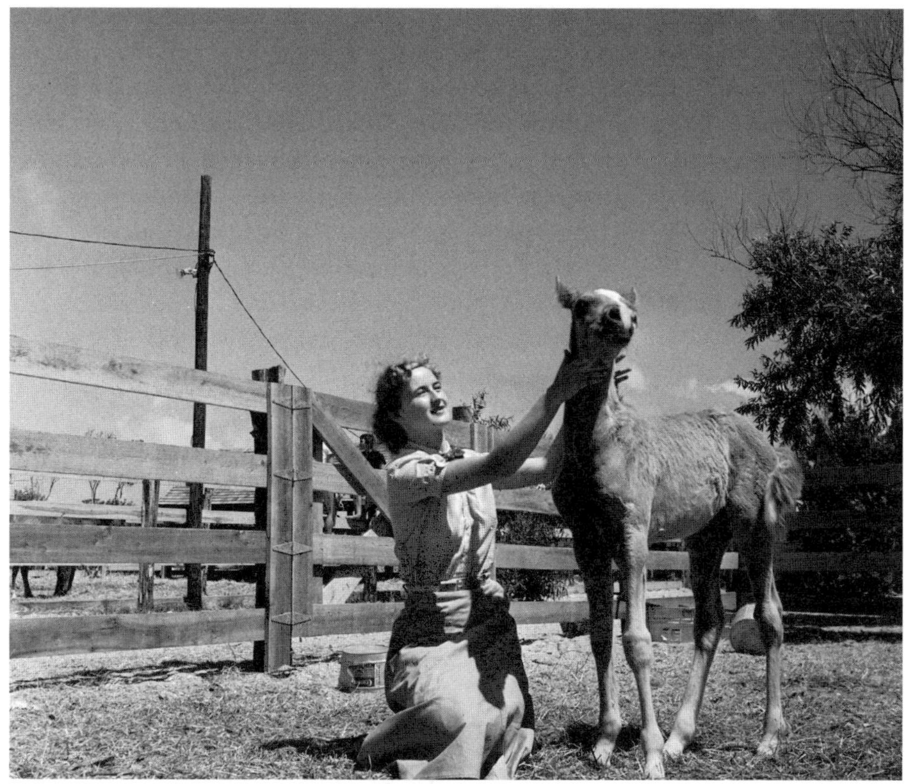

water-scarred workabouts, glide their boats up, docking behind the bar, trading the smell of gas and sea spray for that of cigarette smoke and beer-soaked floors, the jukebox cranking classic country and rock 'n' roll, good old boys and girls talking, shooting pool, and flirting through the smoke, all loving their watery way of life.

On the swing bridge, Aycock drives across the dreamy Roanoke to the Nags Head causeway, loving all the shimmering scenery on either side, including that tiny island with a lone cottage where his buddy Andy Griffith would party down with friends.

Right off the causeway, at Whalebone Junction in Nags Head, Aycock might have smiled at the gas station run by his friend Wally Gray. The junction got its name after Alexander Midgett, in a Model T truck, hauled whale bones off the beach and left them bleaching white in the sun in front of his nearby gas station. The junction is also the site of a Catholic church that was once the Shriner's Club where Andy got his start in the summer of 1952 with his comedic riff on Shakespeare's *Hamlet.* Andy is a big star

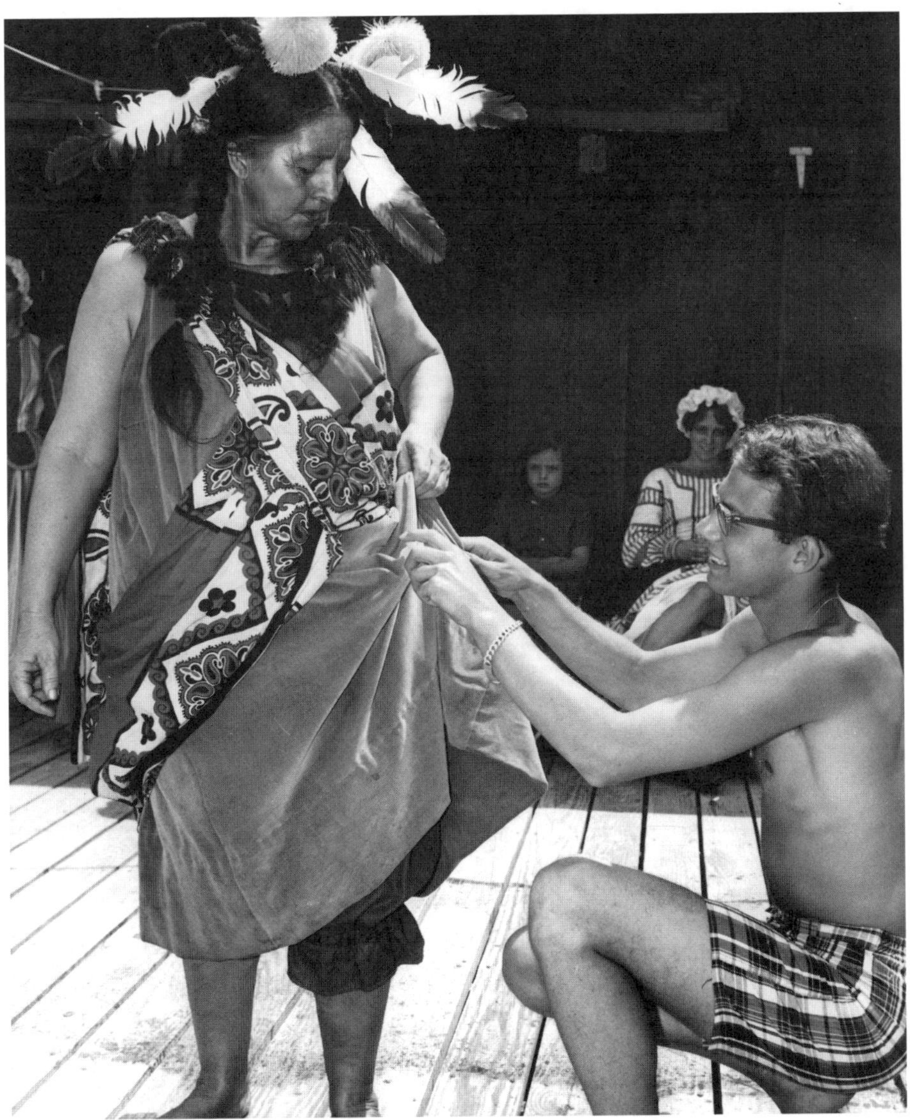

Opposite: Manteo girl Dotty Alford Fry embodied beauty and playfulness, and Aycock used her frequently as a model in promoting the Outer Banks. She is pictured here in 1950 stroking a young Ocracoke pony in the pen at Berkeley Manor Ranchero, established by eccentric Sam Jones. *ABC, OBHC, SANC.*

Above: Dotty's mother, Cora Mae Basnight, played the lovestruck Indian maiden Agona in the Roanoke Island drama *The Lost Colony* from 1957 to 1982, one of the longest runs in U.S. stage history. Her good-natured personality made her a favorite with the cast. *ABC, OBHC, SANC.*

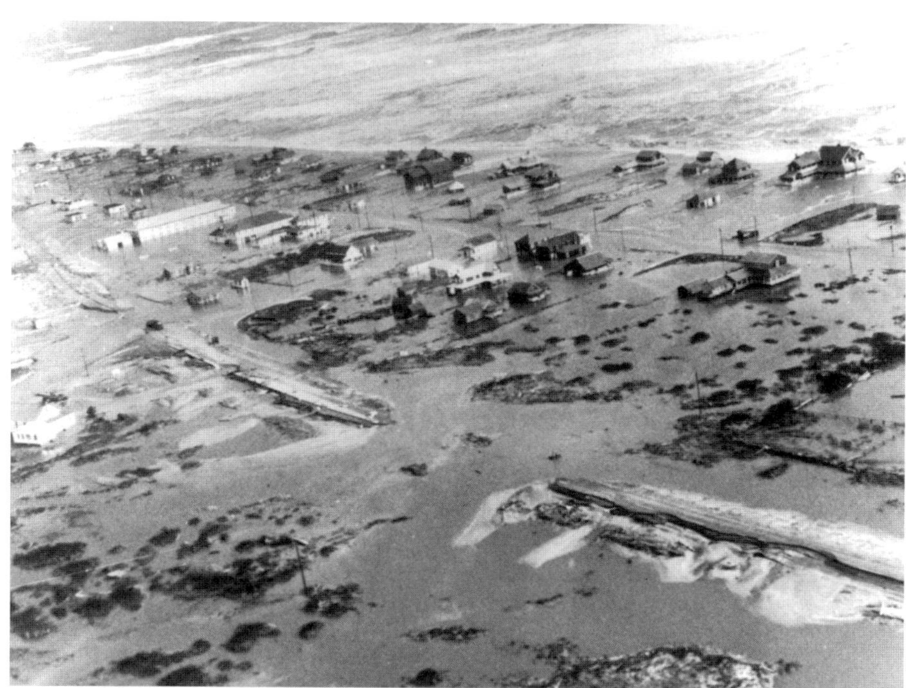

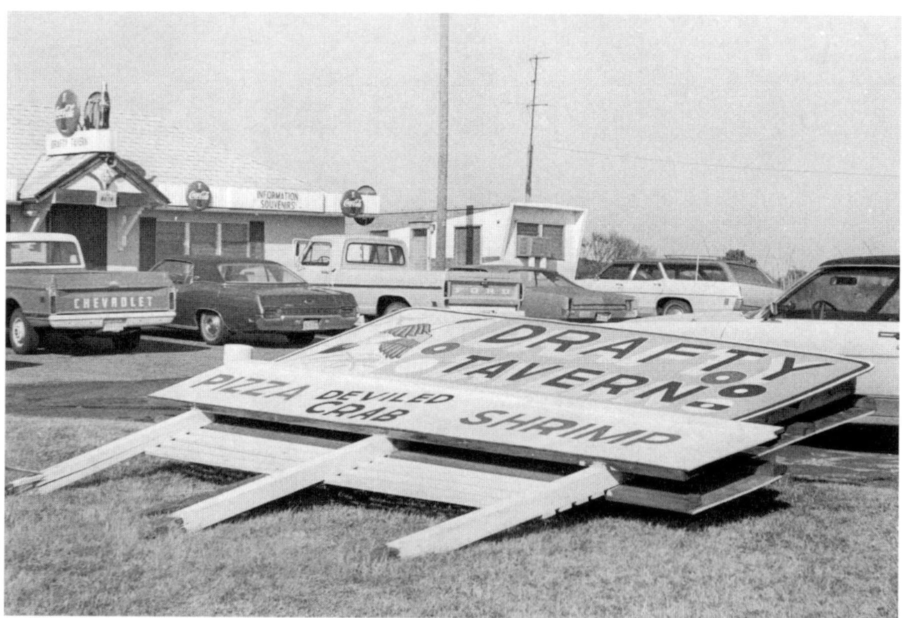
INFORMATION
SOUVENIRS
CHEVROLET
DRAFTY
TAVERN
PIZZA
DEVILED
CRAB
SHRIMP

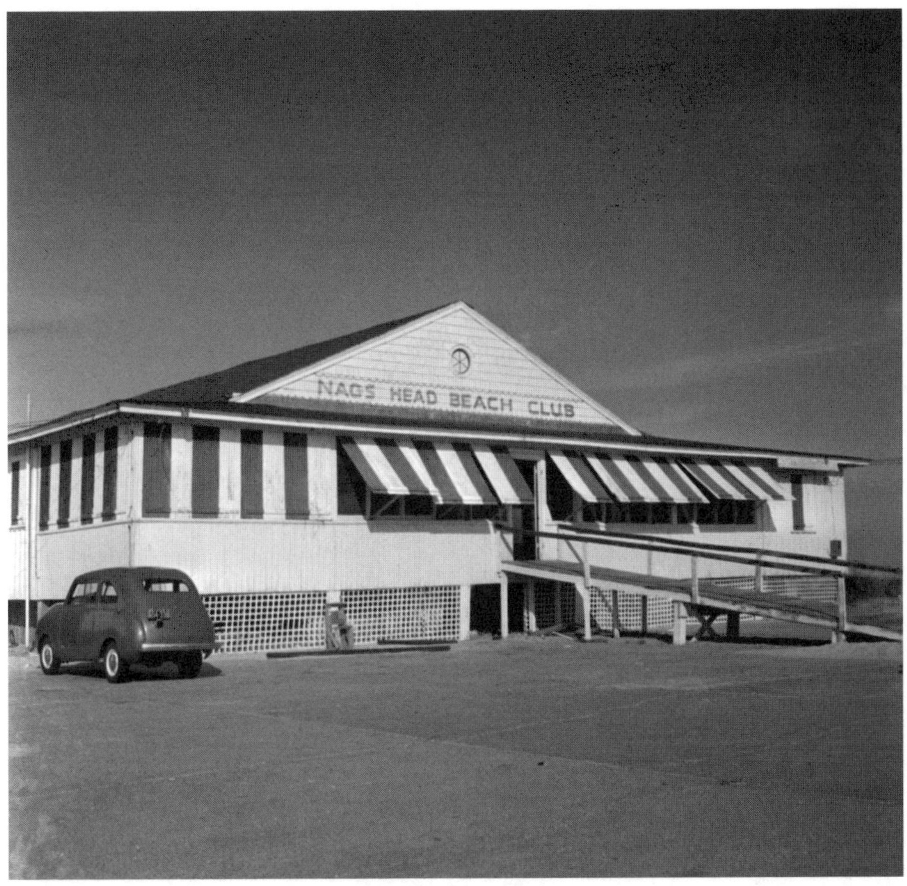

Opposite, top: Airborne Aycock captured this area in Nags Head where ocean and Sound waters met and wreaked havoc. The 1962 extratropical cyclone lasted two and a half days, March 5–7, and Aycock gave it a memorable name, the Ash Wednesday Storm, that stuck nationwide. *ABC, OBHC, SANC.*

Opposite, bottom: An unnamed storm blew down the Drafty Tavern sign, but business went on as usual in the local hangout. Fistfights, almost considered to be a form of entertainment, broke out weekly between patrons. *ABC, OBHC, SANC.*

Above: Andy Griffith performed some of his early comedy acts at the Nags Head Beach Club, including a *Hamlet*-inspired routine that he collaborated on with fellow *Lost Colony* actor Bob Armstrong. *ABC, OBHC, SANC.*

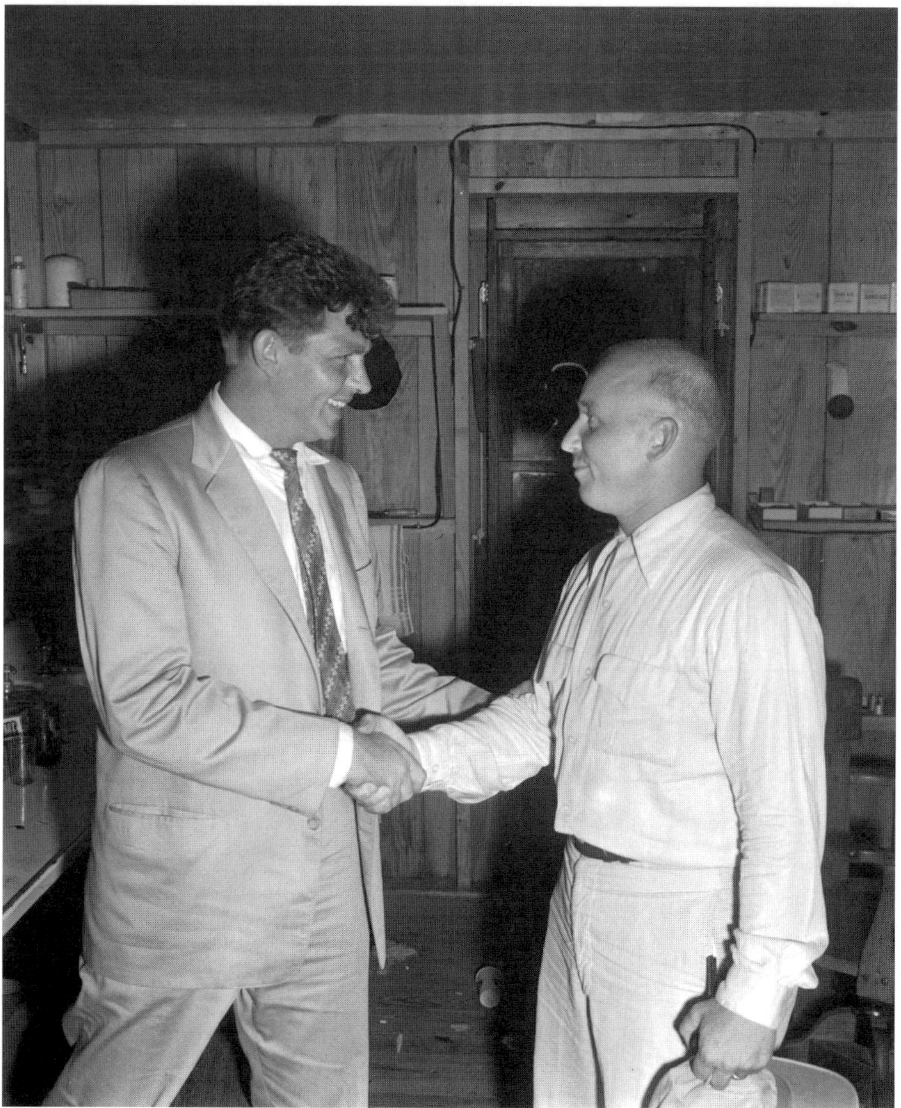

Above: In 1955, Andy Griffith reconnected with Ray Jones of Manteo in *The Lost Colony* green room. His rise to fame in Hollywood was just a few years after his comedic breakthrough in Nags Head, but he never forgot his start at *The Lost Colony*. *ABC, OBHC, SANC.*

Opposite: Wooden shipwrecks were prevalent along Dare County beaches, affirming the region's nickname "The Graveyard of the Atlantic." Some locals have always been "wreckers," taking and repurposing what washes up on the beach. *ABC, OBHC, SANC.*

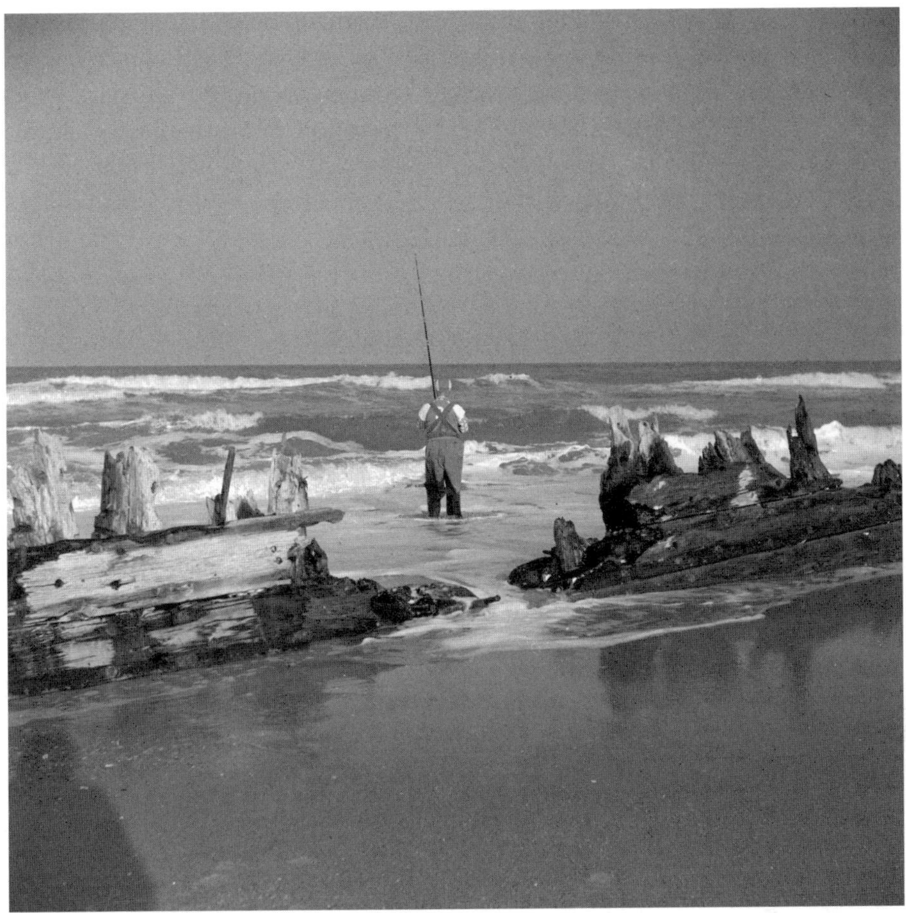

in Hollywood now. When his namesake show first came out in 1960, few locals could easily watch it because TV reception, even with aluminum foil wrapped around the rabbit ear antennas, was sketchy.

Now, with cable TV just kicking in on the Banks, the Norfolk news channels are scant competition for Aycock and *The Coastland Times*. They still routinely scoop the out-of-town papers, *The Virginian-Pilot* out of Norfolk and *The News & Observer* of Raleigh, the latter owned by cousins of the same Daniels family that wields power in Wanchese, the tough fishing community on the south end of Roanoke Island. Aycock mainly feeds his photos and stories to *The Times*, but also sends his work to newspapers nationwide, giving them first to *The Times*, his gentleman's agreement with Francis Meekins.

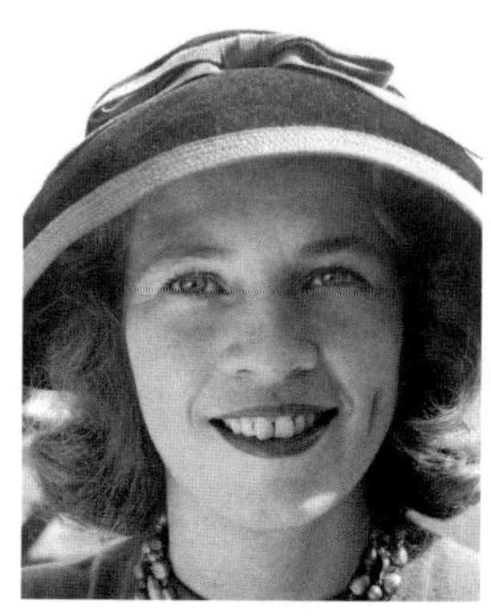

Sarah Alford Owens posed for Aycock long before she worked with him at the Dare County Tourist Bureau. With his small salary, Aycock rarely paid models. *ABC, RV Owens.*

Aycock knows the beach's legendary figures and has elevated some of them to near mythological status. He knows his literature, though he never talks much of it. He might have appreciated F. Scott Fitzgerald's novel *The Great Gatsby*, in which the main character reinvents himself, just as Aycock had, just as many of the legends Aycock promoted are doing. Aycock knows the foibles in his legends and their families. Nathaniel Hawthorne once wrote that "Families are always rising and falling in America." That is true for the Outer Banks. Key families are up and down, just as the sea's shifting currents are constantly covering and uncovering the timbers of shipwrecks, the ebb and flow of life on the Banks.

Aycock drives on. There is Jennette's Pier, the Venice Beach of the Outer Banks, a gathering spot that goes far beyond the fishermen. Surfers are assembling, ready to paddle out and catch waves among the dipping dolphins as bikini-clad girls watch from the shore. Jap Richardson's lifeguards are climbing into their stands.

Just across the street from Jennette's is Sam & Omie's restaurant and bar, the cozy frame shack where Andy and so many others like to eat and drink. Shortly past that is Owens' Restaurant, started shortly after World War II by friends of Aycock. At a young age, his longtime associate Sarah Owens married Bobby Owens and, in a sense, also married the family business. She hostesses there at night in the tourist season after putting in a long day at the bureau. Her children, RV and Lisa, also help out in the restaurant, learning the hard work ethic held by the majority of local youngsters.

Aycock drives on by the ocean, the sea that he has drawn tens of thousands to, but he has an ambivalent relationship with it. In his hilariously quirky style, he once told a reporter about the ocean: "Well, it has always looked filthy to me. Have you ever had a look at some of the things that come out of there?"

Aycock continues north on the Beach Road. He is the king of that road if there ever was one, knowing its residents and business owners better than anybody, having shot tens of thousands of photos up and down it. A few miles north, past the undeveloped Epstein tract, had been the site of the Hayman family's Arlington hotel with its whitewashed beauty and aristocrats hanging out on the wraparound porches, wiped out by a heartbreaking nor'easter in February 1973. Across the Beach Road, the family's Seafare restaurant blossomed, an oasis of a pink stone shimmering in the blonde sand. Aycock loves the boundless resilience of his friends and the fact that they are nurturing a whole new generation of beach business folks.

Aycock might stop if need be and feed coins into one of the pay phones alongside the road to check in with Sarah or relay news tips to the *Times*.

Aycock rides on up the crowded Beach Road, past the "Unpainted Aristocracy," that mile-or-so-long necklace of cottages owned for generations

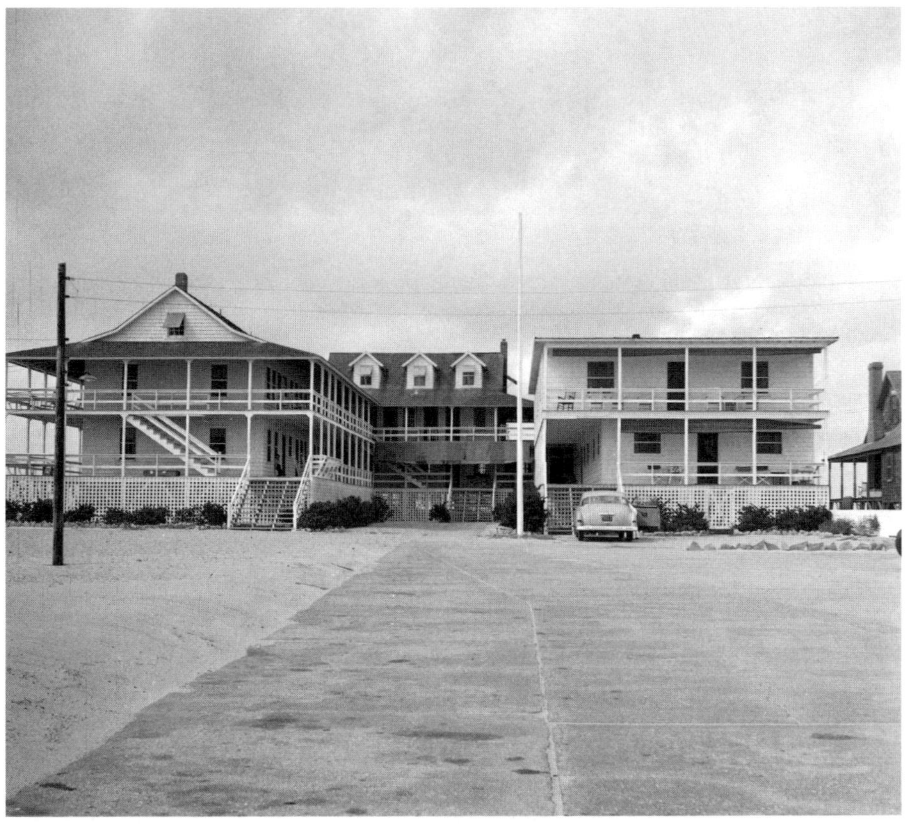

Dewey and Phoebe Hayman bought the Arlington hotel in 1944 and moved it from its Soundside location to the oceanfront. They immediately adopted a high standard of service and hospitality that lasted until 1973, when the hotel collapsed into the stormy sea. *ABC, OBHC, SANC.*

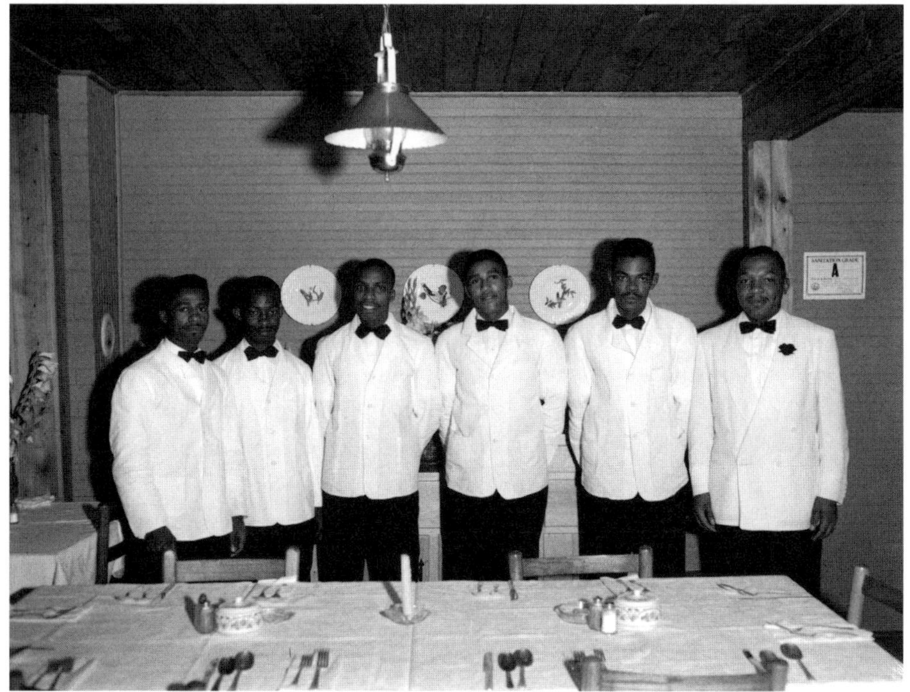

In the 1950s, the Hayman's staff at the Arlington professionally served legendary seafood dishes on china and crystal. A dinner bell announced that dinner was being served in the oceanfront dining room. *ABC, OBHC, SANC.*

by rich boys and girls out of northeastern North Carolina, people whom Aycock worships with at the church in the heart of that area, St. Andrew's Episcopal. He drives by Jockey's Ridge, the big sand dune that had once been as tall as 150 feet or better, although lately the height is receding. But Aycock and the dune, saved from development by fantastic local Carolista Baum, remain legendary, like the fading silent-screen star in the 1950 movie *Sunset Boulevard:* "I *am* big. It's the pictures that got small."

He drives by Harris Grocery, the post office run by the gracious Doll Gray and the seafood store owned and operated by his friends Jimmy and Sandra Austin. He passes the watered-down nightclub that once housed the rowdy Casino where he shot Louis Armstrong blowing his legendary horn, boxers boxing, and real-life fights among Casino owner Ras Westcott, his bouncers, Nags Head Police Chief Donnie Twyne Sr., hippies, and locals; the oceanfront foosball palace by the Nags Head Pier where teens smoked, shot pool, and sneaked beers before graduating to the Atlantis nightclub next door; the grocery store owned and operated by the friendly Bells;

the oceanfront Nags Header hotel, where Steve the Dream pounded the piano; and, across from the hotel, the summer boardinghouse Snug Harbor, nicknamed "Drug Harbor," with hungover surfers stumbling out to "taste the tasty waves." Back in the day, Aycock drank hard and flirted with running illegal booze offshore during Prohibition, just as some young folks were doing now in running pot, pirate style. Aycock never toked. But he might have gotten a kick out of watching the stoners, young Turks challenging the establishment just as he'd once done.

Aycock cruises on by the perfumed Galleon clothing store, owned and operated by his flamboyant buddy George Crocker, along with two

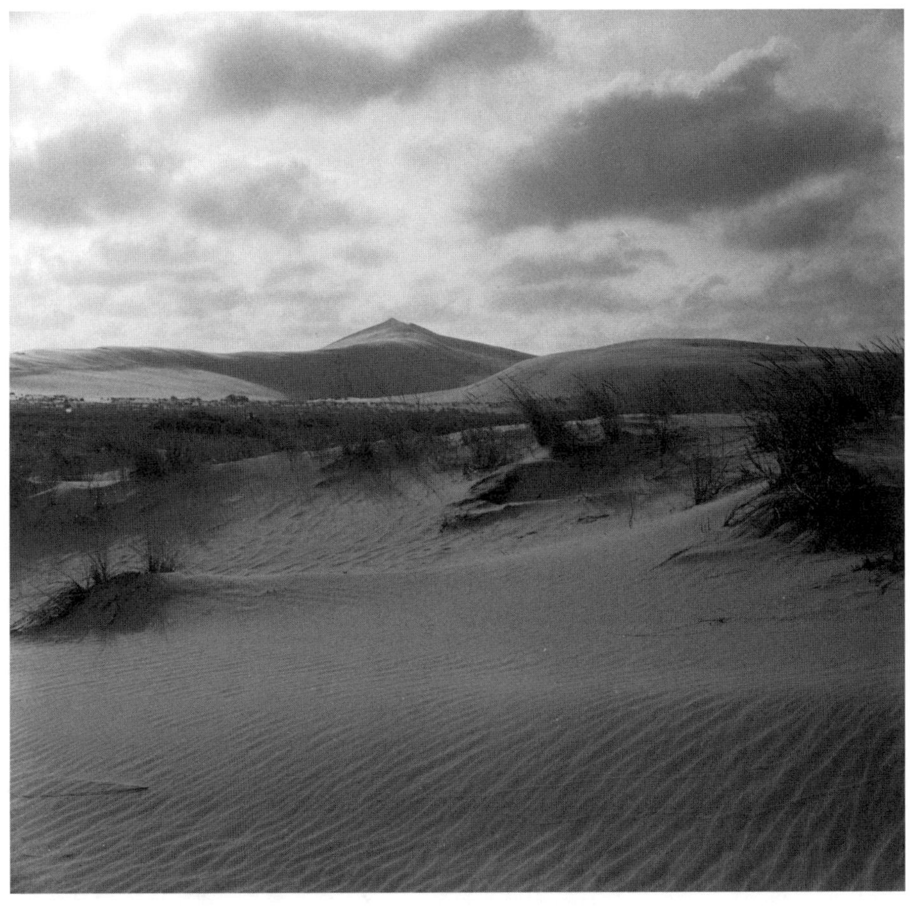

As evidenced by this 1950s photo, today's vacationers are correct when they remember that the sand dunes of Jockey's Ridge used to be higher. An increase in buildings and vegetation prohibit sand from blowing freely and stacking up on the dunes. *ABC, OBHC, SANC.*

hotels and Crocker's namesake restaurant, looking like Rick's place in the film *Casablanca;* Miller's Pharmacy with its fresh-squeezed lemonade; Scarborough's gas station; Gray's Department Store; the Colony theater, where hit movies such as *Grease* are playing; the Carolinian hotel; Nunemaker's grocery store, where his friends Carl and Sally Nunemaker hold court; then on into the town of Kill Devil Hills, past the Ocean House motel his friend Billy Tarkington of Manteo had run. Aycock and Billy, a naval veteran of the South Pacific in World War II, would reminisce about the war. Billy was one of the few people he could talk to about the haunting horror in the eyes of burned survivors of German sub attacks.

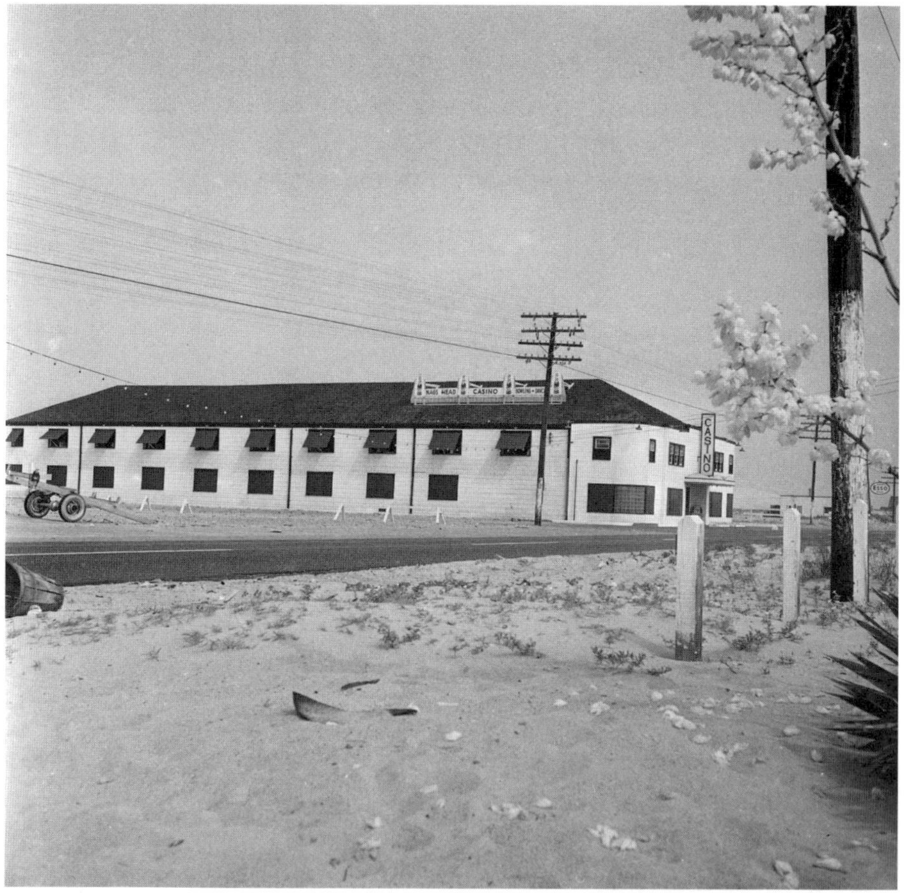

Ras Wescott's Casino in Nags Head was legendary for bowling downstairs, barefoot dancing upstairs, fistfights, and showcasing big-name performers. Wooden shutters were propped high to let ocean breezes in upstairs. *ABC, OBHC, SANC.*

Aycock rides past the old Coast Guard station with its stunning tower of wrap-around windows, now the home of his friend Diane Baum St. Clair. She is from a blueblood Outer Banks family, a businesswoman and former model who resembles Faye Dunaway. Diane is a "looker," Aycock might think with a grin. He passes the Trading Post store, which includes a post office, making the store a daily stop for locals. Aycock drives on, past the oceanfront Sea Ranch Hotel, where owner/operator Alice Sykes had entertained her clients with fine food and beautiful women in an oceanfront restaurant and bar. Just offshore near the Sea Ranch, a hundred yards out or more, are two shipwrecks that divers love to work, one ship having wrecked in 1927 and the second in 1929, cutting through the remnants of the 1927 wreck.

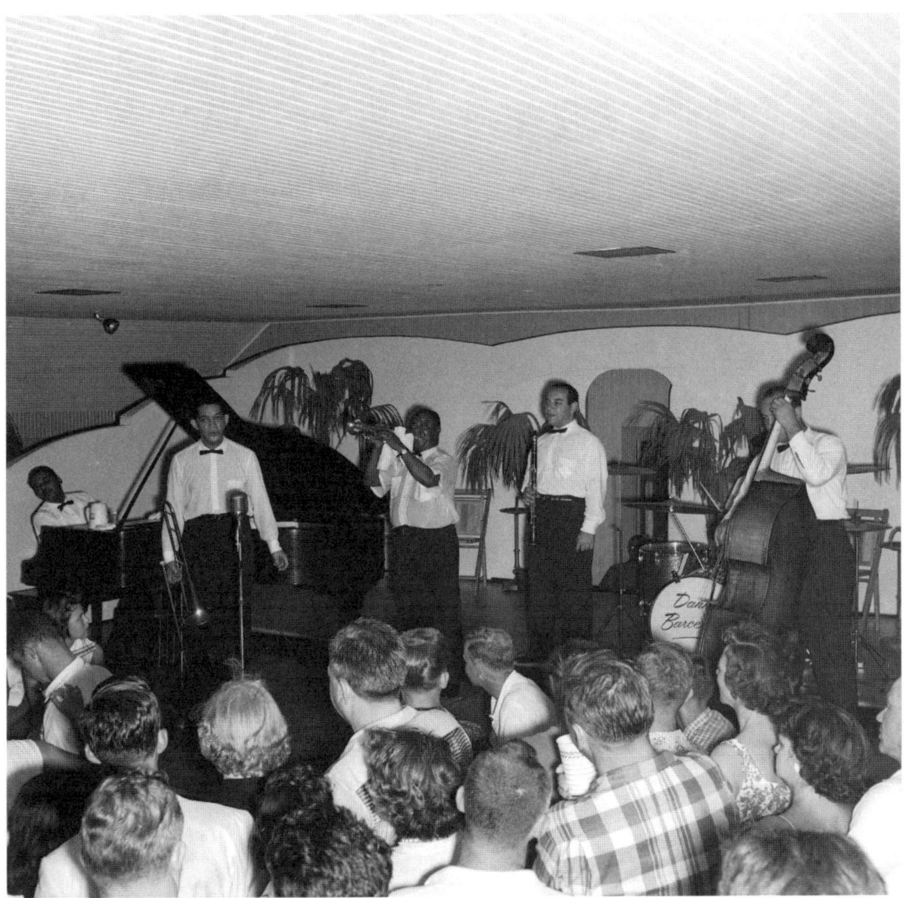

It was standing room only the night Louis Armstrong (*center*) and his band performed at the Casino in 1958. Some wondered if the second floor would hold the weight of the record-breaking crowd. *ABC, OBHC, SANC.*

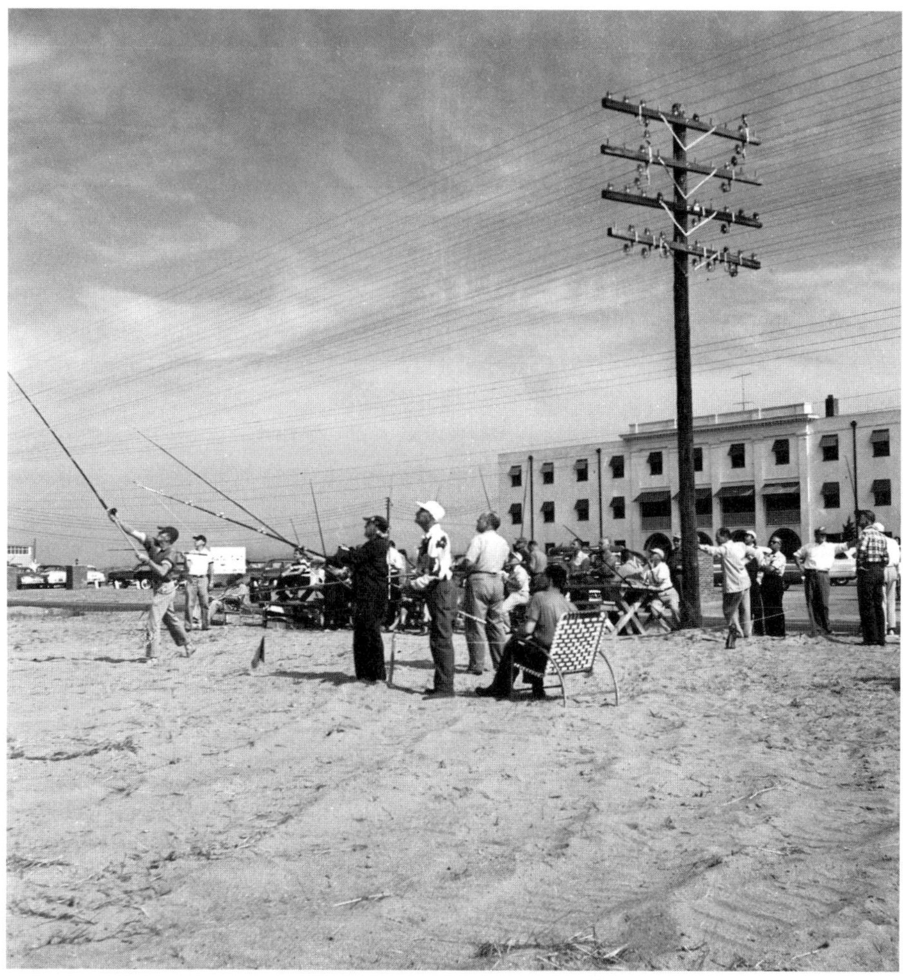

Above: The Carolinian hotel at Nags Head was known for special events. Fashion shows, humorous roasts, awards banquets, and celebrations were hosted in the Dogwood Room. Outside and across the beach road, a casting competition was being held. *ABC, OBHC, SANC.*

Opposite, top: The Carolinian hotel sponsored a Valentine season foxhunt. The day began with a minister conducting a blessing of the hounds before foxhunters began their searches through the marshes and woods of Nags Head. *ABC, OBHC, SANC.*

Opposite, bottom: Alice Sykes built the first iteration of the Sea Ranch Hotel in 1953 in Southern Shores. The architecture was mid-century modern like Florida hotels. It was badly damaged in the Ash Wednesday Storm, but a different version was rebuilt in Kill Devil Hills. *ABC, OBHC, SANC.*

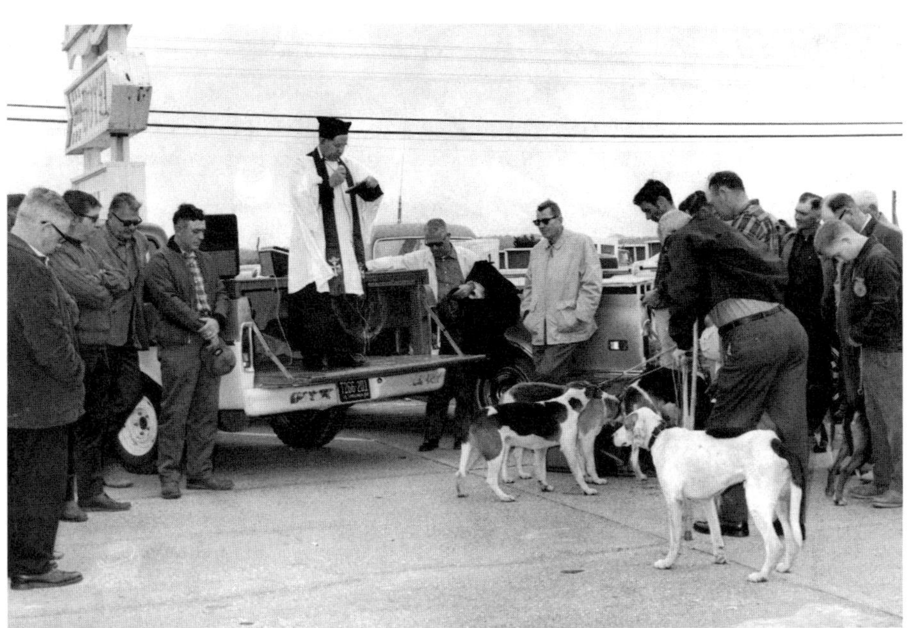

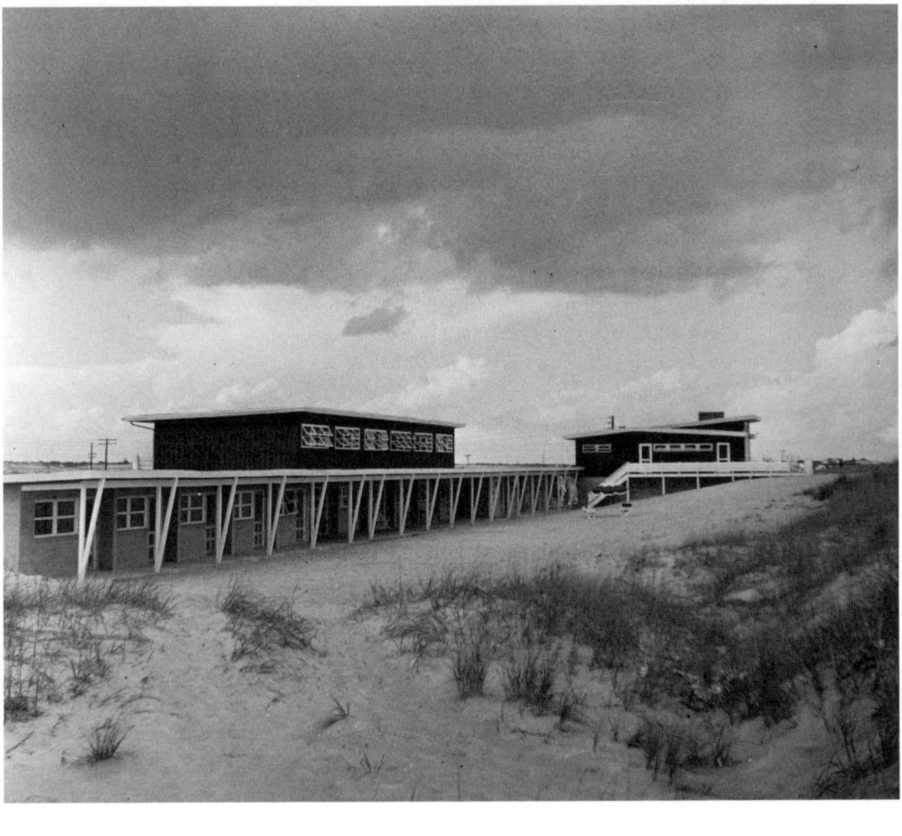

A mile or so on is the Avalon Market, owned and operated by Aycock's friends Lane and Marie Phillips, their daughter Elaine helping out. Up and down the Beach Road are mom-and-pop rental companies that check in repeat customers who have become friends during their dream weeks by the

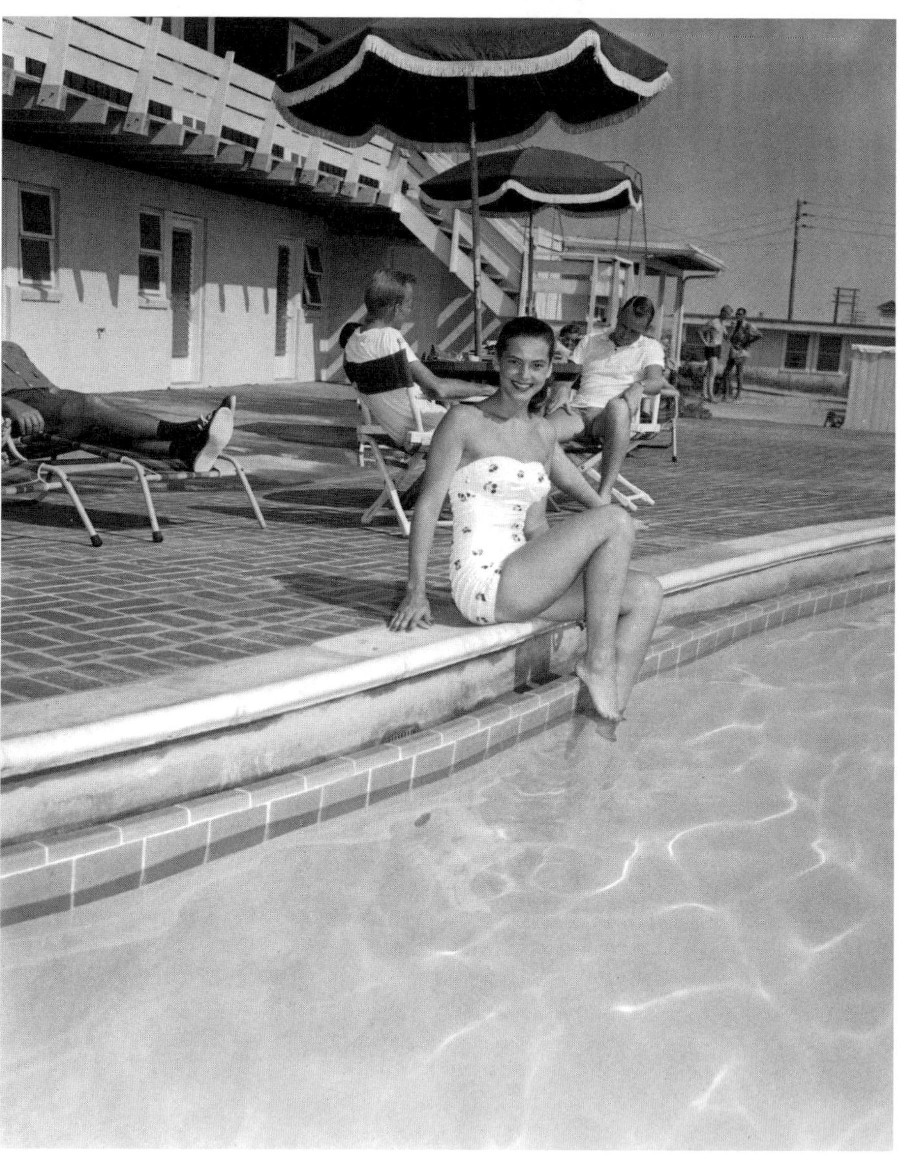

Amenities at the Sea Ranch included a swimming pool in front of the hotel. Aycock noted that the pool was being enjoyed by a "PIKA (Pi Kappa Alpha Fraternity) Dreamgirl." *ABC, OBHC, SANC.*

sea. Aycock drops by these companies, one of his many ways of taking the pulse of the summer.

Aycock continues north, through the eclectic cottages of Kitty Hawk with cool scenes of the ocean peeking through the low dunes; John's Drive-In;

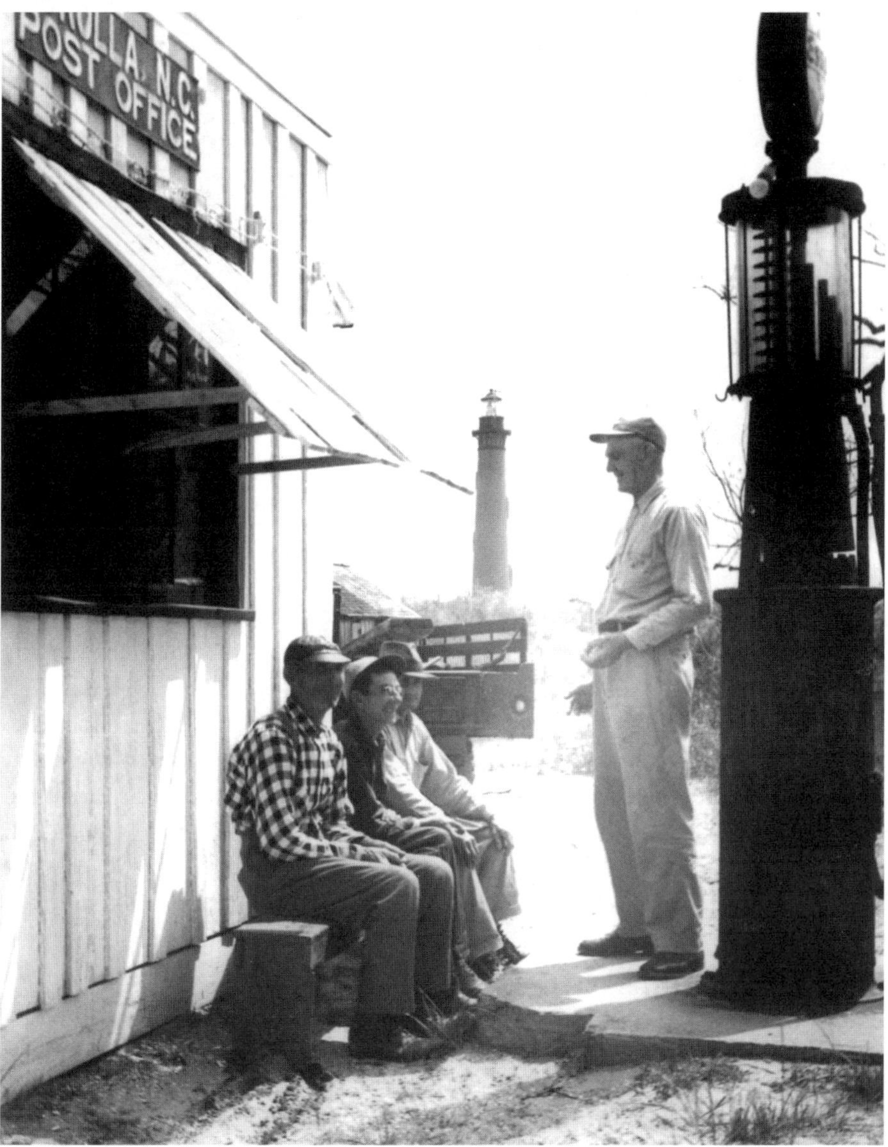

This photograph is one of Aycock's iconic shots summing up life in tiny Corolla in the 1940s: postmaster Johnny Austin amusing the good old boys gathered at the Corolla Post Office with the Currituck Beach Lighthouse in the background. *ABC, Norris and Scott Austin.*

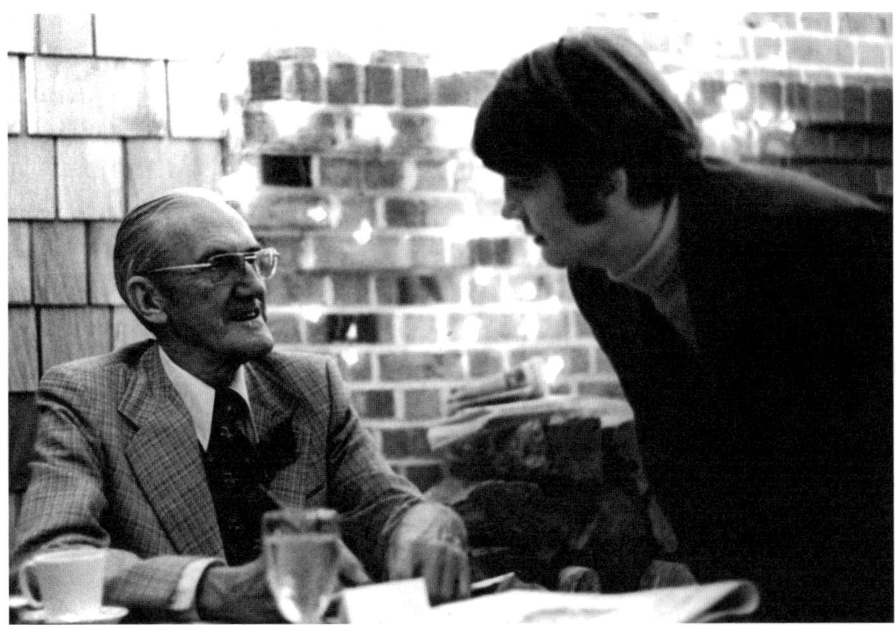

Aycock chats with Mike Hayman at the Seafare Restaurant in Nags Head. Mike grew up at the Arlington and took command of the Seafare after college. He was the consummate restaurateur and made a name for himself and the business. *George Tames, RV Owens.*

Art's cozy restaurant and bar; the flat-topped homes of Southern Shores and on to the town of Duck, scarcely populated save for long-standing residents' houses, a few cottages, and a Winks convenience store. The state road stops at a guard gate just north of Duck, and the pavement ends at the Corolla Post Office, long manned by Norris Austin. After that, there are miles of barren beach to the Virginia state line, an outlaw land, Penny's Hill and Carova, populated by wild ponies and characters such as Ernie Bowden, who runs his cattle through the dunes, and locals with jacked-up old cars who deflate their tires to race down the beach, rarely getting stuck, in sharp contrast to the growing number of tourists in pricey four-wheel drives they sometimes mire in the surf and ruin.

Heading back south to his Manteo home, Aycock might take a detour, a quick trip across the Currituck Sound bridge, which, in 1930, was the first bridge built to link the Outer Banks with the mainland, to sneak a peek at the restaurant at the foot of the mainland side of the bridge that had once been the Point Harbor Grill, owned and operated by his friends Walton and Ruth Griggs, now kept running by new owners.

All the while, Aycock has frequently stopped to talk with locals and meet tourists, snapping photos of them all. He is grinning, taking it all in, smoking his cigarettes, thinking about his thriving friends but maybe a bit sad about the development coming in on top of them and brokenhearted about the recent death of his wife, an Ocracoke Island native. Nobody could believe his story if someone wrote it in a book, he might have thought. Young men and women now coming to the Outer Banks talk of "finding themselves," a phrase popular nationwide. Aycock could identify. He might have thought back on his own lively times.

The Outer Banks blew Aycock away the first time he saw it, on Ocracoke, in 1928. Sand dancing in the screaming wind like banshees. The Atlantic pounding waves on the east and the Pamlico Sound on the west, whipping

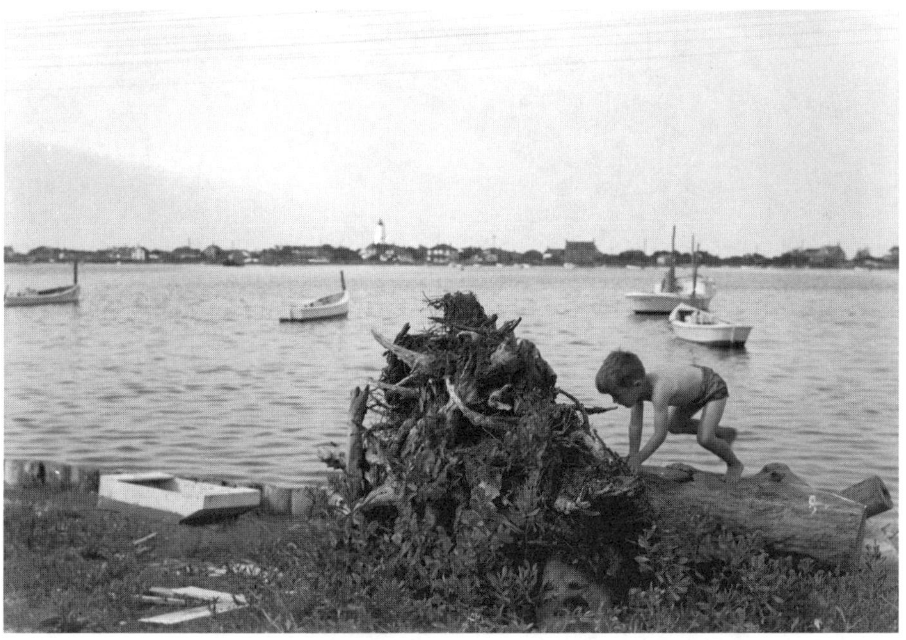

Billy Brown, Aycock and Esther's middle child, explores the edge of Silver Lake harbor on Ocracoke Island in 1943. Ocracoke was quite remote until the nation entered World War II and it became an outpost for U.S. military forces. *ABC, OBHC, SANC.*

whitecaps, the breeze hard and smart and wet with the glorious salt spray, fishing boats out there bobbing and working. And in town nestled around the Silver Lake harbor guarded by the towering old lighthouse, young men tending to their boats and old men watching and telling stories of their glory days, barefoot girls and boys running down the sand streets, some on ponies as their mamas tended backyard gardens and midwives remembered bringing those babies into their island world.

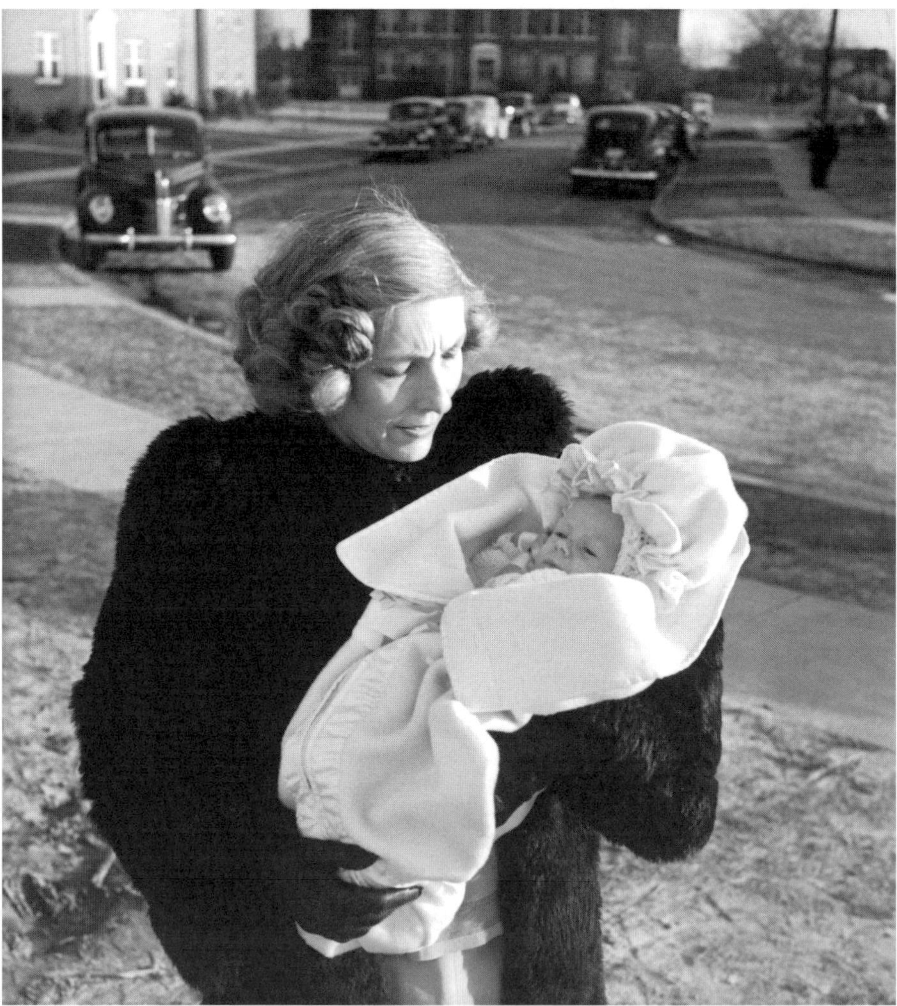

In 1947, Esther Brown held their third child, daughter Esther Gale, whom Aycock affectionately called "Stormy Gale" after losing the battle with his wife to make that the official name on her birth certificate. *ABC, OBHC, SANC.*

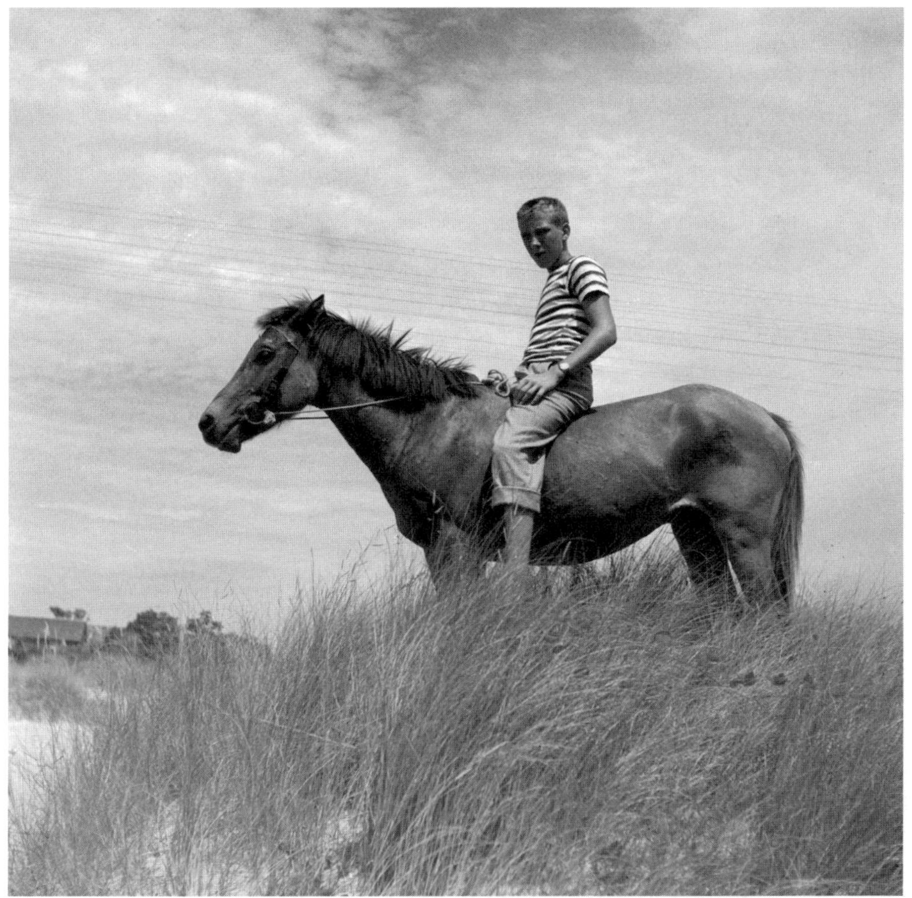

Aycock and Esther's oldest son, Brantley, sits on an Ocracoke pony in the mid-1940s. In 1959, the National Park Service ordered all wild ponies removed because of overgrazing. Some were penned and their descendants remain on the island. *ABC, OBHC, SANC.*

Aycock was twenty-four years old, whip-skinny tough, of medium height and 130 pounds on a good day, having rolled down from the mainland by way of a brief stint in New York City. He instinctively saw it all as pictures, photos, not realizing what it all might mean, just clicking away, digging his bony knees into the sand, and snapping away at this pioneer world few outsiders had seen.

He was tapping into mystic sands. And a few years later, in the World War II days, courage. Just offshore, German submarines were torpedoing our ships. Aycock worked for the military in the grim job of identifying the bodies of U.S. servicemen, merchant mariners, and foreign sailors, later coauthoring a story about it headlined "I Wore a Dead Man's Hands." On Ocracoke, he met Esther Styron, the woman who would become his wife. The Styrons were an old family on the island. Aycock's marriage to her bought him acceptance on the island, whose residents are wary of outsiders. To add to that, Aycock was a charmer who came to understand and respect the islanders, when to shoot pictures and ask questions and when to back off.

He was an old-school romantic, fearless and funny but practical too, one of those rare folk who find themselves at a turning point of history and run with it, a visionary, one able to convey the magic and mystery he was encountering. He was on one of the last frontiers of East Coast

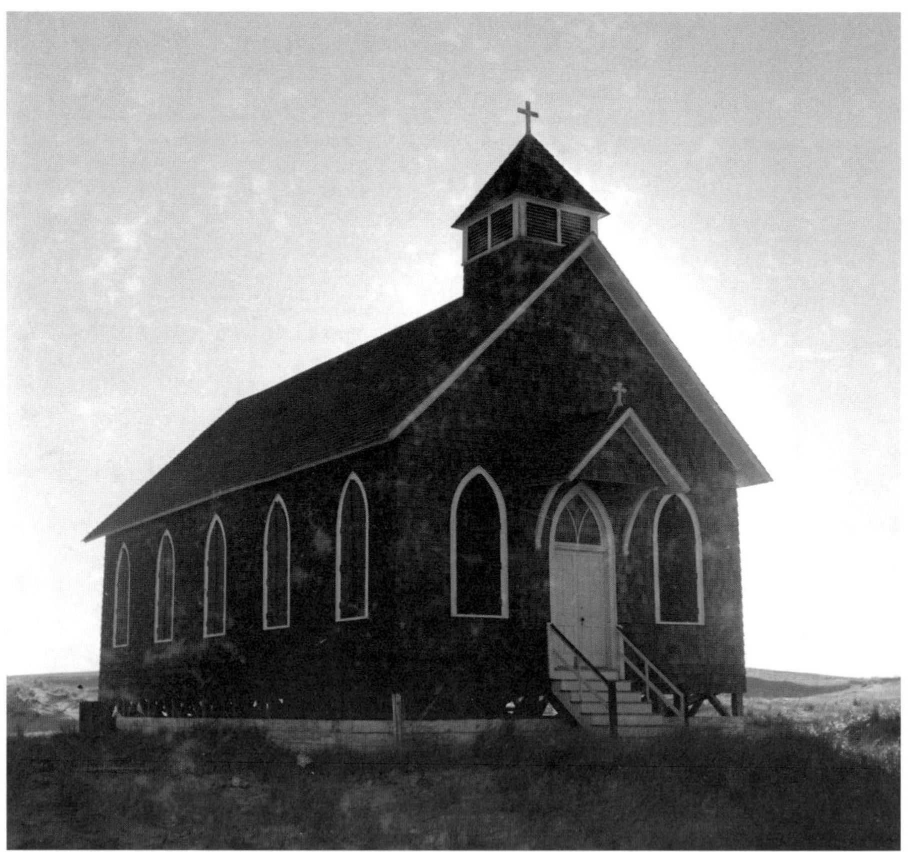

By 1948, the Episcopalian congregation of St. Andrew's By-the-Sea in Nags Head had replaced the door that washed up in a 1916 storm to perfectly fit their large, onion-shaped doorway. A large modern church now surrounds the chapel that was once Soundside. *ABC, OBHC, SANC.*

beaches. The magic surrounded him and seeped into his soul as he and Esther moved from Ocracoke to the southern North Carolina coast, then to Manteo.

Aycock loved looking at the wild water and beaches. He worshiped in a Nags Head church that once had a door from a shipwreck that, incredibly, fit perfectly into the chapel's doorframe. He knew and shot photos of one of the last witnesses of the 1903 Wright brothers' flight. Years later, as he shot photos of soaring pelicans, he watched in awe as fighter jocks tore through the Outer Banks skies in their war birds, roaring out from their naval base in Virginia Beach to the Outer Banks in under five minutes, a car drive of an hour and a half on a good day. We could have used those jets when the

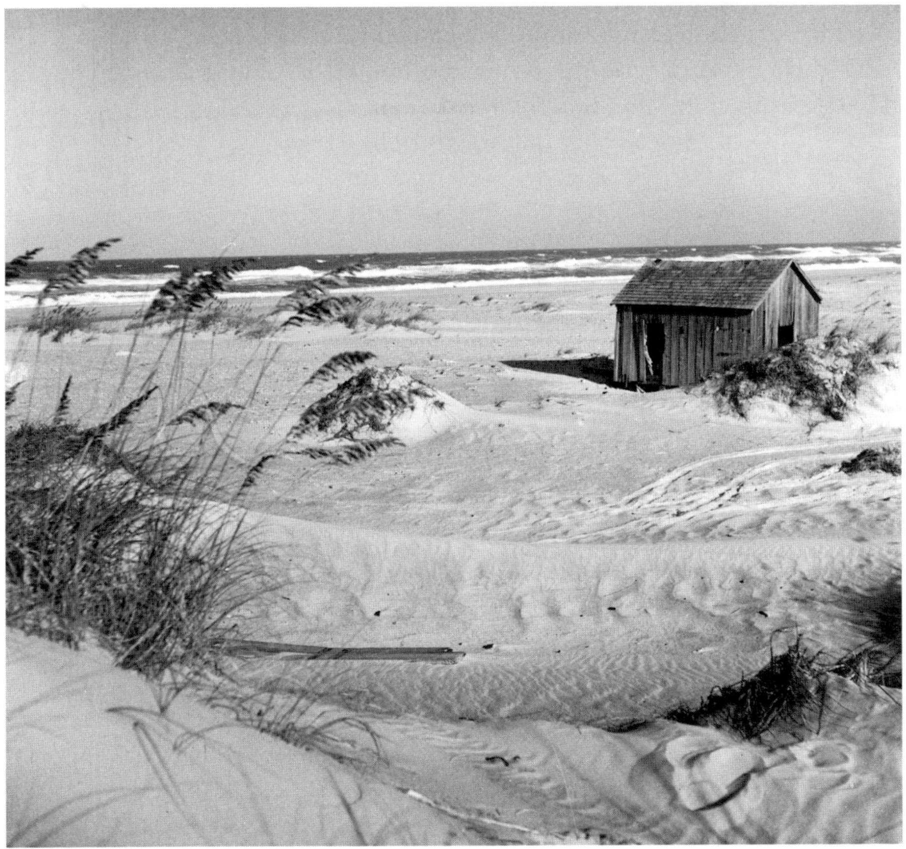

Before native Outer Bankers realized that their quality of life could be greatly enhanced by tourism, they considered the oceanfront, or the "back of the beach" as they called it, to be a wasteland interspersed by shipwrecks and net houses. *ABC, OBHC, SANC.*

Germans were torpedoing the hell out of our boats right here back in 1942, Aycock might have thought of his war days. He camped out by the Wright Memorial in 1969, shooting that glorious moon as the astronauts landed on it. He met astronaut John Glenn and photographed him visiting the Wright Memorial. He intimately knew the magic of the old days on the Banks, when most locals still talked in the Old English brogue— "hoigh toide on the Sound soide"—in the enchanting parallel time.

He was, in his own way, an anthropologist, chronicling a culture and way of life fast vanishing, a filter, a lens, a mirror, a closet intellectual with an impish sense of humor and never-ending wonder almost childlike at times. Once, late in his life, he spent hours riding the beach with a young friend who asked him where seagulls slept, slowing his landboat of a car repeatedly to ask locals that question.

As early as 1972, Aycock sometimes regretted, only half-jokingly, the overdevelopment his timeless photos wrought.

1

AYCOCK'S ODYSSEY TO THE BEACH

Suppose you were looking for the most remote, least visited inhabited spot in the United States east of the Mississippi. My nomination would be the Carolina Outer Banks, where people have been living for more than two centuries, so little noticed by, or noticing of, the outside world that they retain traces of seventeenth century, if not Elizabethan speech.

—Aycock in his journalistic breakthrough, an August 1940 story in The Saturday Evening Post *headlined "Cape Stormy"*

Aycock was born in the North Carolina mountains, in Happy Valley, on October 7, 1904, one of several brothers and sisters. Something special was going on in the Tarheel mountains in October in the early 1900s. Just four years before, Thomas Wolfe, who'd go on to write the classic novel *Look Homeward, Angel*, was born in Asheville.

Aycock was named for one of his father's acquaintances, Charles Brantley Aycock, who served as the governor of North Carolina from 1901 through 1905.

Aycock's father soon moved the family down to Orange County, near the University of North Carolina at Chapel Hill, where he oversaw a farm. Aycock, in one of his first acts of reinvention, soon shortened his name to Aycock Brown. The governor he was named for would, more than a century later, be discredited for his white supremacist views. Aycock, who never wrote or spoke much about his namesake, was long dead by then.

When Aycock was thirteen, a cyclone blew timbers from a horse barn through the bedroom where Aycock and a brother had been sleeping. Aycock suspected "the urge to write was born of his desire to express all the terror that the cyclone spread for him and his family," according to a newspaper account.

Soon thereafter, he got his first look at the ocean, at Wrightsville Beach in southern North Carolina. "It was a real thrill," he would later say. "There was the sea and the fishing boats and the old Lumina [dance pavilion] was going full blast."

As a young adult, he went to work in Elizabeth City in northeastern North Carolina for the Elizabeth City *Independent* under renowned editor W.O. Saunders. Facing firing for his inexperience, he quit, borrowed $500, and set off for New York City, inspired by one of Saunders's flapper daughters with whom, he once said, he had "kind of fell in love."

Kinda, maybe, sorta? Aycock rarely let up on his garrulousness, but he could be coy.

In New York, Aycock enrolled at the prestigious Columbia University to study journalism. He lived in Greenwich Village, gathered with artsy types, and probably loved the Bohemian lifestyle, hanging out in bars, talking literature, but mainly just listening to stories. Aycock had what the novelist James Jones, who would become most famous for the World War II novel *From Here to Eternity*, called "this f—— ear," a fascination with dialogue heard from people of all stripes.

Aycock's school money ran out. He worked as a longshoreman and then worked shoveling snow. He was a door-to-door salesman. He unloaded goat hides from a ship, as he later told *The News & Observer* of Raleigh:

> *Loading goat hides was smelly work. I'd work during the day and go to classes at night. I began to notice that no one wanted to sit near my desk when I arrived in the classroom. I finally discovered what it was. Actually, I smelled very pleasant to me.*

After eleven months, he scuttled, crab-like, back to North Carolina.

That was in the late 1920s. Aycock returned to newspapering on the coast. The time was more than forty years before the glory days of journalism, when the work of *Washington Post* reporters Carl Bernstein and Bob Woodward on President Nixon's Watergate scandal led thousands of young men and women to enter the field. But journalism had always been a haven for restless adventurers, and Aycock embraced that. He worked briefly for a Durham newspaper, then for newspapers on the southern coast of North Carolina, in Beaufort and Morehead City. He was drinking, as a North Carolina reporter wrote soon after that time:

> *This was the period in his life when journalist Brown confused getting relaxed with getting stiff. He drank enthusiastically and with a steady-minded purpose, a fact that strained his relations with his employers. They didn't know what he would do next and they shuddered when they contemplated what he had just managed to do.*

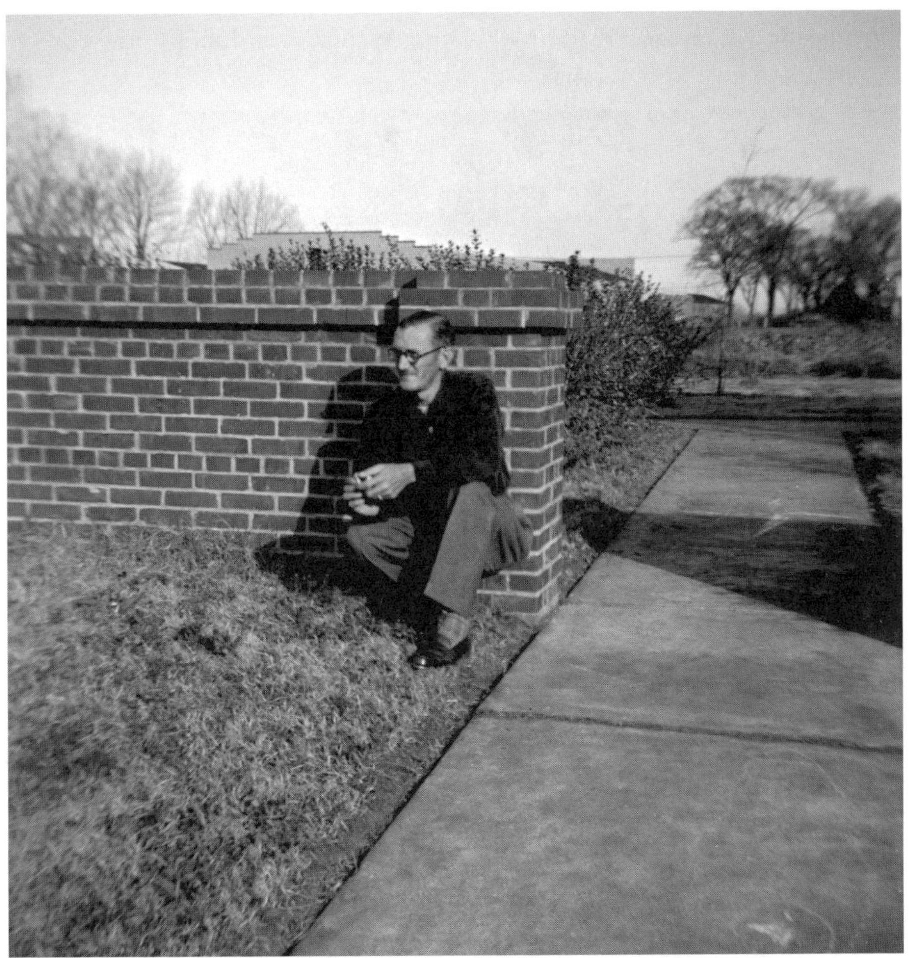

Aycock squats in front of a wall in New Bern, North Carolina, in the early 1940s. His civilian service in the military helped him find his niche in newswriting, reporting, and photography. *ABC, OBHC, SANC.*

By then, he was supplementing his newspaper work with public relations. There has always been a symbiotic relationship between journalists and PR folks, a relationship that is sometimes ambivalent, with PR types dependent on journalists to act on their tips and transform them into stories, thus satisfying the clients who pay them. Journalists often use the tips but just as often resent public relations, complaining that the PR folks are pushing weak stories on them, free advertising instead of the paid ads on which newspapers depend. Many journalists, however, eventually entered the PR field for the better money but didn't openly engage in PR while acting as journalists, usually a no-no in mainstream journalism. Starting early in his career, Aycock was doing both. For his

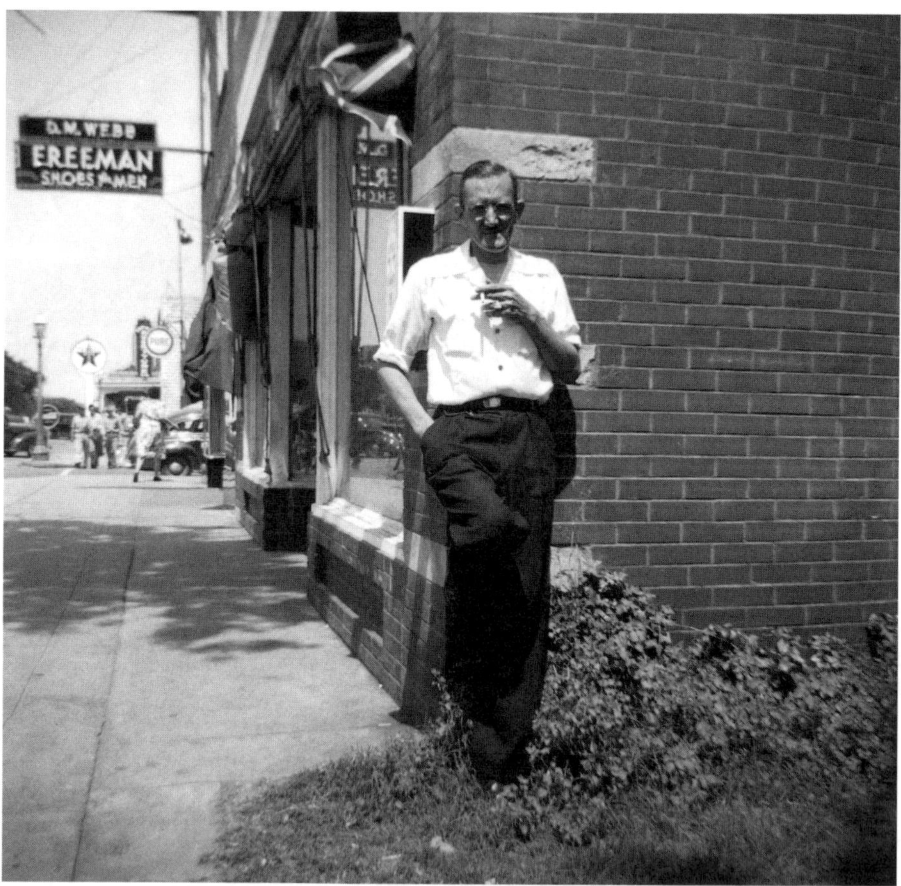

Although his pose in downtown Wilmington suggests an air of nonchalance, Aycock Brown's journalistic inclination always had him looking for the next story. *ABC, OBHC, SANC.*

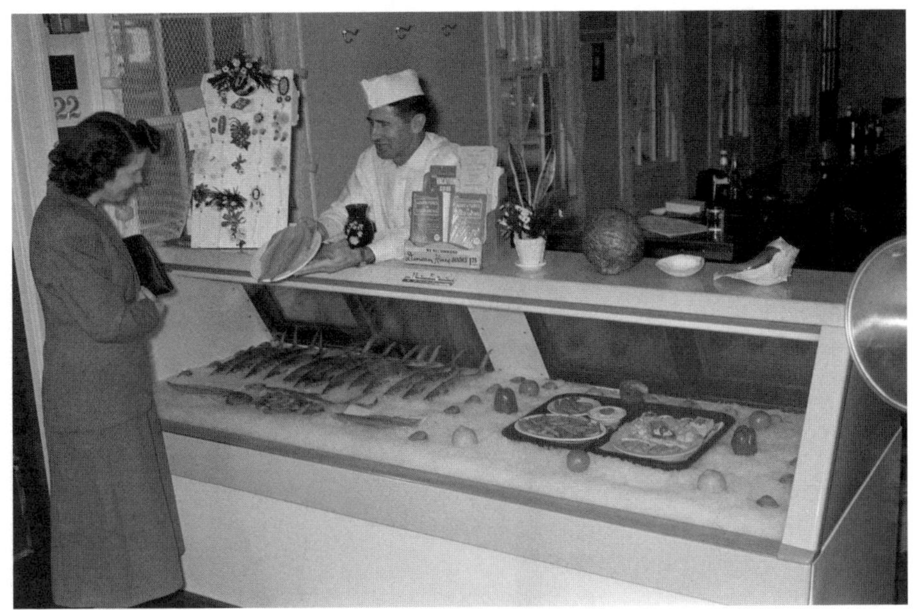

Aycock worked as a press agent for Tony Seamon (*right*), owner and operator of The Sanitary Fish Market and Restaurant. His efforts made the Morehead City, North Carolina restaurant one of the best known on the East Coast. *ABC, OBHC, SANC.*

part, later in his career, Aycock identified himself as a "press agent," not a "public relations man." The words have become interchangeable, but Aycock maintained that "a public relations man sits back and tells people what to do. A press agent goes out to do it." That he did.

In 1928, he moved to Ocracoke for a few weeks. By one of Aycock's accounts of his Ocracoke arrival—he told a few—"I was headed for Cuba on a public relations job but decided to visit Ocracoke. Heard it was a wide-open place."

It's tempting to imagine what might have happened if Aycock had gone to Cuba. One can see him wearing a beret—which he occasionally did—and riding motorcycles with rebel leader Che Guevara. He might even have built a life there, enhancing that island's tourism. Fortunately, he chose Ocracoke. "After a few days, I just stayed on and began writing stories about Ocracoke," he once said.

By the most widely accepted account, he came to Ocracoke to generate publicity for the venerable Pamlico Inn in exchange for free room and board. At one point, he nearly drowned in the ocean and gave up swimming in it for the rest of his life. "I got caught in a riptide and

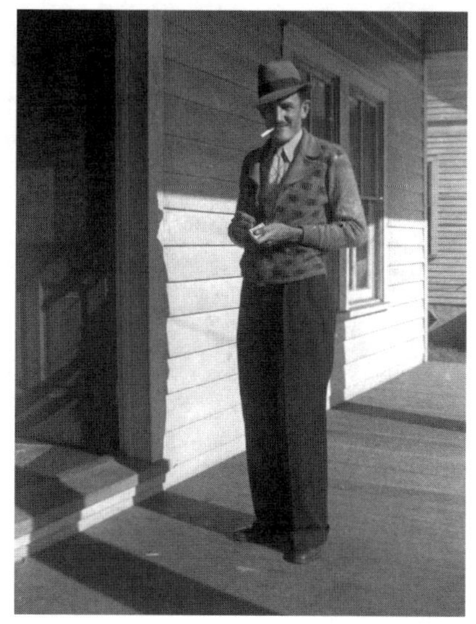

liked to not got back to shore," he said in one of his colloquially charming twists of phrase.

In addition to writing, he used "odd jobs" to make ends meet. "It was while working one of these 'odd jobs' that he met his wife [Esther Styron]," Shawna Hubbard wrote in a 2013 paper for R. Wayne Gray's English class at the College of The Albemarle in Manteo. Esther was barely five feet tall, beautiful with high cheekbones and a deceptively tough style all her own. "He said, 'I was bootlegging booze…and when our boat pulled into the dock she was standing there. She was so pretty I forgot about the booze."

This was during Prohibition, when most alcohol was prohibited in the United States. Aycock was hustling to make a living, preceding in his own small way the outlaw Captain Harry Morgan in Ernest Hemingway's 1937 novel *To Have and Have Not*, set between Key West and Cuba, as well as the tension between the rich and the poor depicted in the book.

Aycock said, late in his life, that he "never exactly bootlegged, but I always knew where you could get a drink, and I gave a lot to my friends. As long as you give it and don't sell it, it's not bootlegging, is it?"

"I was drinking pretty heavily in those days," he acknowledged. At a party on a boat one night, he fell overboard. Friends pressed him to calm down.

During his time on Ocracoke, in search of stories, Aycock sometimes made the short motorboat ride across Ocracoke Inlet to Portsmouth Island, a once thriving community that was quickly becoming a ghost town. In a May 1974 interview, Aycock told a longtime friend, Outer Banks historian David Stick, much about Portsmouth and the rest of his time on Ocracoke:

> *I remember one of the early trips that I made, and this was 1928, I went to Portsmouth. I'd say there were 40 or 50 people out there. There might not have been that many because I remember I went there and there was a Mrs. Dixon who was teaching in the school, and the strange thing about the school was it didn't have* [but] *about five or six pupils. And I made a picture of it and said it was one of the smallest schools in the state….*

Stick: Well, now, was there much communication between Portsmouth and Ocracoke then?

Brown: Yeah, Portsmouth and Ocracoke, they got along pretty good together. And the McWilliams family used to live over there at Portsmouth. As a matter of fact, one of the McWilliams was an officer in charge of the Coast Guard station. One of the big things that happened at Portsmouth, two or three things have happened there, but one was the wreck of the Vera Cruz. *The* Vera Cruz *came in, and that was in 1904. I believe it was 1904. She was a Portuguese ship that had sailed from the Cape Verde Islands, and she was loaded down with about 300 immigrants.*

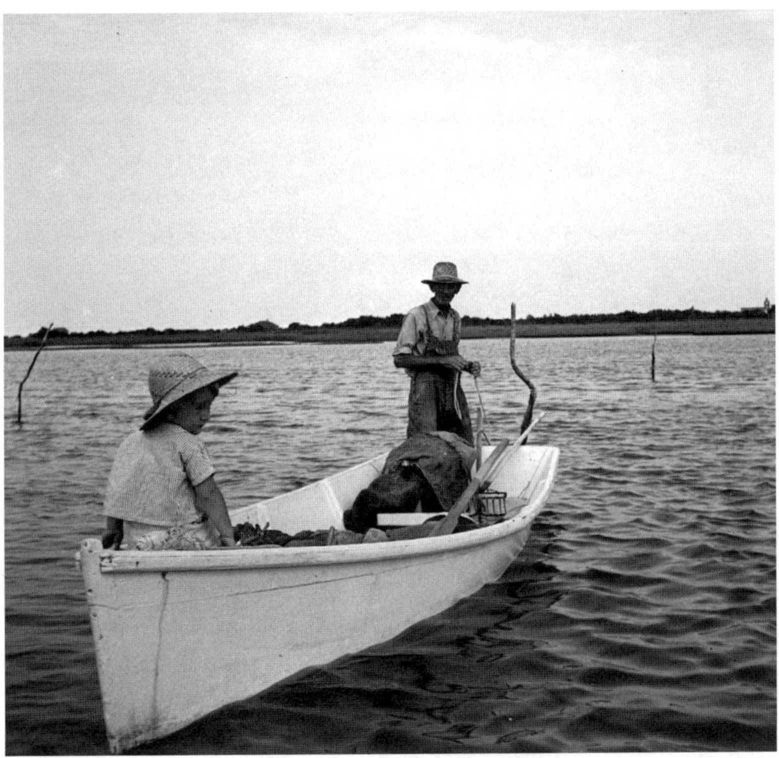

Opposite: Aycock stops to light a cigarette on an Ocracoke porch. Richard Gonder, public editor of *The Virginian-Pilot*, once marveled that Aycock came up with so many newsworthy events in such a small world. *ABC, OBHC, SANC.*

Above: A Portsmouth Island man is pictured here returning from poling his skiff out to meet the mail boat on its way to Ocracoke in the 1940s. On this trip, there was a special young passenger going along for the ride. *ABC, OBHC, SANC.*

You've heard this story, 300 immigrants from the Cape Verde Islands. And none of them had any papers to get in the country with, so they were taken ashore at Portsmouth, and a revenue cutter came down from New Bern. That's where they had a revenue cutter station there at the time. He came down and got them off the island. Well, some of those people apparently were able to stay in the country, but a lot of them were sent back. And the man on the Vera Cruz, *the captain of the* Vera Cruz, *he went ashore at Ocracoke and got Lum (?) Gaskill to take him over to Belhaven where he could send a telegram to his [boat] owners. Or, that was a pretense he was going down there. He paid him $50, I believe, to take him over there, which was big money in those days. And he carried*

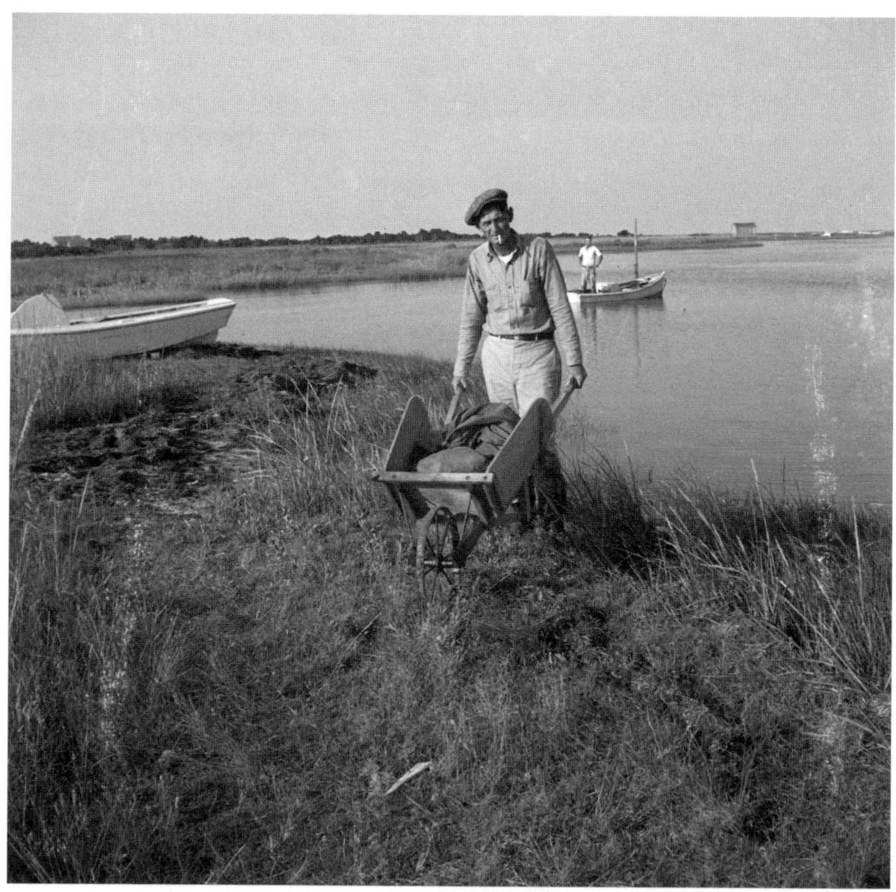

Mailman Carl Dixon wheelbarrowed letters and parcels from a skiff to the post office in Portsmouth village in the 1940s. With no electricity or phone service, the tiny population depended on the mail for communication with the outside world. *ABC, OBHC, SANC.*

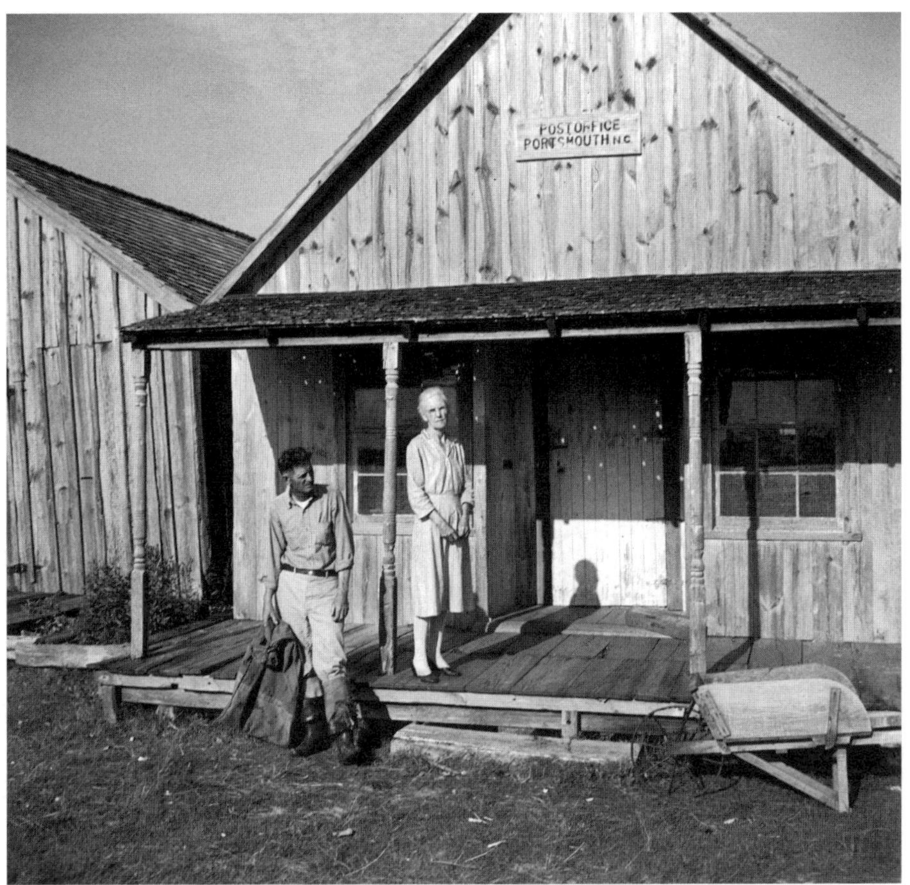

An empty mailbag and wheelbarrow indicate the mail was safely delivered to the Portsmouth Island Post Office, or "Mrs. Salters' Post Office," as Aycock labeled this 1940s photograph. The island is now part of the Cape Lookout National Seashore. *ABC, OBHC, SANC.*

> *him over to Belhaven on the pretense of sending a telegram. Well, when he got over there, this was the captain and the mate, I believe, both went. And he* [Gaskill] *kept waiting for them at the boat, but they didn't come back to the boat. They kept going. And they tell a story, you know, that he went up to Bedford, New Bedford, Massachusetts, and he shipped himself out of the country by hiding himself in a whale oil barrel. I don't know whether that's true or not.*

The Graveyard of the Atlantic Museum has this to say about the *Vera Cruz*. It corrects Aycock by a year—1903 instead of 1904— and does not include most of Aycock's details:

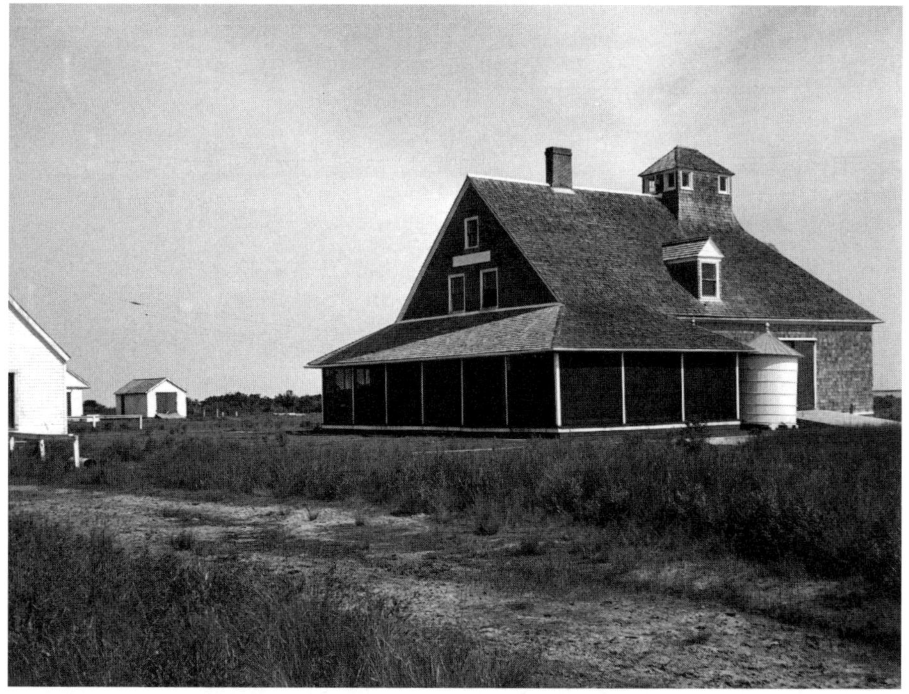

The Portsmouth Island Lifesaving Service Station once housed a crew to assist vessels when the island was on a critical shipping route. Both Portsmouth and Ocracoke villages provided pilots to navigate tricky waters. *ABC, OBHC, SANC.*

> *On May 8, 1903, the barkentine "Vera Cruz" was traveling from the Cape Verde Islands to New Bedford, Massachusetts when she drug her anchor and went into the breakers. She stranded on Dry Shoal Point with 22 crew and 399 passengers on board. The 29-year-old ship was carrying 214 barrels of whale oil valued at $6,000. The Portsmouth Life-Saving Station crew brought 23 women, three children and two men in by surfboat.*
>
> *The following morning, the sea was getting rough. Several surfboats were used to take the remaining 371 people to Dry Shoal Point. A wreck report from the U.S. Life-Saving Service indicates that the "shoal was covered with water before we got them all off and had to be very watchful to keep them from sinking the boat." The Portsmouth community baked bread to help feed the survivors.*

The account does not say what became of the immigrants. Stick continued the interview:

Stick: Well, did they make any whiskey on Ocracoke?

Aycock: No, they made meal wine. Meal wine was the preliminaries to whiskey. You'd make it out of meal and sugar and raisins and stuff of that kind. I remember the first time I ever drank it, and it tastes quite good if a person knows how to make it. And they made it all up and down the Outer Banks. So these boys came to see me, Bill Garrish and one of the Styron boys…came to see me. By that time I got to Ocracoke, you know, and they extended the warm welcome to me. They asked me if I ever took a drink. I said, "Oh, yeah, once in a while." So I went out with them to take this meal wine. I drank it, and I'd never drank any before, and it tastes almost like a carbonated drink to me, though, see? But they give you a nice teacup full of it. So I drank a nice teacup full of it. They said, you like it? I said, yeah. They said, well, yeah, let's give you another glass. By the time I drank those two glasses, the next thing I knew was next morning, they'd carried me home.

[David Stick laughs] *It really knocks you out.*

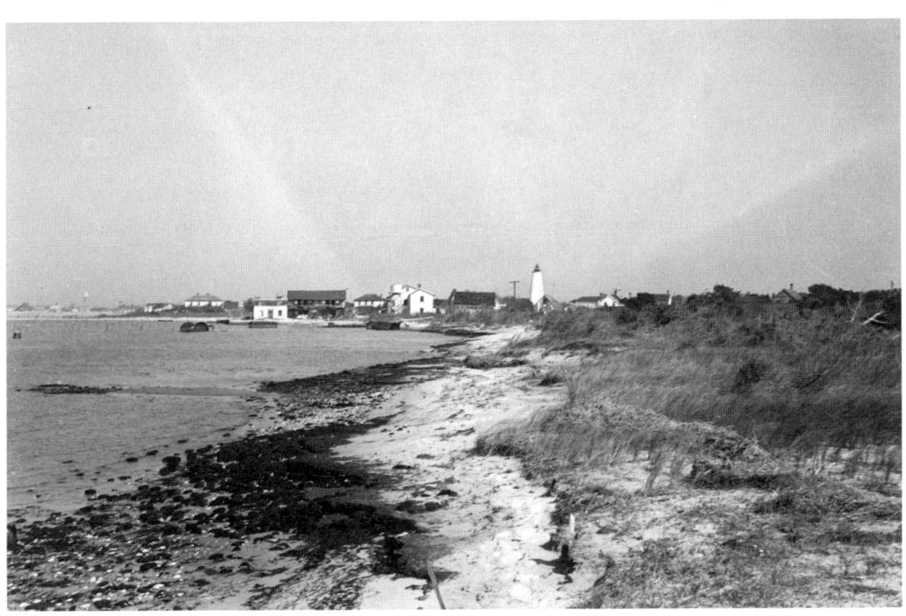

Jobs were hard to find on Ocracoke Island by the time Aycock arrived. Piloting and shipping waned as shifting shoals caused trade routes to change. Commercial fishing was unreliable because of a lack of markets. Tourism became the new economic base that Aycock helped expand. *ABC, OBHC, SANC.*

Aycock: Meal wine.

Stick: Did they make this in secret, or did they make it out in the open?

Aycock: Well, some of them made it. They didn't make it out in the open. They just made it in the smokehouse or the net house or something like that, see? I never did learn how to make it, because I wasn't an expert at it, and there were too many experts down there, so in case you're wondering, I didn't have to drink very much after that. I mean, I got my fill of it.

Aycock and Esther Styron, the daughter of a Coast Guardsman, married on Thanksgiving Day 1929. She settled Aycock down a bit, at least as much as anyone could ever settle him. They lived on Ocracoke for seven

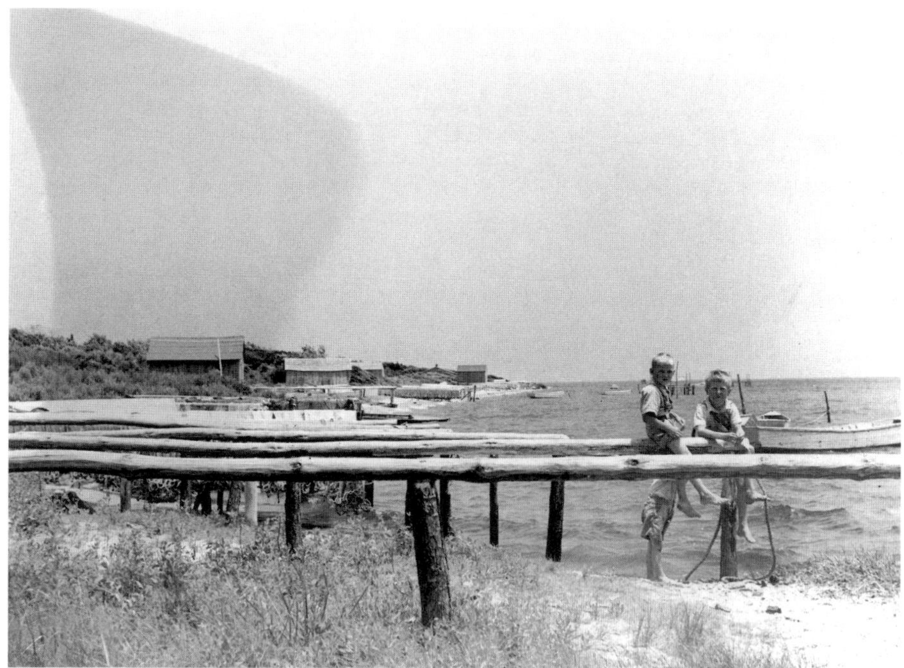

It is uncertain if this photograph was taken on Ocracoke, but it shows a shoreside scene of net-drying racks and net-storage houses. Even though Aycock was a native mountaineer, he integrated himself into the coastal way of life. *ABC, Lisa Griggs.*

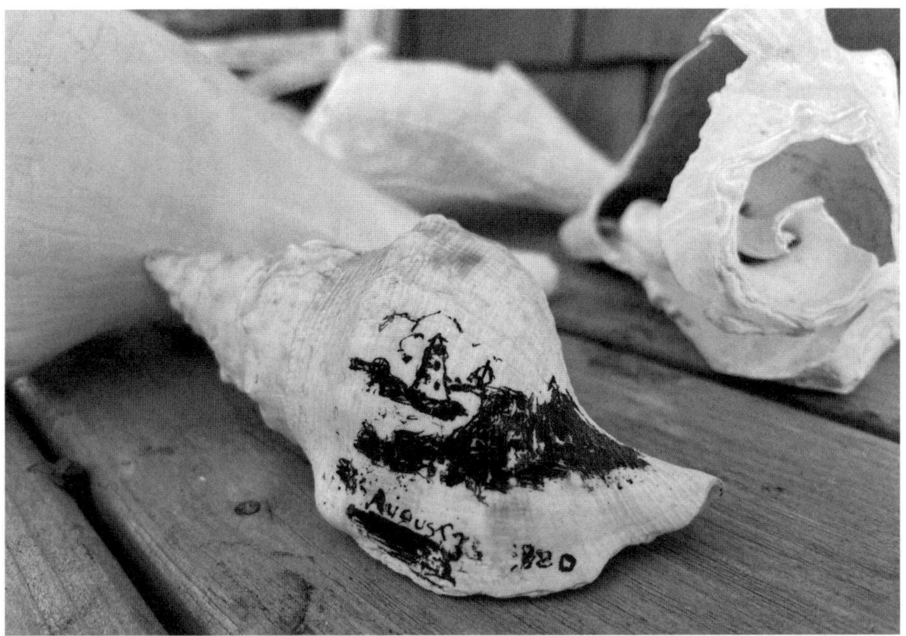

When Aycock told his young friend about the drawings he made on shells forty-five years earlier to sell to Ocracoke tourists, she insisted on one. Aycock sketched a lighthouse with seagulls and a sailboat on a conch that is now treasured by Angel Ellis Khoury. *Nancy Beach Gray.*

years, with Aycock constantly sending out stories about the island and ferrying north across Hatteras Inlet to report on the culture of Hatteras Island, including its tradition of honoring "Old Christmas" in January. He also sold ink drawings of lighthouses on whelk shells. "The drawings were awful," Aycock later told *The News & Observer*, "but I had discovered that a tourist will buy anything."

During the Great Depression, Aycock left home like millions of his counterparts, stomaching the time away from family to make money for them. He took a job laying pipe from a dredge in the Delaware River. Injured on the job, he said, he landed in a military hospital on Ellis Island in New York "in a ward alongside West Indian Negroes, German sailors who did not approve of Hitler, Russians and Chinamen." Aycock obviously loved their stories, continuing to expand his open mind.

He came back to Ocracoke, and he and Esther soon moved to New Bern, while Aycock continued his newspapering and press agentry, both for the Beaufort/Morehead City area and the Outer Banks. His stories included popular ones about scuba fishing and others that played a big role in popularizing the Sanitary Fish Market and Restaurant in Morehead City, still a tourist-magnet to this day.

In 1940, Aycock made his national debut. A friend at *The Saturday Evening Post*, with a nationwide circulation of more than three million, asked Aycock to show one of their photographers around Hatteras Island for a story to be told through photos. Aycock agreed to do so and cajoled his way into writing the text for the spread. Through Aycock's efforts, the photo spread grew into a story with photos. In a flip that would contradict all his future work, Aycock was the writer on the story instead of the photographer.

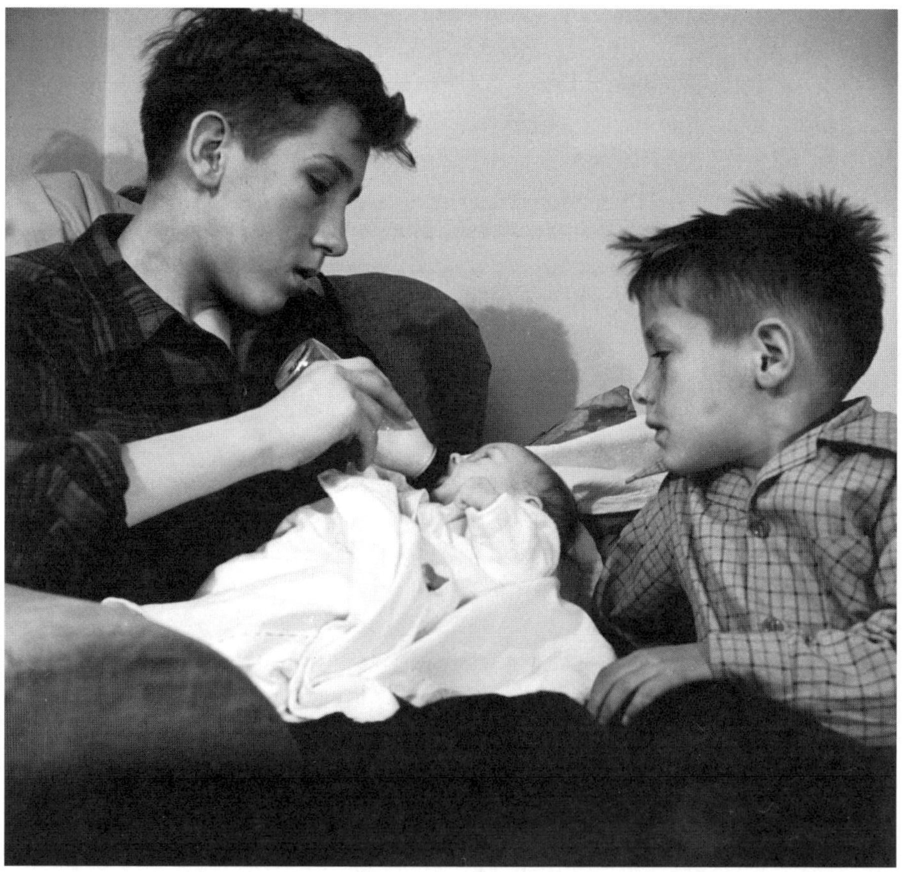

At their home in New Bern, North Carolina, the Brown boys look as if their baby sister had been keeping them awake. Aycock's children were born roughly seven years apart: Charles "Brantley" in 1932, William Kenneth "Billy" in 1940, and Esther "Gale" in 1947. *ABC, OBHC, SANC.*

The story, headlined "Cape Stormy," came out in August 1940, stylishly tucked amid ads for Lucky Strike cigarettes (sans filters, of course) and an essay warning of the dangers of Hitler. The photos by a photographer simply identified as "Pinto" were good, although Aycock could have shot better. From the start of the story, Aycock's writing was transformative. While focused on Hatteras, it also included much about the Outer Banks north of Hatteras:

> *Suppose you were looking for the most remote, least visited inhabited spot in the United States east of the Mississippi. My nomination would be*

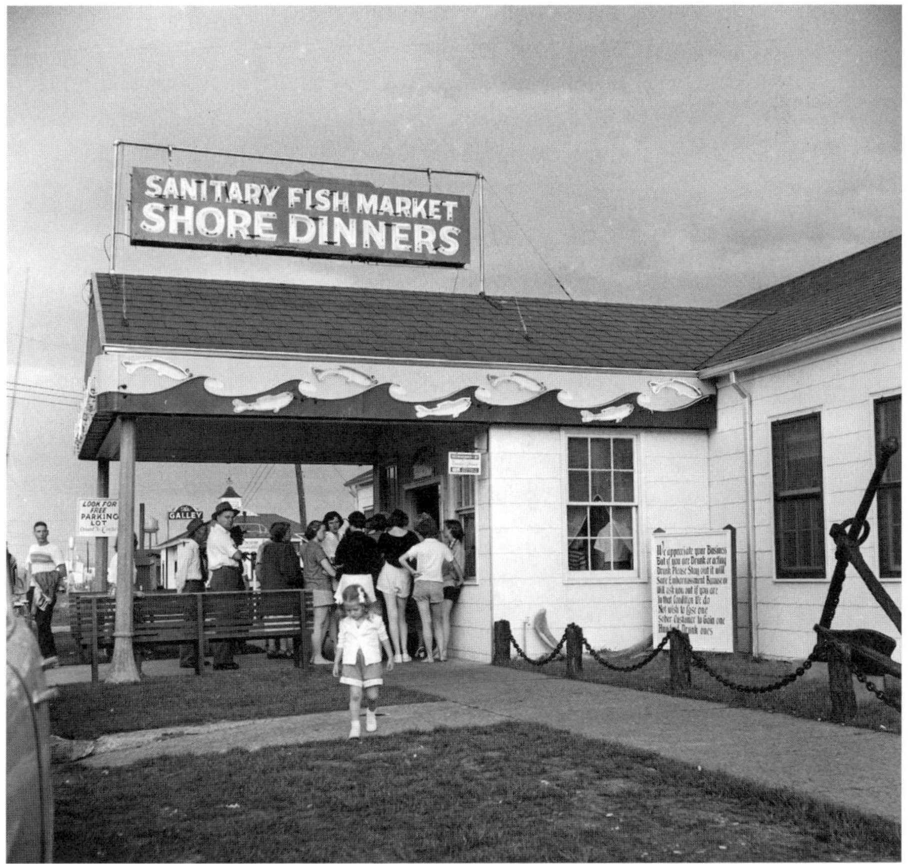

Customers queued up at the Sanitary Fish Market and Restaurant in Morehead City, North Carolina, in the 1940s. Aycock promoted the business as a public relations gig. He highlighted the sign that read "If you are drunk or acting drunk please stay out." *ABC, OBHC, SANC.*

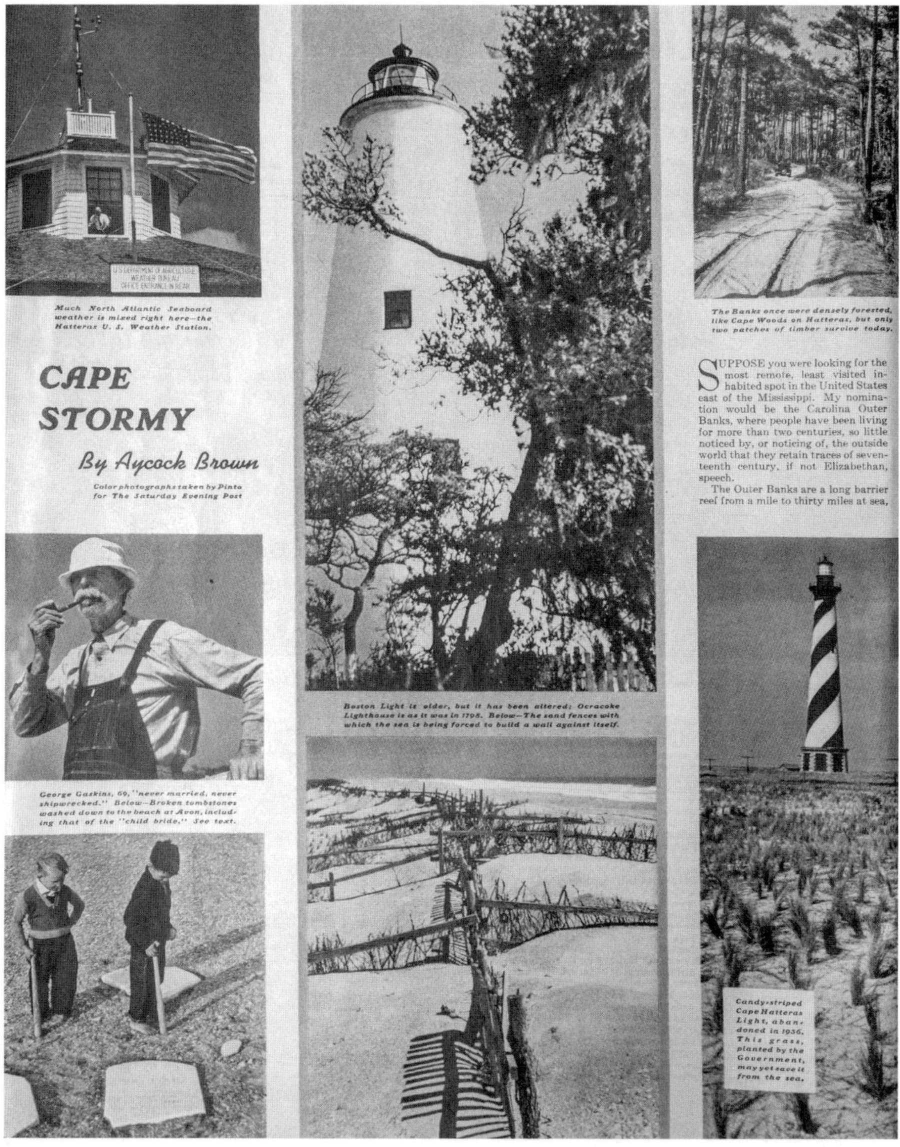

Much North Atlantic Seaboard weather is mixed right here—the Hatteras U. S. Weather Station.

CAPE STORMY

By Aycock Brown

Color photographs taken by Pinto for The Saturday Evening Post

George Gaskins, 69, "never married, never shipwrecked." Below—Broken tombstones washed down to the beach at Avon, including that of the "child bride." See text.

Boston Light is older, but it has been altered; Ocracoke Lighthouse is as it was in 1798. Below—The sand fences with which the sea is being forced to build a wall against itself.

The Banks once were densely forested, like Cape Woods on Hatteras, but only two patches of timber survive today.

SUPPOSE you were looking for the most remote, least visited inhabited spot in the United States east of the Mississippi. My nomination would be the Carolina Outer Banks, where people have been living for more than two centuries, so little noticed by, or noticing of, the outside world that they retain traces of seventeenth century, if not Elizabethan, speech.

The Outer Banks are a long barrier reef from a mile to thirty miles at sea,

Candy-striped Cape Hatteras Light, abandoned in 1936. This grass, planted by the Government, may yet save it from the sea.

Above: *The Saturday Evening Post* published Aycock's extensive article "Cape Stormy" in its August 3, 1940 edition. The seven-page spread (including twenty-five photographs and a map) expertly captured the unique culture of pre–World War II Hatteras Island. *Francesca B. Marie.*

Opposite, top: On Ocracoke beach, Aycock (*left*) explores the wrecked bow of the schooner *Carroll A. Deering*, which was uncovered by a storm in 1940. It has been called a ghost ship because a 1921 rescue crew found it eerily deserted, except for a cat. *ABC, OBHC, SANC.*

Opposite, bottom: With no paved roads, an almost-every-time occurrence when traveling on Hatteras Island was getting stuck in the sand like these travelers near the Bodie Island Lighthouse in 1950. Passengers were expected to help dig or push. *ABC, OBHC, SANC.*

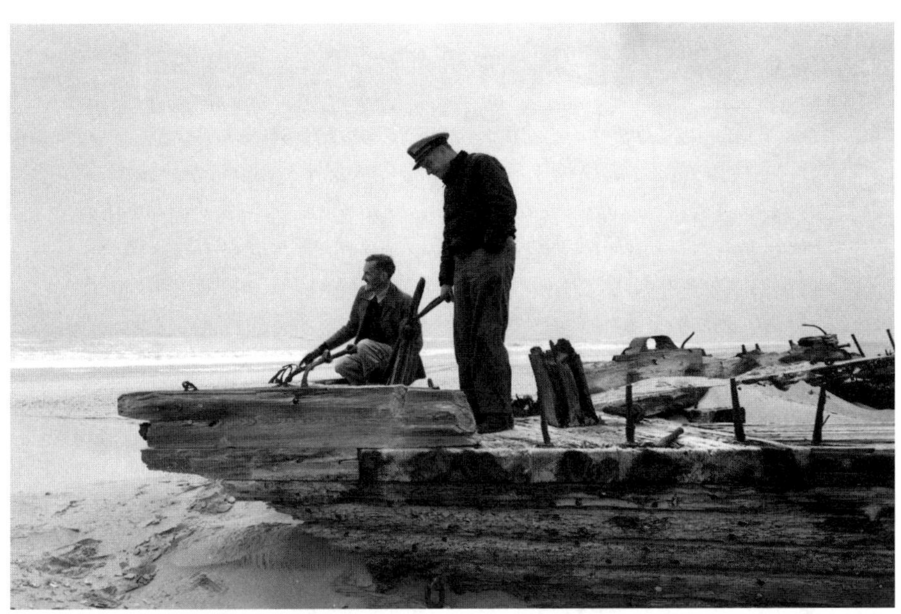

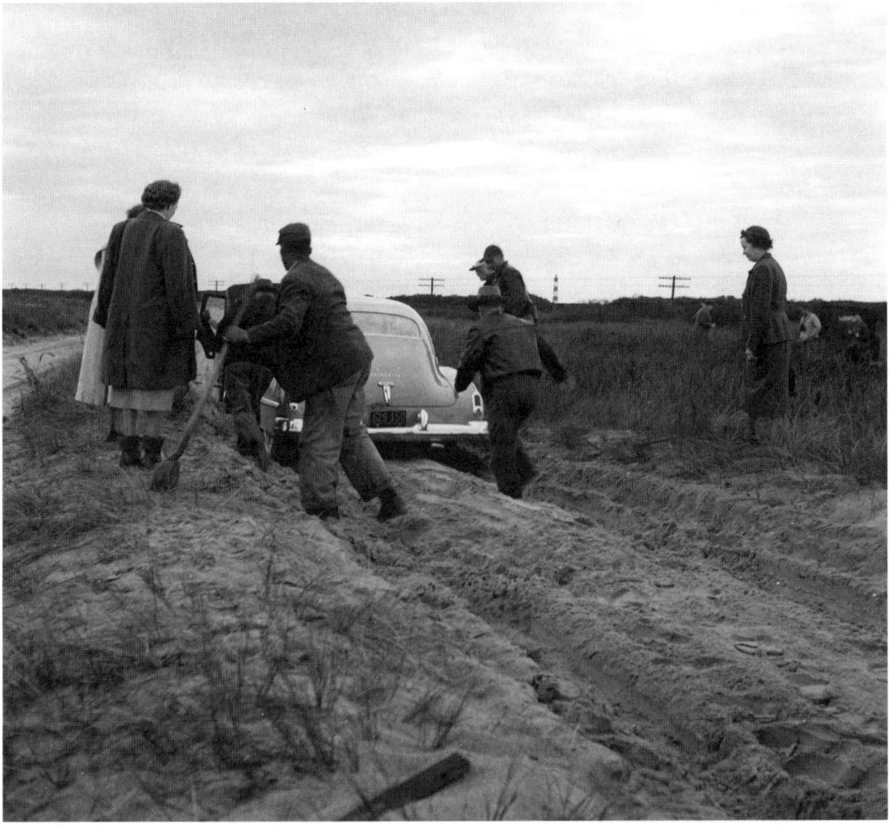

the Carolina Outer Banks, where people have been living for more than two centuries, so little noticed by, or noticing of, the outside world that they retain traces of seventeenth century, if not Elizabethan speech. The Outer Banks are a long barrier reef beginning in Virginia and extending more than half of the length of North Carolina, cut up occasionally into islands by inlets where the sea has burst through in storms.…Kitty Hawk, where the Wright Brothers first flew, is on the Banks, but in the past ten years the Currituck Sound has been bridged in the north and a paved highway carried as far as Roanoke Island, where the first English colony in America vanished between voyages of its supply ships. You drive to Roanoke Island as simply as to Atlantic City.

But from there south there are no roads. You can travel by boat.… You may even drive, if you know the trick of getting through deep and treacherous sand, or ride the daily station-wagon stage which struggles through the sand from Manteo to Hatteras, there connecting with a ferry to Ocracoke Island. You may, but very few do it, and so Hatteras and Ocracoke are what is known as unspoiled. There are half a dozen villages on Hatteras with 1,154 persons in all, by the 1940 census, and the one village of Ocracoke, on the island of that name, population 492. The only other settlement south of Roanoke Island is the dying village of Portsmouth, on Core Banks, which once was to have been a great port.…

Hatteras is the Cape Stormy of the Atlantic Coast, and there are few on the Banks who are not descendants of shipwrecked sailors, or of deserters from pirate ships, who first peopled [the Banks]. *In the lee of Ocracoke is Teach's Hole, where Edward Teach, otherwise known as Blackbeard, used to rendezvous and caulk his pirate ship, the* Queen Anne's Avenger [Revenge]. *He is supposed to have had the protection of Charles Eden, governor of the colony of Carolina, until Governor Spotswood of Virginia sent Lt. Robert Maynard* [of the Royal Navy] *and a sloop of war after him in 1718. Maynard sailed back to Williamsburg with Teach's severed head attached to the prow of his sloop, and thirteen prisoners in the hold, all duly tried and hanged.*

William Howard, who had been a quartermaster on Teach's craft, remained behind on Ocracoke with a handful of beached seamen. Twenty-one years later an Arab sailor named Wahab washed ashore from a wreck, the only survivor. These [folks] *began to find wives on the mainland. A daughter of William Howard married a son of the first Wahab and the Wahab-Howards became the first family of the Banks. Hatteras was peopled in the same fashion. There the most numerous clan today is the Midgettes, formerly spelled Midyettes.*

The National Park Service preserved large parts of Hatteras Island. As with any large-scale federal action in a remote area, it was not without controversy, as Aycock noted in the story.

One of the first acts of the Park Service was to banish the beach ponies from Hatteras, in the conviction that they were eating and trampling down the cover needed to hold the sand in place. Ocracoke has been allowed to keep its ponies and about one hundred of them roam the fourteen-mile length of the island. Their origin has been forgotten. They are hardy and easily

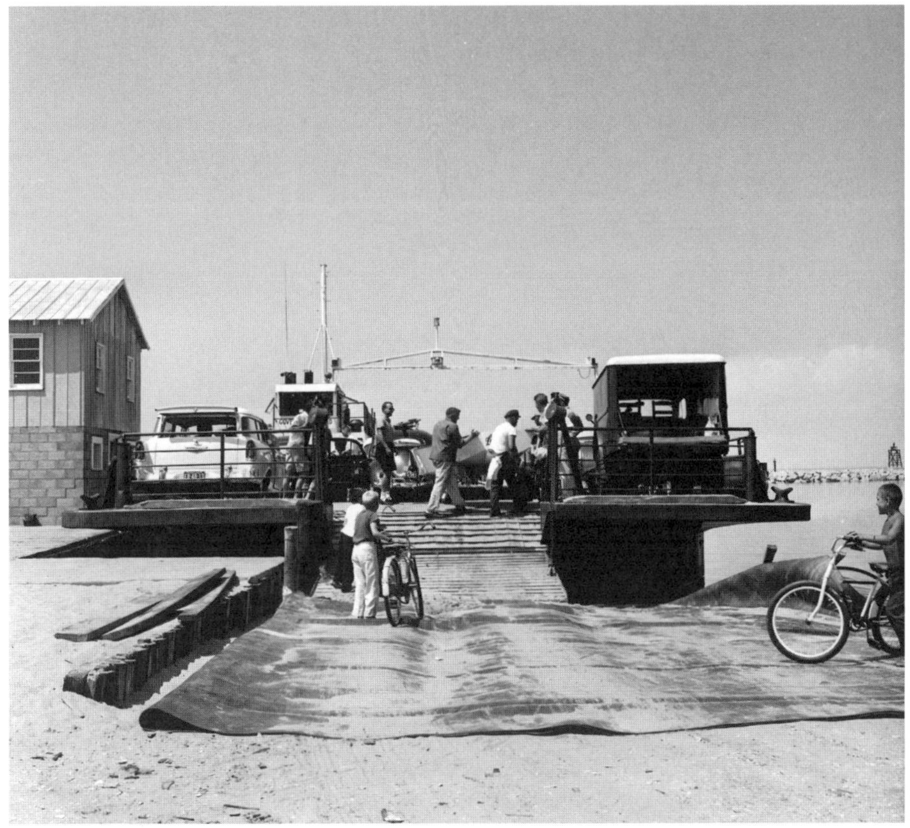

Aycock was on the beat when the National Park Service acquired land to form the Cape Hatteras National Seashore, which eventually opened in 1953. Transportation was greatly improved, including state-run ferries to Ocracoke. *ABC, OBHC, SANC.*

> *domesticated and are allowed to roam wild as cattle were in the West, with an annual roundup—penning—on July Fourth, when the owners of branded animals mark the spring's colt crop.*

In the story, Aycock gives scant treatment to the long and rich history of African Americans on the Outer Banks, writing only, in a tone sadly reflective of the time:

> *Probably there never was enough wealth or agriculture on the Banks to support slavery and there is only one Negro family on Ocracoke, none on Hatteras, though far up the island, at Pea Island, is the only Negro Coast Guard crew in the service, and a very good crew it is.*

Indeed. Starting with Captain Richard Etheridge's men in the late 1800s, the Pea Island crew held their own with the all-white crews all around

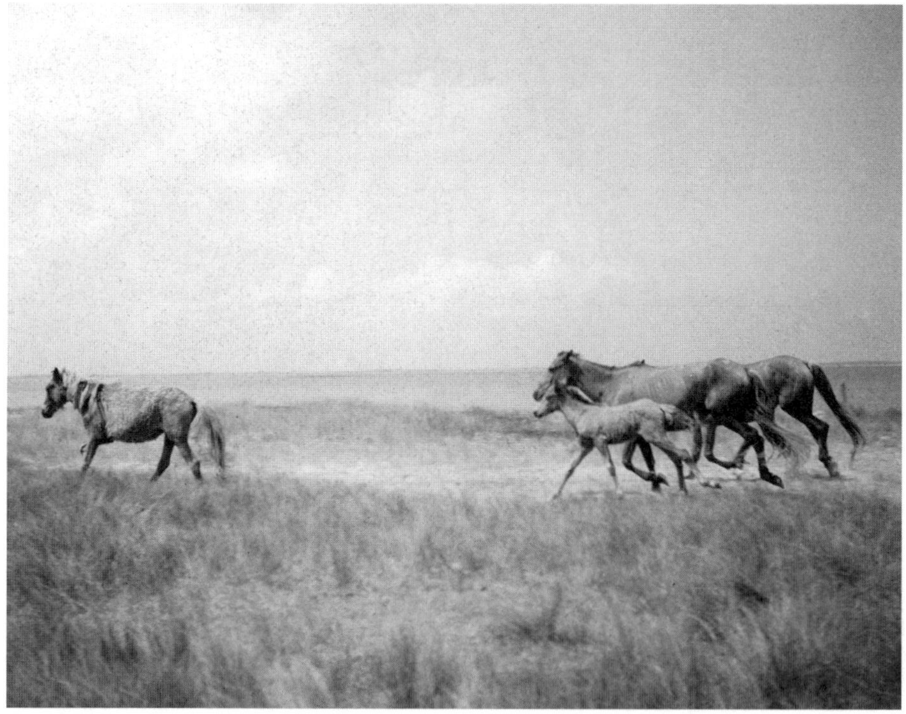

Possessing a knack for knowing what people wanted to see, Aycock photographed the scruffy wild ponies of Ocracoke Island in 1947 before they were an obsession with tourists. *ABC, OBHC, SANC.*

them, braving their lives to save numerous souls. And in the Civil War, Union General Ambrose Burnside led a legendary assault on Roanoke Island, a campaign that's still studied by the U.S. military today, seizing the island for the Union. The federal government established a freedmen's colony on the island, giving the formerly enslaved people land. As in the rest of the South, the colony died as Reconstruction did. But some proud Blacks held fast on Roanoke Island, establishing a strong community in Manteo called California.

Aycock was on firmer sand in writing about the Coast Guard on the Banks in general:

> *Relative to the population, the Banks have sent more men into that gallant service than any other region in the country. The reasons are two: With so little other opportunity, it is the ambition of three boys in four to enlist, and here is the greatest concentration of the Coast Guard—there are*

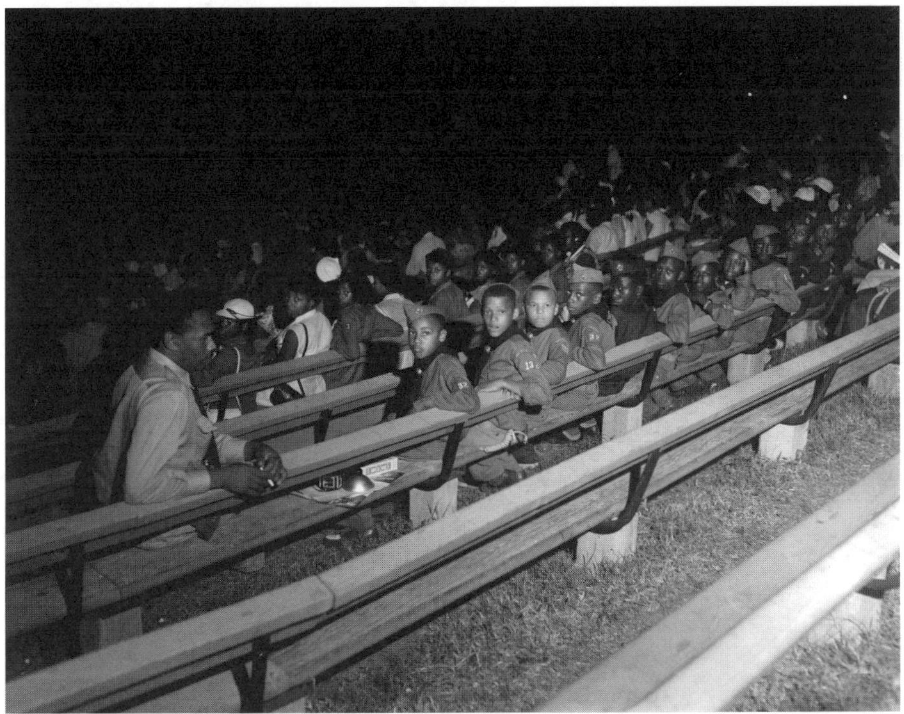

Aycock photographed this Boy Scout troop at Waterside Theatre listening to community speeches and attending a performance of *The Lost Colony* drama on African American Citizens Day in 1953. *ABC, OBHC, SANC.*

thirteen stations from the Virginia line to Beaufort [North Carolina]*; and there were twenty up to 1931. To be a great surfman, the natives agree, is the ultimate test of a man. In good weather and bad, surfmen patrol the beach nightly, like sentries walking posts. It takes courage and knowing how to walk the beach in a howling nor'easter with a hissing storm tide threatening to sweep across the Banks into the Sound, opening great gullies in their paths. It takes nine giants to launch a 3,000-pound lifeboat through brawling breakers; brawn and skill, too, where the least hesitation might slam the heavy boat down upon their broken bodies.*

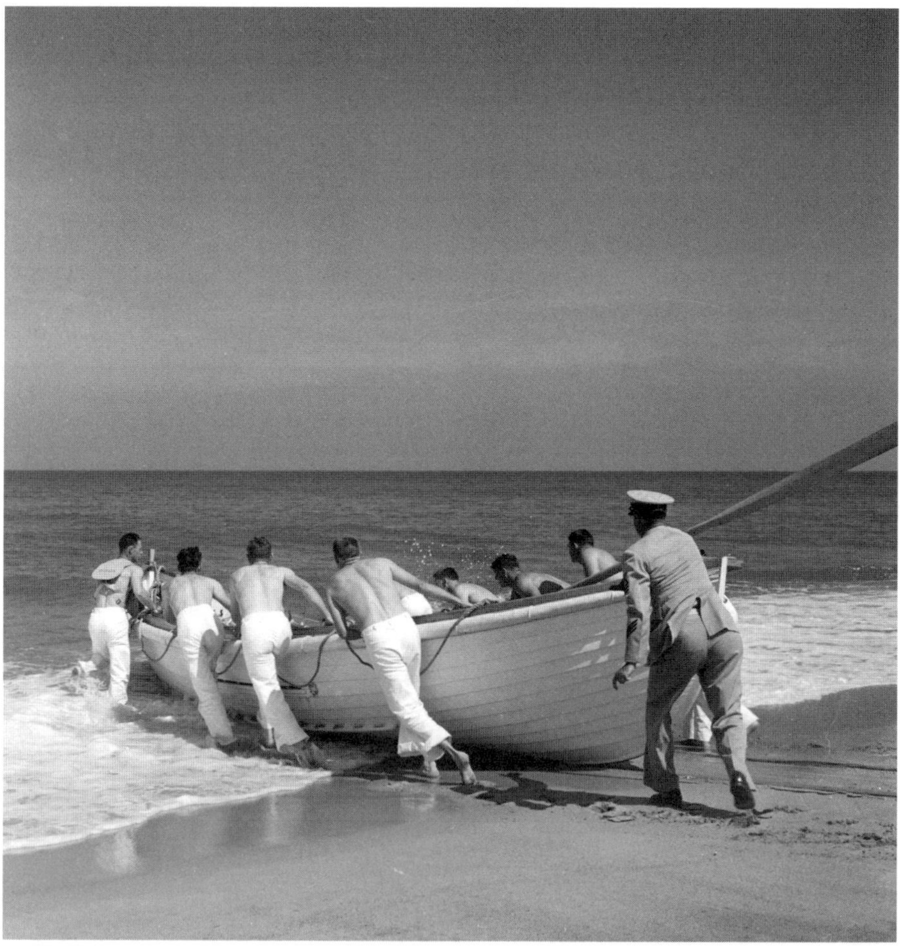

During a 1953 Coast Guard celebration, guardsmen reenact a rescue at sea. They must have been reminded of the strength and bravery of their Lifesaving Service predecessors when they launched the heavy wooden surfboat. *ABC, OBHC, SANC.*

Aycock's writing makes clear he'd come to intimately know the Coast Guardsmen and their courageous work. In his next passage, he refers to the precursor of the Coast Guard, the U.S. Lifesaving Service:

> *It was the Banks which gave the Service its unofficial watchword. One night when a vessel was breaking up on the outer reef at Hatteras and a crew was preparing to launch its surfboat, a rookie turned to the bos'n, saying: "I believe we can get out there, cap'n, but I don't believe we ever could get back."*
>
> *The bos'n spat away from the wind. "Don't fret about that, Bub," he answered. "All the regulations say is we got to go out there. The regulations don't say a damn thing about having to come back."*

Aycock wrote on:

> *Hatteras just doesn't happen to be stormy. Its restless weather is due to the meeting of the Gulf Stream with the waters of the North Atlantic just offshore, the closest approach the Stream makes to land north of southern Florida. From here it veers far to sea. Its nearness gives the Banks a winter climate many degrees more moderate than the nearby North Carolina mainland.... This is the farthest north you will find Spanish Moss, the growth of that air plant being governed by nearness to the sea as well as by latitude. The palmetto and yucca grow profusely amidst live oaks, red and white myrtles, cedars, yaupons and fig trees. The flood tides are death to flower gardens, but the late Joe Bell, a retired jeweler who sought peace and contentment at Ocracoke, brought one packet of Gaillardia seed with him and it has spread astonishingly. To natives it will always be "Joe Bell" flowers....*
>
> [The islanders] *live by the tides rather than by clocks or calendars, for fishing, commercial or sport; crabbing, hard or soft-shelled; clamming; are governed by the tides. Because the tides are governed by the moon, the moon is supreme in their folklore. They believe implicitly that death comes on the ebb tide.... You will look a long while before you find a clock, or a man or a woman who can name the day of the month. Meal hours vary, according to the tide, fishermen watching the water rather than the sun. In the Pamlico Inn, at Ocracoke, the only clock is one by which the cook boils the eggs.*

Aycock wrote of the challenges of driving in sand and the practical joys of going barefoot:

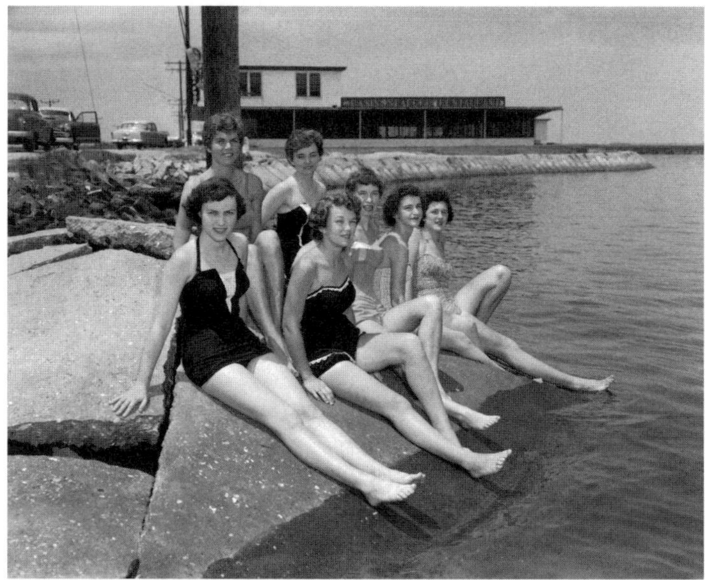

In 1955, waitresses in swimwear pose on the Nags Head Causeway with the Oasis Restaurant in the background. As a come-on for more business, the Oasis advertised that its waitstaff served their tables while barefooted. *ABC, OBHC, SANC.*

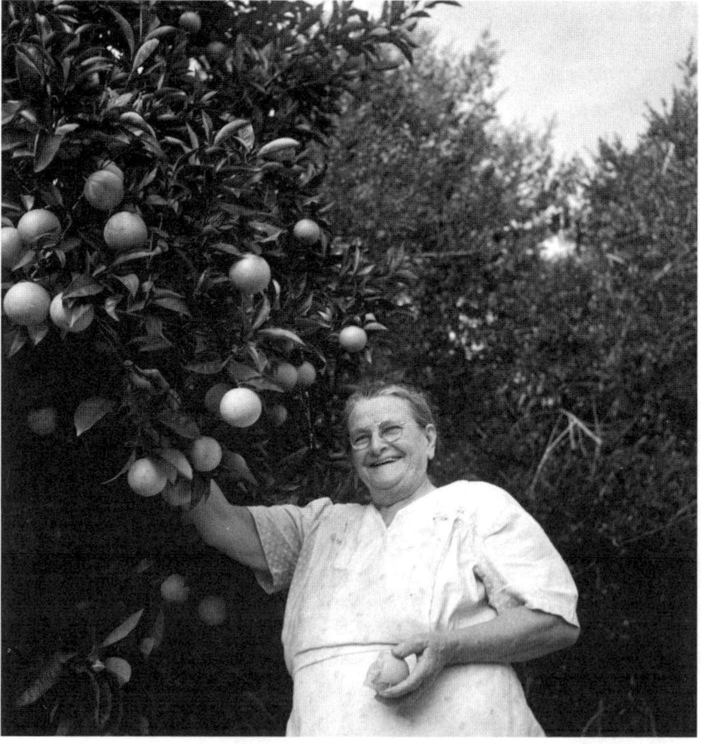

A Mrs. Barnett of Buxton proudly shows off her orange tree full of fruit at her home in 1954. Many residents of Hatteras Island have been able to grow citrus and tropical fruit trees because of warm Gulf Stream breezes. *ABC, OBHC, SANC.*

> *As on the prairie before roads were graded, a driver follows the last passer-by's tracks as long as they seem passable, and makes a new track when older tracks look forbidding. On the Banks, men, women and children usually go barefoot from May until October, not so much to save shoe leather as because walking in sand is less laborious barefooted.*

It was Aycock at his best, an amateur anthropologist showing sand-smarts and subtle love for his adopted home.

Outer Banks vacationers had been mostly limited to wealthy landowners from northeastern North Carolina who could afford long vacations and access by slow steamboats. They started staying on the Soundside in Nags Head and then gradually moved to the oceanfront. The Currituck Sound bridge began to change it all in 1930. With speedier access, blue-collar and middle-class families streamed onto the Banks, staying in mom-and-pop hotels and cottages rented by the week that quickly sprouted up to accommodate them.

But there was nothing like the overdevelopment hitting beaches in the coastal states north of Carolina such as the Jersey shore. *The Saturday Evening Post* story was a breakthrough in introducing Northerners, and the rest of the world, to the Outer Banks, laying it all out mystically and magically, a fantasyland.

The article was also Aycock's personal breakthrough. After the story came out in August 1940, he heard from the governor, he told David Stick in the 1974 interview:

> *The governor of North Carolina, Clyde Hoey, his secretary, Bob Thompson, called me up and said, "Mr. Hoey thinks that's the best story that's ever been written about the Outer Banks." I guess it was up to that time, because there hadn't been too many stories written about the Outer Banks.... The photographs were terrific. So he* [Thompson] *said, "He wants to do something for you, and what he wants you to do is to take the state boat, the* Hatteras*"—that was the name of the state boat they had at that time, it was a 75-footer converted Coast Guard boat. "He wants you to take a cruise up through the waters of North Carolina. All expenses. You don't have to buy anything at all." I said, "Well, I don't know whether I can do that now, because my wife's pregnant and she's going to have another baby," and I said, "I don't know whether I can do that." So he said, "Well, see if you can't arrange it. Get a doctor to go along with you." I said, "Well, that's an idea. I've got a*

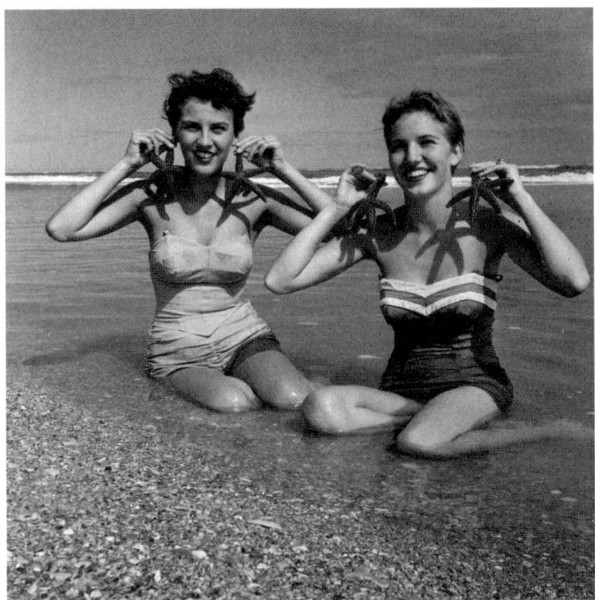

Promoting a new kind of "ear ornament," *(from left)* Shirlie Barnett and Connie Basnight of Buxton helped Aycock compose the kind of gimmicky shot that would make editors look twice and run his photos in their papers. *ABC, OBHC, SANC.*

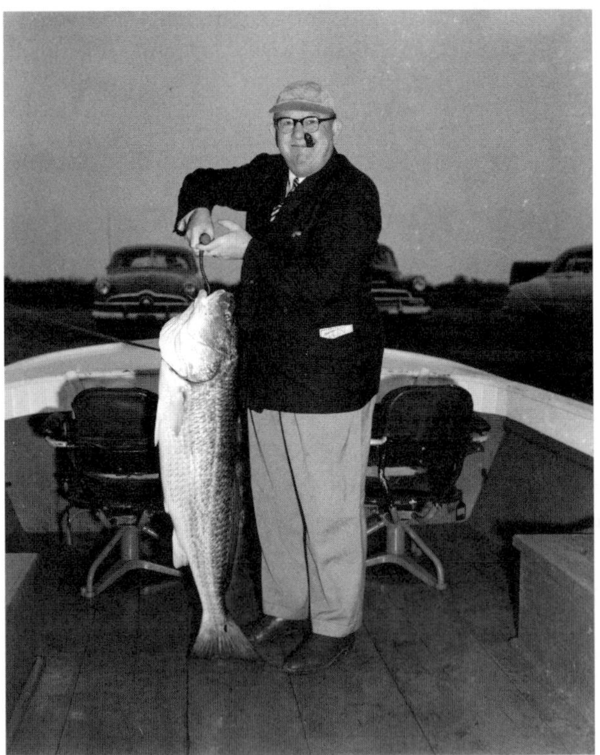

With a grin and a celebratory cigar, U.S. Senator Homer Capehart of Indiana displays a huge drum in 1953. Senators were invited to fish offshore to introduce them to the new Cape Hatteras National Seashore. *ABC, OBHC, SANC.*

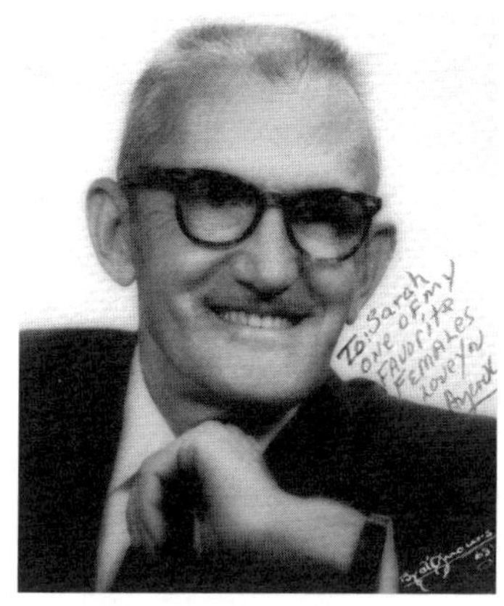

As was the practice of the times, Aycock inscribed his portrait by writing directly on the photograph. He was obviously joking with his coworker and longtime friend Sarah Owens. *Charles D'Amours, RV Owens.*

friend here [in Beaufort], *a doctor who's working himself to death, maybe he needs a vacation." So I went to see Dr. Moore....He said, "Well, you know, I think I will go."... We left Morehead City on the boat and got to Ocracoke. I was expecting to be a big hero over there, but, God, the people...just saw me coming, and they walked away. I didn't last very long.*

The News & Observer later reported:

"You said we don't have a clock on the island," someone accosted him. "I've got a clock." Aycock tried desperately to explain that he had tried to infer that Ocracoke tells the time more by tide than by clock. In fact, he had suggested a title, "Where Tide Means Time."

Aycock, like many journalists before him and after, was shot down after an initially warm reception for one of his biggest stories. Perhaps he couldn't help feeling that he'd failed some of his most valued sources, his wife's fellow islanders, the ones from whom he'd expected and needed praise. There's an old saying in newspaper work: Reporters don't have thin skins. They have no skins.

But things got better, as the Raleigh paper reported: "Any ruffled feelings caused by his incisive observations about Ocracoke customs and manner of speech were soon erased by the influx of vacationers and the accompanying cash."

All in all, history would smile on "Cape Stormy." Aycock would never again write anything close to its length or power. It's like he was channeling Robert Louis Stevenson of *Treasure Island* fame, maybe one of his idols. "Cape Stormy" would become Aycock's bible of sorts, his foundation for introducing the world to the marvtastic seashore on which he'd been lucky enough to land. He nicknamed his daughter "Stormy Gale" in honor of the story.

He'd learned from the story's reception, listening all the more closely to his sources. It would be disingenuous to say that Aycock didn't continue to exploit his sources for the outside world. He did. Often, if not usually, his sources were in on the exploitation and Aycock's often gimmicky shots to promote them. He was bringing them much-needed tourist dollars.

Aycock would build on "Cape Stormy" in the years ahead. But first came World War II and the war off our Banks.

2

"THE HORROR IN THEIR EYES"

Off the Outer Banks
1942

Up and down the Outer Banks, gunfire and explosions punctuated the rumble of the surf, burning ships illuminated the nighttime horizon, oil fouled the waters, and debris littered the beach.
—David Stick in An Outer Banks Reader

Aycock, in his mid-thirties as World War II broke out, couldn't serve in the military because of faulty eyesight and the injury he sustained laying pipe in the Delaware River. But he and other heroes would rise on the home front.

One of Aycock's many newspaper contacts, Davenport Steward of Acme Newspapers, anticipated in a March 22, 1941 letter to Aycock what he might encounter on the Outer Banks:

> *There's more than a bare possibility that a German submarine may poke its snout into your harbor one of these days. At the moment, there's no reason to expect that your town will be shelled; but there's every chance in the world that some U-boat may be disabled and chased inside by some British or Allied craft operating just off the coast. So—and please keep this letter handy—if a German sub actually does show up, we'll appreciate your remembering ACME Newspapers.*

The Japanese military attacked Pearl Harbor on December 7, 1941, prompting President Franklin Roosevelt to declare war on Japan, which had joined Germany in the Axis powers.

Aycock secured a job as a civilian intelligence officer in the Navy, working off the Outer Banks. On January 26, 1942, he signed a contract with Naval Intelligence to perform "Coastal Information duties and other duties of Naval Intelligence as may be assigned."

Navy officials recognized Aycock's burgeoning photographic talents and his knowledge of the North Carolina coast. "The Navy hired his talents ($325 a month and a liberal expense account) as a civilian agent," a North Carolina journalist later reported. "He was one of the few men employed in that capacity by the Navy during the war."

Aycock knew that close to five hundred ships had been lost off the Outer Banks since the late 1500s in the Graveyard of the Atlantic. He knew that in World War I, German U-boats sank American ships off the Outer Banks. Now the Germans were returning. (U-boat and submarine are often used interchangeably for the German subs in both world wars. U-boat came from the German word for submarine, *Unterseeboot* or "undersea boat.")

Aycock covered the attacks of German submarines on merchant and Navy ships off the Outer Banks. He bore witness to an unbelievable nightmare, at one point telling someone on the mainland: "If you don't

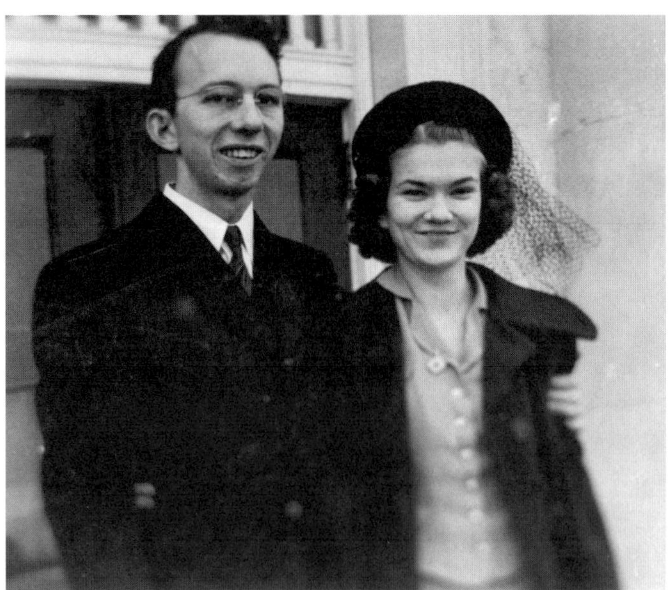

Perhaps historically inaccurate in this instance, Aycock labeled this photograph as the first man drafted in World War II. Looking shockingly young, John Edward Lawton and his wife posed in Morehead City, North Carolina, in 1941. *ABC, OBHC, SANC.*

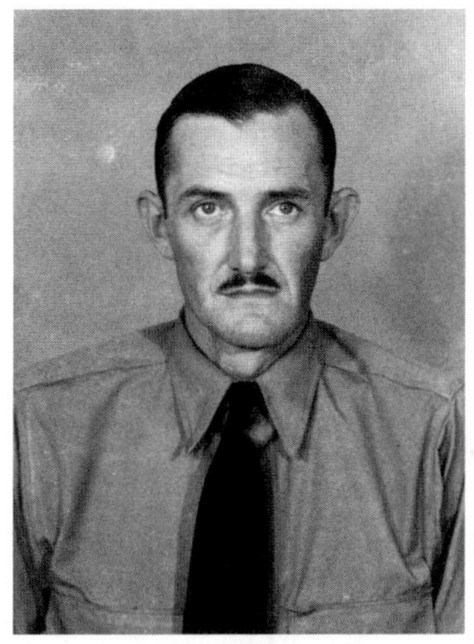

Aycock posed for his military identification picture with a somber expression and no glasses. Serving the Navy as a civilian agent, he would use his photographic skills and his familiarity with the coast to help the war effort. *ABC, OBHC, SANC.*

believe it, I'll hold the telephone out the window and you can hear the booms."

Despite all the books and articles about the war off our coast, it's still horribly incredible to consider, and many of our children have no idea that a world war came home to us. Outer Banks houses were often rattled by the reverberations of German subs torpedoing our ships and those of our allies. Parents and their children saw night skies glow orange in the aftermath of attacks offshore. Headlights on cars were masked, leaving small holes for the beams. At night, residents were required to pull shades over their windows so the German couldn't spot their lights. Residents posted Army-issued signs on their property:

HELP
Save the Lives
of
Our Men at Sea
Pull Shades All the Way Down
When Lights Are on –
Turn Off All Lights
When Leaving
Room

As the war began, one of Aycock's possible heroes, the journalist-turned-novelist Ernest Hemingway, was cruising out from his Cuban home aboard his boat the *Pilar* in a fruitless hunt of German submarines that was maybe more about getting scarce gas to hunt marlin. Hemingway would go on to put his boots on the ground in war coverage in Germany. But in 1942, Aycock beat him to the punch in risking his psyche and soul.

Aycock reported submarine sightings, shot photos of torpedoed ships, and examined bodies recovered and washed ashore, using photos, fingerprints, and interviews with survivors to identify them. He also arranged for burials.

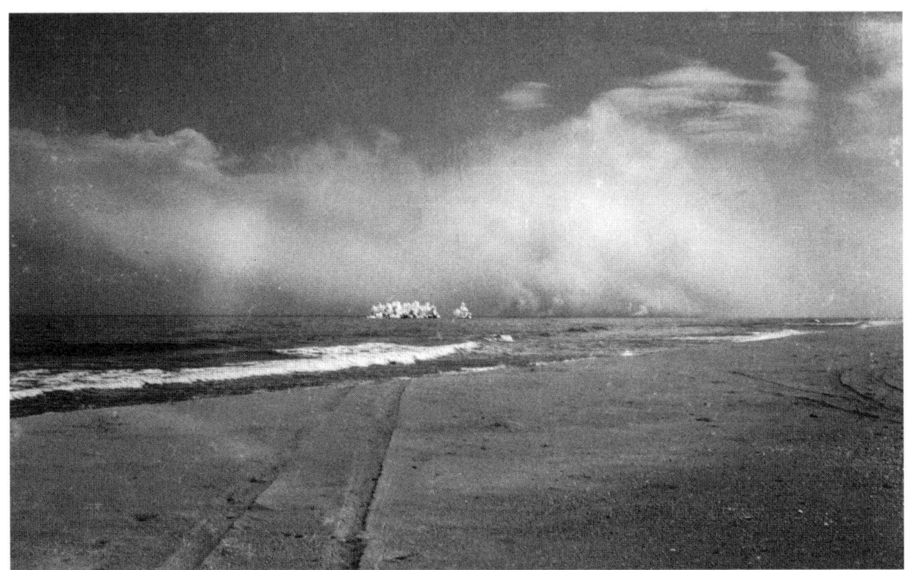

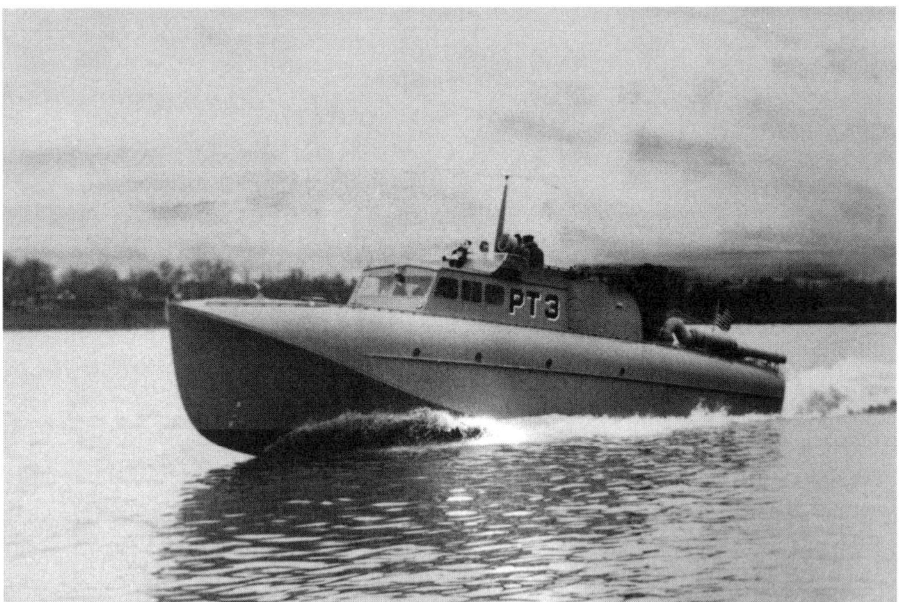

Top: A 1942 explosion was captured off Ocracoke. The nation was broadsided by Germany's U-boat assaults making U.S. coastal shipping lanes a sea of death. Seagoing men soon nicknamed the hammered area "Torpedo Junction." *ABC, OBHC, SANC.*

Bottom: PT (patrol torpedo) boats, made to speed to wreck sites, were constructed for the war effort at Manteo Boatbuilding Corporation. Ocracoke's Silver Lake Harbor was dredged deeper to handle military boats. *ABC, OBHC, SANC.*

The war off our shore was accelerating, as David Stick noted in *An Outer Banks Reader* and *Graveyard of the Atlantic:*

> *In the first six months of 1942, the handful of submarines involved in* [the Germans'] *Operation Drumbeat cut a frightful swath through Allied shipping, sinking more than five dozen vessels in North Carolina waters alone. Before long, the area around Cape Hatteras earned an unflattering nickname, Torpedo Junction. Up and down the Outer Banks, gunfire and explosions punctuated the rumble of the surf, burning ships illuminated the nighttime horizon, oil fouled the waters, and debris littered the beach.*
>
> *Simply stated, the reason for this early success by Nazi submarine raiders was that the Germans had concentrated on the development of U-boat warfare while this phase of naval preparedness was relegated to a comparatively unimportant status by the United States. Thus, the outbreak of war in December 1941 found Hitler with a large and fully trained undersea fleet, and when this fleet attacked shipping along our coast it had about a hard a time of it as a hunter shooting into a pool of tame ducks.*

Aycock typed several pages on his work, calling it the "War Diary of Agent Aycock Brown." In the decades after, numerous articles and nonfiction books were written about the war just off our coast, as well an iconic novel for young people, Nell Wise Wechter's *Taffy of Torpedo Junction.* Aycock's diary remains fascinating because it is fine contemporaneous writing by an insider. His diary writing is markedly different from his newspaper writing. It is, by design, matter of fact, devoid of his usual color and hyperbole. In its tone, it's reminiscent of the early journalism of Hemingway: You can read much between the lines, including the pain Aycock must have felt viewing the corpses, suppressing that pain to do his job.

He wrote about the deaths, and he wrote about "briefing" survivors, often wounded in torpedo attacks, gathering any intelligence to help the Allied effort. His job also entailed investigating reports of suspicious citizens, usually ones with German names. On the West Coast of the United States, Japanese American citizens were being interned in prison camps. In sharp contrast, that never happened to Americans of German descent. But along the Outer Banks, suspicions raged. Aycock investigated several rumors.

From his 1942 diary:

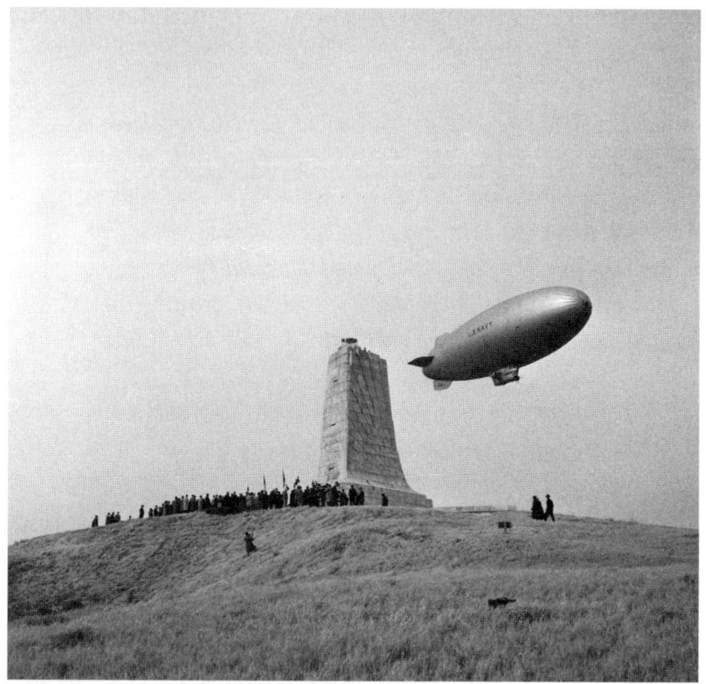

Outer Banks residents saw U.S. Navy airships during World War II patrolling the coastline, looking for enemy submarines below the water's surface. This blimp was present at the celebration of fifty years of flight at the Wright Brothers National Monument in 1953. *ABC, OBHC, SANC.*

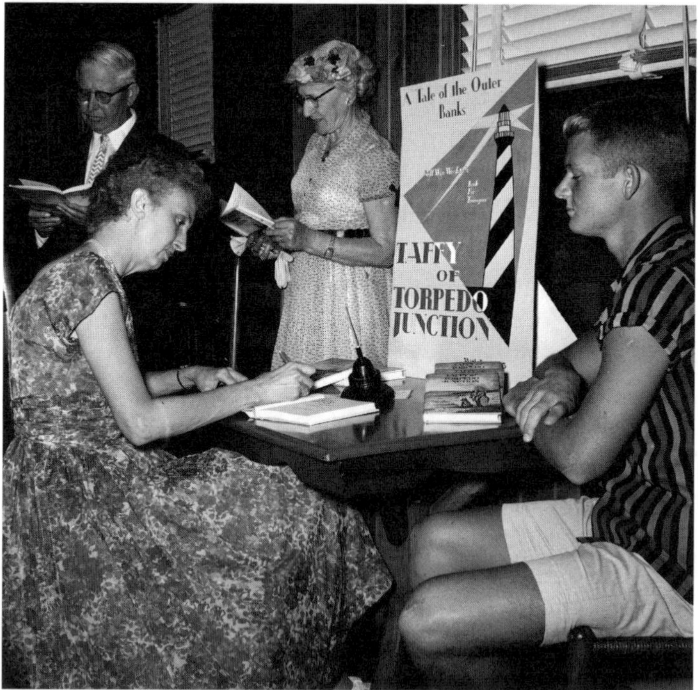

In 1957, Stumpy Point resident and schoolteacher Nell Wise Wechter signs her newly published book *Taffy of Torpedo Junction*. It is a fictional account of a Hatteras girl who helps capture Nazi spies during World War II that is still read today. *ABC, OBHC, SANC.*

> *31 January: Rumors were spreading on Harkers Island* [south of the Outer Banks] *that —— a teacher at the island's public school was possibly connected with subversive activity. Investigations revealed that the rumors were false. Similar rumors were current in Swansboro, N.C., that ——, a German-born merchant, was an enemy agent, that he was selling "white gas" from a container marked "aviation gas," that he had made mysterious trips to lonely Bear Island near Bogue Inlet, no doubt for the purpose of contacting submarines or supplying them with fuel or provisions. Following a most careful investigation during which time Bear Island was visited by this agent, the results of investigation proved negative.* [The suspect], *however, will be kept under surveillance by the Army patrols, State Highway patrol officers and contacts of this agent.*
>
> *17 February: In Swan Quarter and Engelhard, N.C., have started investigation of —— and members of his family (who according to rumors are suspicious characters) and* [another man] *German born (and one-time-machine gunner in the German army).* [They] *were kept under surveillance for a number of months, were investigated by FBI and state law enforcement agencies and also Naval Intelligence. Results of all investigations were negative.*

Rumors abounded, including one that some crewmen off a German submarine sneaked onto Nags Head one night and partied at the Casino, a nightclub that had opened in 1937 and quickly became a beach bedrock. And some locals swore that a couple of German submariners—or spies—had ventured onto Roanoke Island, where they watched a movie at the Pioneer Theater in Manteo.

Aycock's work soon became consumed with identifying those killed in ships torpedoed by German subs, whether those bodies were found at sea or washed ashore. It was dangerous, haunting work. Military pilots flew Aycock over torpedoed ships so he could shoot photos of the burning carnage in the waters he'd come to love.

In peacetime, he'd come to know that these waters could churn into huge waves that wrecked ships, but this was his descent into the hell man could unfurl.

From his 1942 diary:

> *12 February: Have interviewed Captain Cornelius Sanders, skipper of the fishing trawler* Two Sisters. *A few days previously he had rescued… survivors from a tanker (*Empire Gem*) which had been torpedoed off*

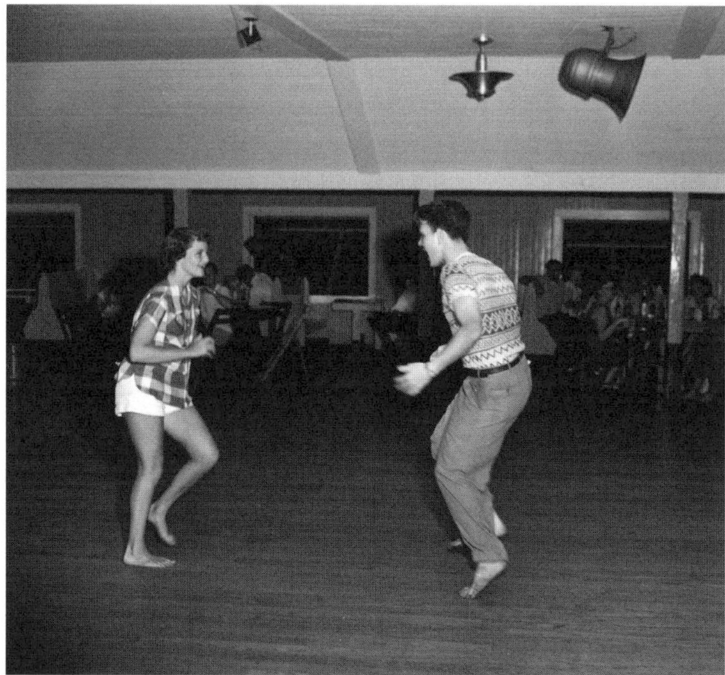

Rumors began flying during wartime. Stories circulated that German U-boats would surface off Nags Head at night so the sailors could listen to music from the Casino. There were also tales of Germans swimming ashore to enter the dance hall. *ABC, OBHC, SANC.*

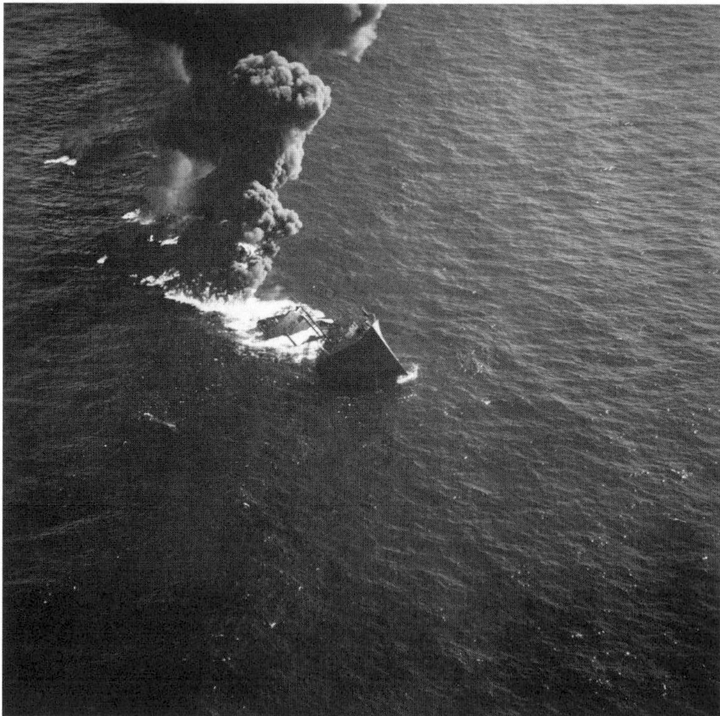

The British tanker *Empire Gem* was less than a year old when German *U-66* torpedoed it off Diamond Shoals on January 24, 1942. The ship was fully loaded with gasoline. Only two of fifty-seven crewmembers survived. *Naval History and Heritage Command.*

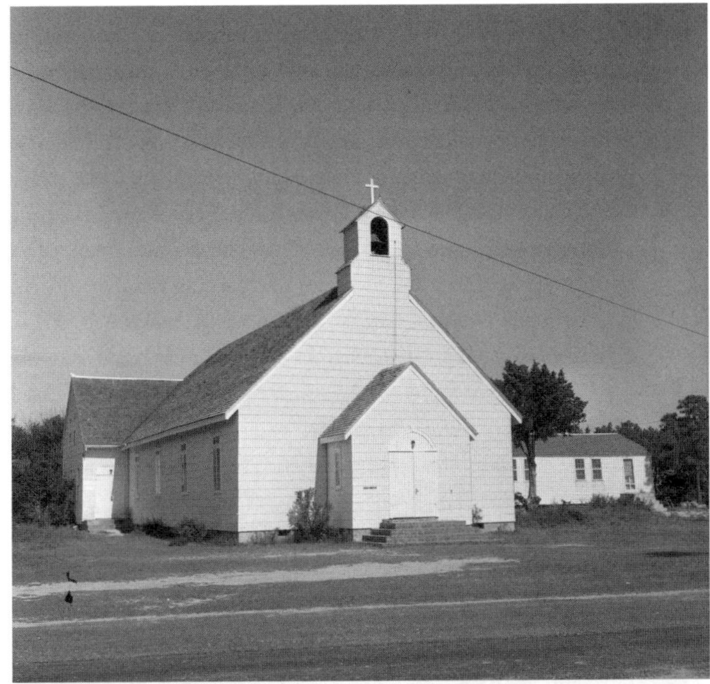

The war became more personal for Ocracokers when Jim Baum Gaskill was killed while serving on the torpedoed merchant ship *Caribsea*. A cross made out of a salvaged wood from *Caribsea* stands on the altar of the Ocracoke United Methodist Church in Gaskill's honor. *ABC, OBHC, SANC.*

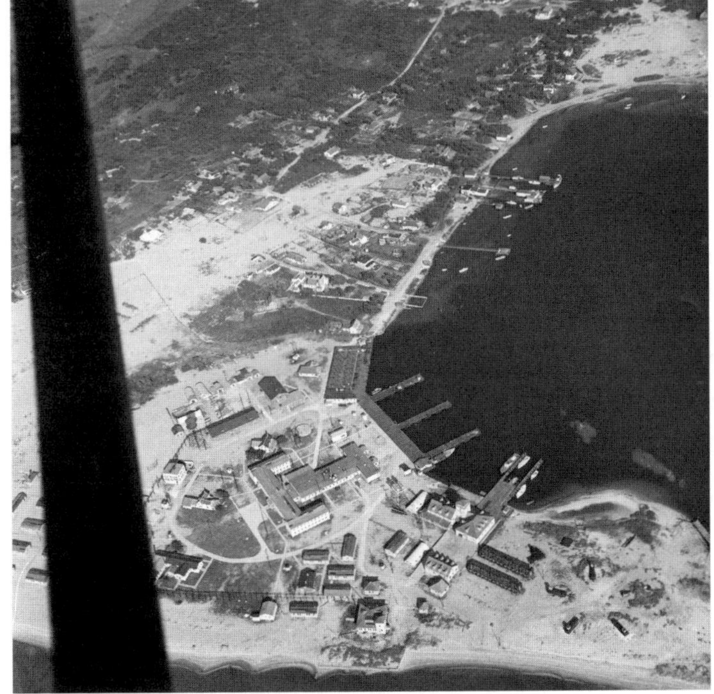

The Ocracoke Naval Station Base was constructed in 1942 as support for an anchorage at Hatteras. An influx of military men caused Ocracoke's population to double. The Navy built the island's first concrete road, from the station to an ammunitions dump. *ABC, OBHC, SANC.*

Cape Hatteras. Captain Sanders expressed the opinion that southbound trawlers from the Norfolk area had been followed at night by "submarines with running lights reversed." This report could not be verified.

The tail end of the report could not be verified, but the bombing of the *Empire Gem* was fact. Aycock reportedly shot aerial photos of the tanker ablaze. His work continued.

11 March: On this date the S.S. Caribsea [of the Merchant Marine], *a small American ship of 1,610 tons, was torpedoed and sank in 9 fathoms approximately 13 miles east northeast of Cape Lookout. On the streets of Beaufort, N.C., the news was spreading that the torpedoing had taken place. C.G.* [Coast Guard] *lifeboats were searching the area for survivors or bodies. The ill-fated little ship had sunk in less than two minutes. Five survivors were taken to Norfolk for* [military] *briefing.*

13 March: While Coast Guard lifeboats were still in the area where the S.S. Caribsea *was torpedoed two days ago, a frame containing the Mate's License of James Baum Gaskill washed ashore on Ocracoke Island, 30 miles up the coast. Gaskill was 2nd Officer aboard the ship. It was an ironic twist of fate that the license of Gaskill should come ashore on Ocracoke, because Ocracoke was his home.*

Outer Banks author Charles Harry Whedbee, referring to James Gaskill as "Jim," known and loved on the island for his "sunny disposition," courage, honesty and loyalty, wrote in 1966 that the nameplate of Jim's boat washed up at the dock of the Pamlico Inn on Ocracoke, which Gaskill's parents owned and where Aycock had gotten his start on that island. The nameplate apparently surfaced shortly after the license. In his book *Legends of the Outer Banks and Tar Heel Tidewater*, Whedbee wrote:

To Jim, the sea was a way of life. That ocean near his doorstep was always referred to as "she" or "her," never as "it" or "that." The sea was both a generous mother and a raging she-devil, depending on her mood.

Whedbee continued:

The Caribsea *was not a fighting vessel. She was slow, fat and clumsy, but she could do the job for which she was built and could help to fill a need more urgent than most Americans knew* [to help keep the lines of supply open]. *A machine gun on her foredeck and a hastily installed small cannon on her stern comprised her only armament and her sole protection during her assigned travels in the offshore waters of the eastern seaboard.*

Before the war, Aycock might have wondered what kind of people might be manning the ships he'd see on the horizon. Now, he came to briefly know some of them, ones who spoke English and others who spoke in foreign tongues, bonded by endurance and courage, bearing witness to watery flames.

16 March: Assisted in briefing survivors from torpedoed tanker Olean *when they were brought to Section Base, Morehead City. In the crew of 39 there were four dead, two missing and four hospital cases. Following briefing of survivors this agent went to* [the] *morgue, fingerprinted, photographed and succeeded in identifying the bodies of four persons from* Olean.

17 March: Assisted in briefing survivors of Greek ship Kasanda Louloudis *which had been torpedoed off Cape Hatteras.*

18 March: The tanker E.M. Clark *was torpedoed off Ocracoke Island on this date. Fourteen members of the crew were brought to Morehead City where this agent assisted in briefing them. Of the crew of 41, one person was reportedly killed.*

19 March: The S.S. Liberator, *an ore* [earth metals] *carrier was torpedoed and sank off Cape Hatteras this date. The survivors were transferred first to Ocracoke C.G. station thence to Morehead City where this agent assisted in briefing.*

23 March: The S.S. Naeco, *a tanker which had sailed from Bolivar Roads, Texas, was torpedoed off Cape Lookout on this date. Of 38 crew members only 14 survived the torpedoing. The survivors were brought to Morehead City, N.C., where this Agent assisted in the briefing. Four bodies were also brought to port and prepared for burial.... The bodies were photographed and fingerprinted by this agent. (On April 5, the nude body of a man, wearing a life jacket bearing name of S.S.* Naeco, *washed ashore near Cape Lookout. The body was in such an advanced stage of decomposition it was impossible to secure fingerprints or make identification. Upon instructions of the ship's owners, the body was buried in Morehead City on or about 15 April.)*

24 March: A tanker, the Nashville, *broke in half after being torpedoed southwest of Beaufort on 23 March. The bow sank but the stern remained afloat and was towed into Morehead City early tonight.*

> *In spite of the* [conditions] *this Agent boarded the half ship, searched the engine room crew quarters, confiscated letters and forwarded them.... This half-ship remained in Morehead City for several weeks, was finally towed to Norfolk.*

Aycock made no mention of the obvious danger he'd undertaken in roaming around on a "half-ship."

> *25 March: A bullet-riddled life raft from the S.S.* Olean *was towed to Fort Macon Coast Guard Station today. The* Olean *had been sunk by the enemy off Cape Lookout on 16 March. Photographs of the raft were made upon the supposition that the enemy sub which sunk the* Olean *may have machine-gunned the survivors after they were adrift in the raft.*

Aycock left it at that. But with his writer's heart, he must have been imagining those men on the life raft in their last terrible moments, having survived a bombing only to be mercilessly shot. He must have wondered where their bodies went. That was his job, whatever it meant in a world

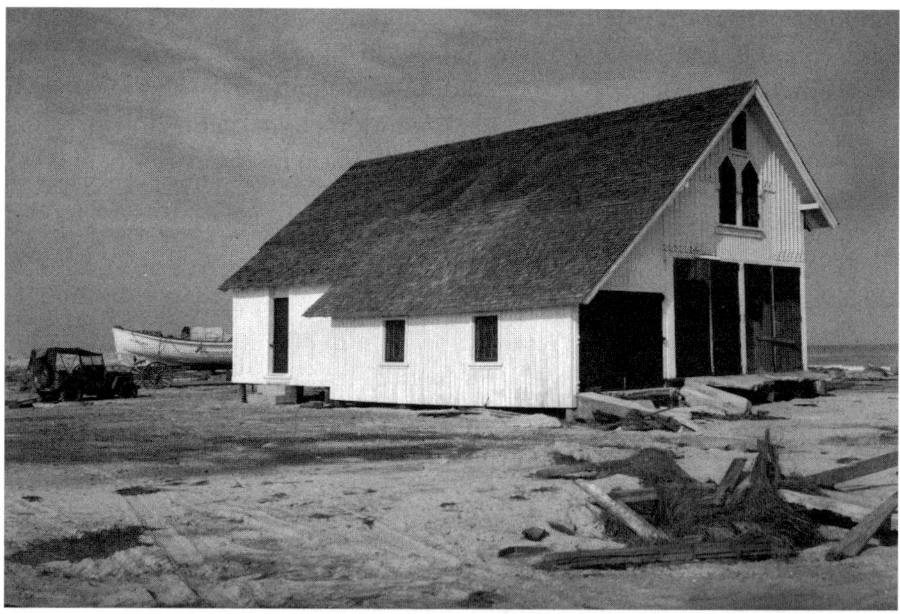

This photo exhibiting the effects of war on Ocracoke Island shows faint numbers on the roof of a Coast Guard boathouse. In the rear, a wooden rescue surfboat cradled in a horse-drawn cart stands in contrast to a military Jeep. *ABC, OBHC, SANC.*

turned upside down, just to identify the lifeless shells of the war-dead souls and let their survivors know closure but not peace.

> *10 April: On this date the S.S.* Tamaulipas *was torpedoed off the North Carolina coast. Of 37 crewmembers, two were reported missing. Nine of the crew were wounded and had to be entered at Morehead City hospital. The survivors were debriefed by this agent and* [other] *personnel...upon their arrival in Morehead City.*
>
> *10 April: The S.S.* Atlas, *torpedoed off Cape Lookout on 9 April, had a crew of 34 persons of which two were lost. The survivors were taken to Morehead City and briefed by this agent and* [other] *personnel. The two bodies were brought to Morehead City and photographed and identified by this agent. There were five hospital cases.*
>
> *10 April: The British Tanker* San Delfino, *laden with high-test gasoline and bound from a Texas port to Great Britain, was torpedoed off Cape Hatteras on this date. Of a crew of 49, 28 were reported missing, the survivors were brought to Morehead City...and interviewed by this Agent and* [others]. *There were several hospital cases. A number*

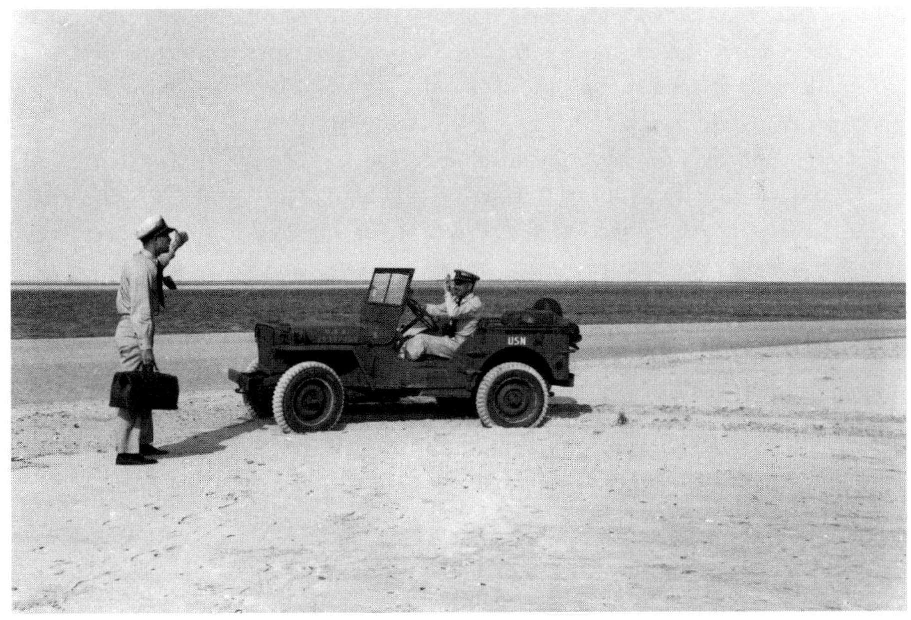

Humor helped servicemen cope with loneliness and stress. In 1942 on quiet Ocracoke, there was no outlet for the men. No entertainment, no liquor, and a lack of available women made it a place few wanted to be stationed. *ABC, OBHC, SANC.*

> *of bodies washed ashore after this sinking, one being Maldwyn Jones, a soldier and member of the gun crew, two other bodies were G. Fisher and R. Watt.*
>
> *11 April: Assist*[ed]*…in briefing survivors of torpedoed tanker Harry F. Sinclair Jr. This ship with crew of 37 was torpedoed off Cape Lookout, with loss of two crewmembers known dead and eight missing. The two bodies which had been brought to the morgue in Morehead City were photographed, fingerprinted and identified by this agent.*
>
> *14 April: In Hatteras a group of enterprising fishermen had salvaged certain articles from the S.S.* Australia *which had been torpedoed near Diamond Shoals on 17 March. They had taken the salvaged articles… to Norfolk and as they were attempting to find market for same, various enforcement agencies including Coast Guard, FBI, Customs and Naval Intelligence had temporarily placed a restraining order prohibiting sale due to the fact it had been salvaged from a British ship.*

Aycock was called in to investigate. In his summary of the incident, he applied his knowledge of Outer Banks traditions:

> *It was learned that the fishermen never gave a thought that perhaps they were doing anything wrong; that they were merely acting in the role of "wreckers," an honorable profession of their forefathers along the coast at Hatteras.*
>
> *22 April: Conduct an extensive investigation of Ensign* —— [who had a German name], *engineering officer aboard a vessel being outfitted in Elizabeth City. It had been reported to FBI that this officer may have subversive tendencies, that he "owned a short-wave radio set" etc. It developed following a thorough investigation that the rumors started about* —— *were unfounded, that he did own a short-wave set (it was a Boy Scout practice set) and that he was a good officer who had become the victim of idle gossip.*
>
> *29 April: Russian ship* Ashkhabad *torpedoed off Cape Lookout. Forty-seven survivors brought to Morehead City Section Base and briefed. On the following day before ship had finally sank, this agent was flown to scene of torpedoing to make aerial photographs.*
>
> *On 7 May, this Agent flew to Cape Hatteras to identify and bury a body which was in an advanced state of decomposition and had been discovered by a fisherman on the beach that morning.*

In 1955, Aycock wrote, with coauthor Ken Jones, an article for *Male* magazine with the sensational headline "I Wore a Dead Man's Hand" about identifying that body. Much of the purple prose apparently flows from Jones. The story, while morbidly fascinating about the specific case, also relays stark detail about Aycock's war work in general. It was written in Aycock's first-person voice, starting with his visit to the Cape Hatteras Coast Guard Station:

> *The* [dead] *man would likely be one of three things: a member of the British or American military, a British or American seaman, or an enemy*

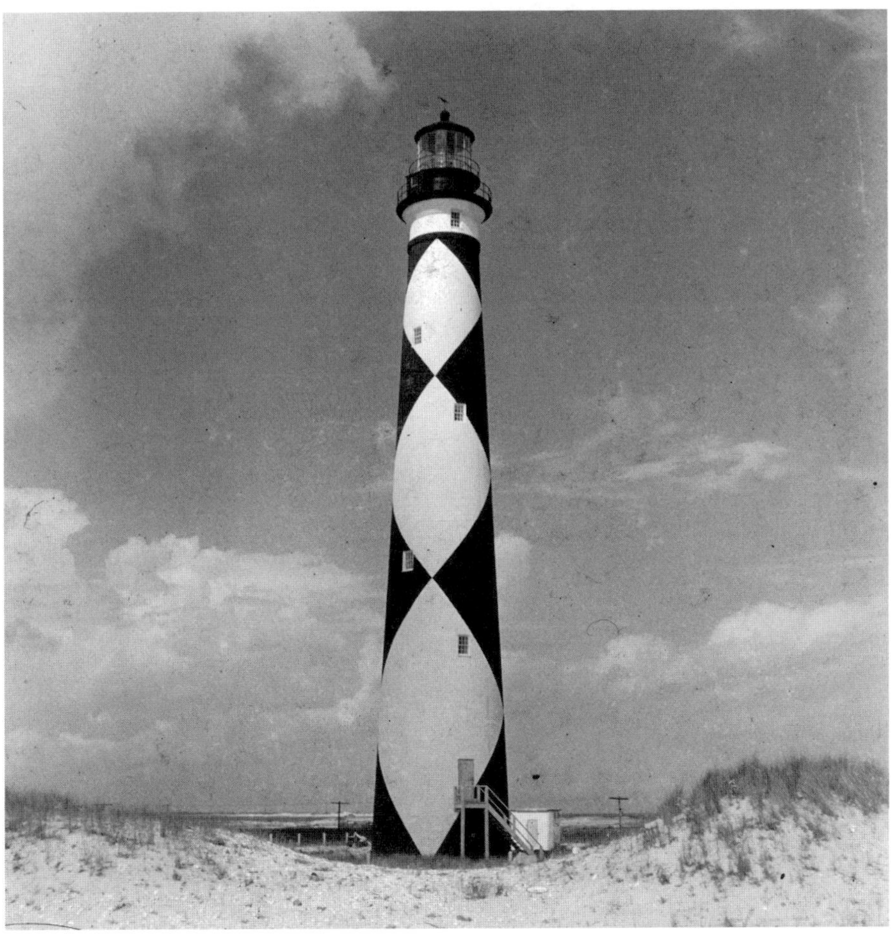

The lighthouses along the Outer Banks are painted with different patterns so that mariners can use them as aids to navigation. German U-boat captains knew them, too. Aycock photographed the Cape Lookout Lighthouse in 1949. *ABC, OBHC, SANC.*

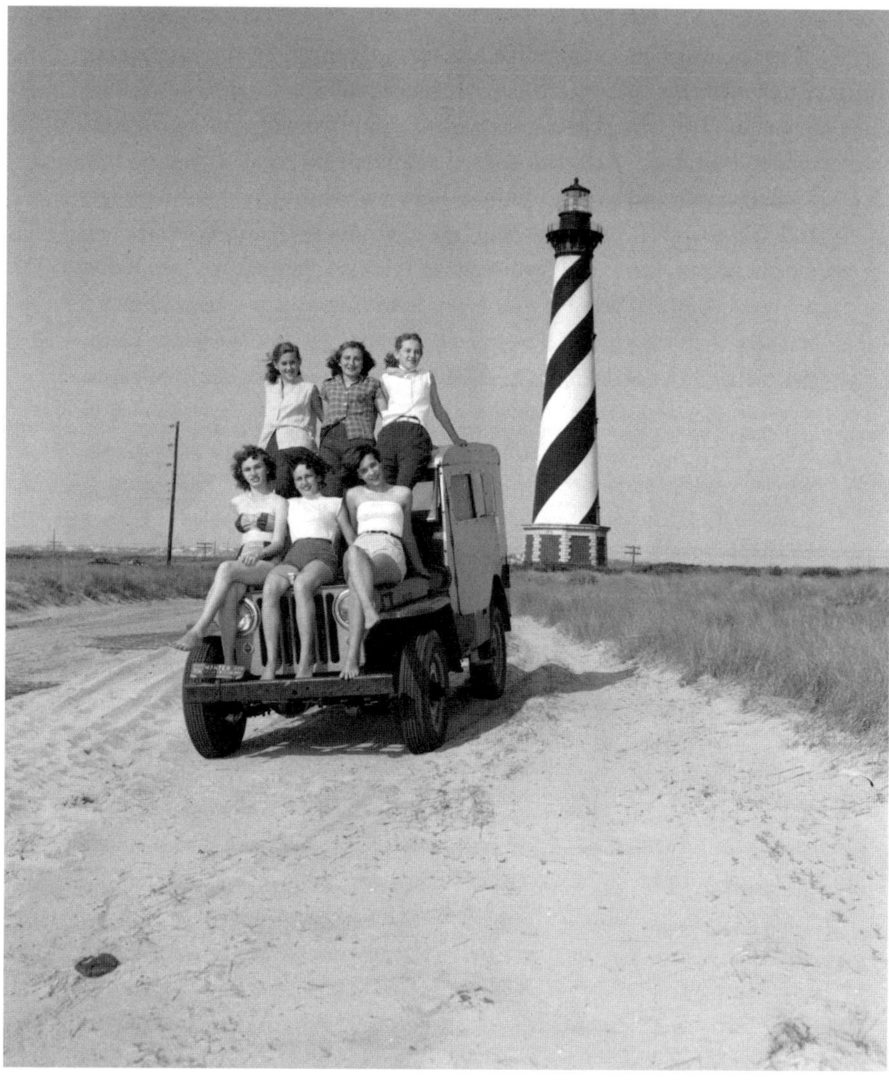

Above: In happier postwar times, Aycock had a red-and-white 1952 Willys Jeep. In 1953, he persuaded Hatteras girls to climb aboard. Top row *(from left)* Jeannie Gray, Yvonne Hooper, and Connie Gray. Bottom row *(from left)* Christine Gray, Gwennie Gray, and Barbara Midgett. *ABC, OBHC, SANC.*

Opposite, top: This shot is too good for Aycock not to have framed it and posed in it. The Ocracoke Lighthouse, the American flag, a grassy spot, and hands firmly on the wheel are all compositional elements pointing to a man who knew what made a great photograph. *ABC, OBHC, SANC.*

Opposite, bottom: Like the eight other Coast Guard stations on Hatteras Island, the Cape Hatteras Station provided a variety of services to travelers and locals such as emergency communications, medical assistance, and shelter for the displaced. *ABC, OBHC, SANC.*

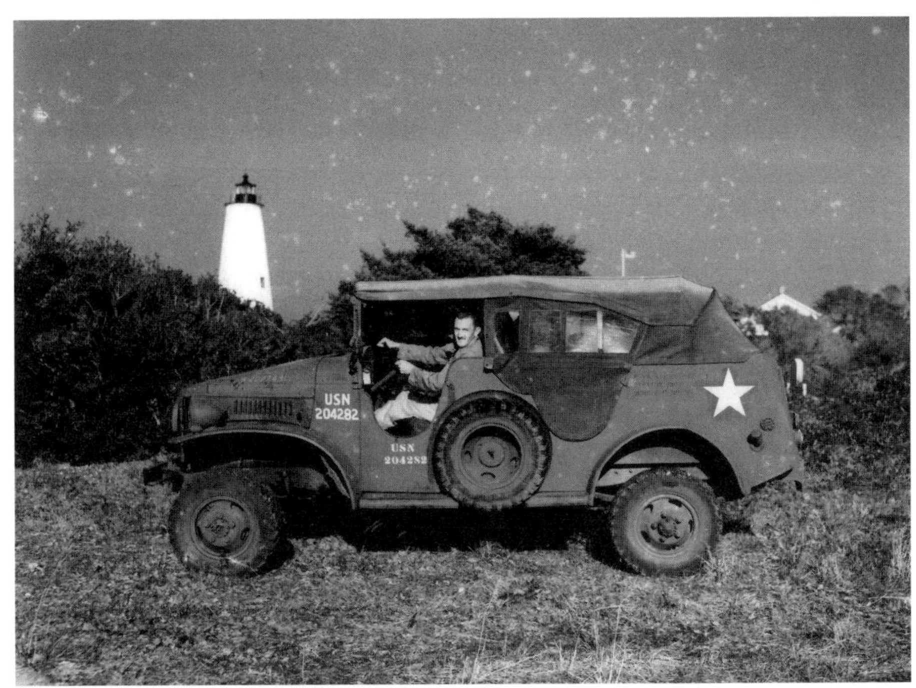
USN
204282
USN
204282

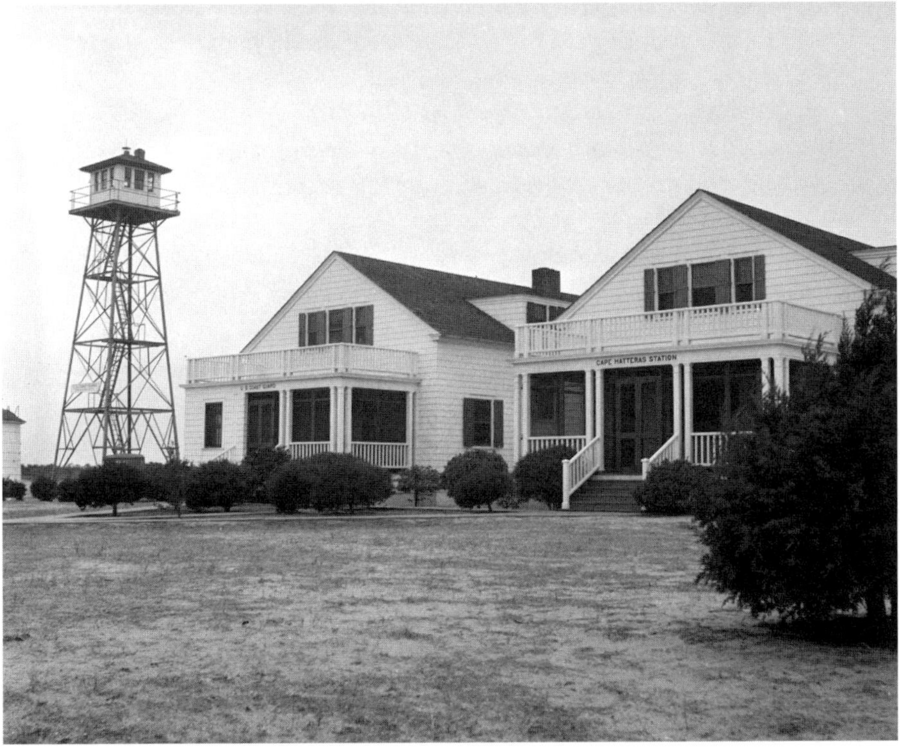

agent. I had to know which and the subject himself couldn't tell me in his present condition.

The gloom of the unlighted interior and the smell of death of days, perhaps weeks old, cut sharply, like a knife, across the threshold of the equipment house. Outside, the fresh air stirred with a lively rustle, and the bright summer sun reflected from clean white sand. Stepping through the door, I saw the dim outline under a tarp on the floor in the furthest corner. I crossed quickly to it, raised one edge of the canvas, and contemplated the job before me.

The man's face was disfigured to a degree which rendered it a mask stamped with a vacant horror. The body was naked, and there were no identifying dog tags.... The hand was missing from the stump of the left wrist, which stuck out awkwardly and stiff almost on a line with the shoulder. The knees were drawn up as if locked in bitter protest against an unbearable cramp. But all of this was nothing compared with the right hand which held my fascinated gaze.

The right arm was thrust upward and partly out until the hand was just below the chin. And the black, bony fingers were gnarled and twisted into a claw more forbidding, more frightening than anything I've ever seen. My job was going to be a tough one, because, quite apparently, fingerprints would be the only possible means of identification.

Unlimbering my portable fingerprint kit, I reached for the dead man's hand. As I touched it, a shudder of revulsion passed through my whole body, and I drew back with a quick, spasmodic gesture. But that one touch had told me one thing I needed to know. Those fingers, bent as they were into an iron claw, could never be printed. Again I forced myself to shake hands with the dead, and this time I had a crazy notion: Maybe the fingers would come off!

The fingers wouldn't come off. But as I stood there holding it I became aware of another value: Despite the rigidity of the bones, the skin of the fingers was loose! Could I...? Yes, I could, and I did! Fighting back an understandable disgust and an unreasoned fear, I slid the skin casings from those fingers, one by one. Then, holding them in the palm of my hand, I bolted through the door and back to the world of reality where the truck waited to drive me to my plane.

There was another problem.

I had the skin finger casings, complete with the fingernails, but how could I preserve them until I found an opportunity to finish my weird experiment in post-mortem fingerprints? Alcohol sure. But I didn't have any alcohol—or did I? After all, there was my bottle of bourbon. In they went!

As I flew back in the plane with my bottle, I thought about other grisly things I'd had to do to identify the dead. And no matter how I did it, it was important that it be done—at all costs.

Meanwhile, Aycock continued to work the April 10 torpedoing of the British tanker *San Delfino*:

Although the San Delfino*'s master managed to launch boats and rafts before she went down in the night, there was considerable loss of life in the disaster. The survivors, picked up at sea by surface craft, were taken directly to Norfolk for interrogation by the Office of Naval Intelligence. Some days later I received an urgent call to go to the morgue at Morehead City to try to identify two bodies. I found the bodies in excellent condition— fully clothed, and with identification papers. One was a British seaman. The other was a member of the British Army gun crew aboard the tanker.*

Now, Aycock, wrote, he turned "'to the job of burying the dead reverently,' as my orders read." For that, he needed two British flags. He made his way to the HMS *Bedfordshire*, in for coaling at Morehead, and soon found top officer Tom Cunningham. Cunningham said the flags would be no problem, Aycock wrote, and invited Aycock to have a drink while he had Union Jack flags "brought up."

Cunningham told Aycock that his wife was pregnant, as was the wife of another top officer on the ship, R.B. Davis. "When the babies came, Cunnigham said, the *Bedfordshire* would be holding a party that he was certain Morehead City would never forget," author Homer Hickam Jr. wrote in his 1989 book *Torpedo Junction*. "Would Brown be interested in attending? Aycock Brown said he would, indeed, and hoped to see Cunningham before that as well."

Aycock wrote in his article:

Tom Cunningham and I had a drink and a talk and we were very merry for a brief time. I wished I could meet him again after the war. It's not very often that you make friends like him so readily. Finally, with the British [flags] *under my arm, I went ashore and arranged the burial.*

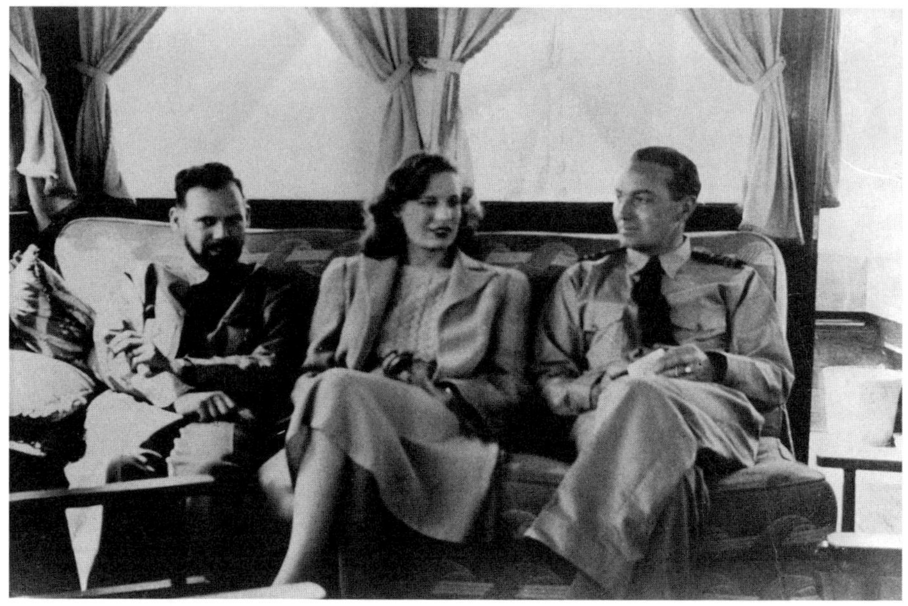

A few weeks later, Aycock wrote, on May 16, he was at the Ocracoke Coast Guard station consulting with Captain Homer Gray about two recently recovered bodies. "I don't see how you'll ever identify this pair!" Gray told him. Aycock continued:

> *I had been summoned to look at two bodies picked up at sea by a patrol boat and brought to the Ocracoke station. Homer and I stood in the boathouse, and he held up one corner of a dirty tarpaulin, revealing the bodies of two men. They were nude, in rather bad shape, and there was little apparent means of identification. But as I looked at the faces of the two men, the strength seemed to flow out of my body.*
>
> *"I'm afraid it will be easy to identify these two men," I said. Homer looked at me.*
>
> *"I know this man," I said finally, when I could control my anger at an enemy who fired torpedoes. With my foot I indicated the nearer of the two bodies. "He's Tom Cunningham, of the HMS* Bedfordshire.*" The same Cunningham I'd talked and drank with in borrowing the British flags.*

In his diary, written years before Hickam's book during the war, Aycock, dispassionately adhering to the official record, left out his feelings about his friend's death:

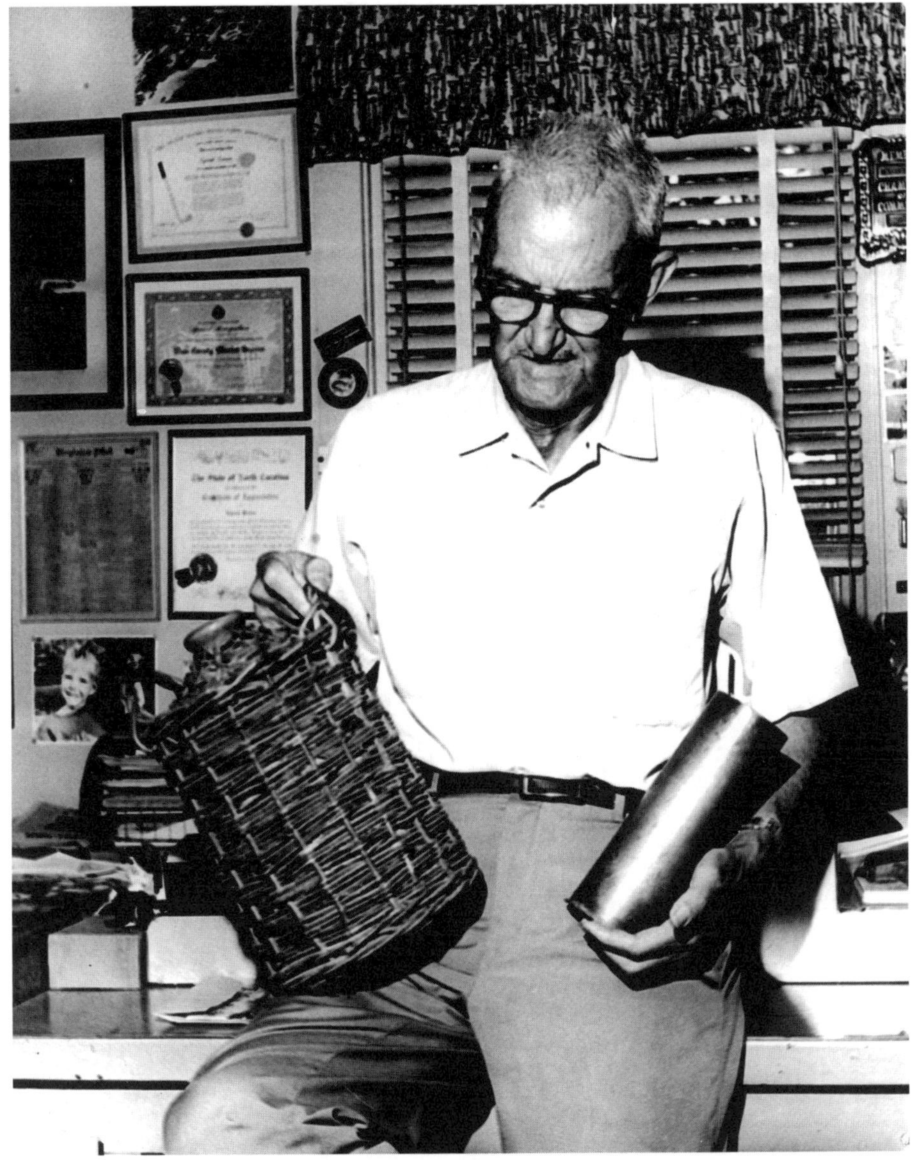

Opposite: Sublieutenant Thomas Cunningham (*left*) met with Aycock in Morehead City in 1942. His assignment was to a former commercial fishing trawler, the HMS *Bedfordshire*, which the Royal Navy specifically outfitted to fight German U-boats. *ABC, OBHC, SANC.*

Above: Years after his wartime service, Aycock holds gifts from Thomas Cunningham, a shell casing from the HMS *Bedfordshire* and the rum jug that he helped drink dry on the night they met. The rum jug still holds pride of place in Aycock's grandson's home. *Patrick Byrd.*

11 May: On this date, His Majesty's ship Bedfordshire *was last heard from and it was determined later she had apparently been torpedoed with all hands lost. On 16 May this Agent was ordered to Ocracoke to identify two bodies which had washed ashore during the previous night. Identification was made, the bodies being Sub-lieutenant Thomas Cunningham and Stanley R. Craig, an able-bodied seaman. They were members of the crew of the* Bedfordshire, *which had last been heard from on 11 May. After the bodies were identified, coffins were constructed of old duck hunting sink boxes and the services of a local minister were obtained to construct a Christian burial.*

Homer Hickam added this:

The funeral was solemn and dignified, as befitted two heroes who had come from a foreign land to protect American lives and property. Plots were donated by the Williams family beside their own in the little Ocracoke cemetery. A United States Coast Guard honor guard acted as pallbearers, and the caskets were draped in two of the Union Jacks that Cunningham had given Brown. Amasa Fulcher, a lay preacher for the Methodist Church in Ocracoke, conducted the service and even sang an appropriate hymn. It was, in many ways, a typical Outer Banks funeral given by a people who had known all their lives the hardships rendered by the sea.

Eventually, a sign was posted by the graves, words from the English poet Rupert Brooke, who died of illness during World War I:

If I should die, think only this of me:
That there's some corner of a foreign field
That is forever England

Years later, Outer Banks author R. Wayne Gray added this about the burial:

A week later two more men were picked up by a patrol boat at sea, but they were never identified. It was assumed, however, they were from the Bedfordshire *because of the Royal Navy blue turtleneck sweaters they were wearing. They were buried in the same cemetery as Cunningham and Craig. Aycock was in charge of the funerals.*

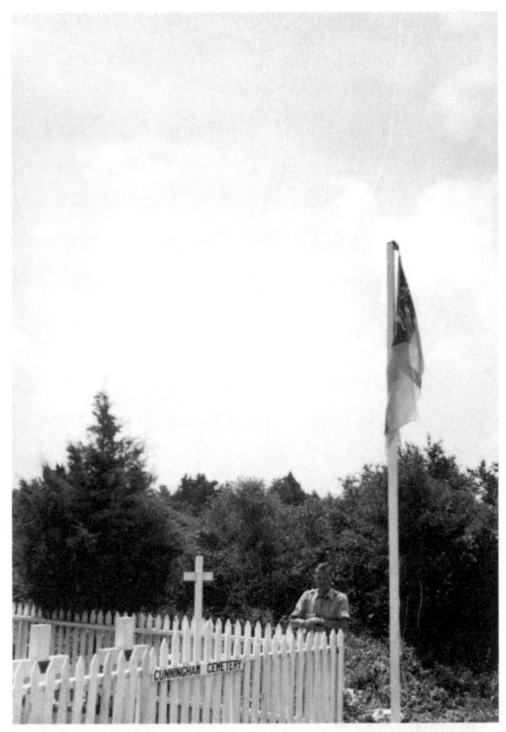

Right: In a show of compassion and solidarity with our British allies and men at sea, the citizens of Ocracoke provided improvised coffins and land to bury the Englishmen. A sign on the picket fence displayed the original name of Cunningham Cemetery. *ABC, OBHC, SANC.*

Below: Cunningham, Stanley Craig, and two other English seamen were laid to rest in what is now called the British Cemetery on Ocracoke Island. Other Ocracokers who had met Cunningham—Wahab Howard and Jack Willis—remembered his coal-black beard and gold watch and ring. *ABC, OBHC, SANC.*

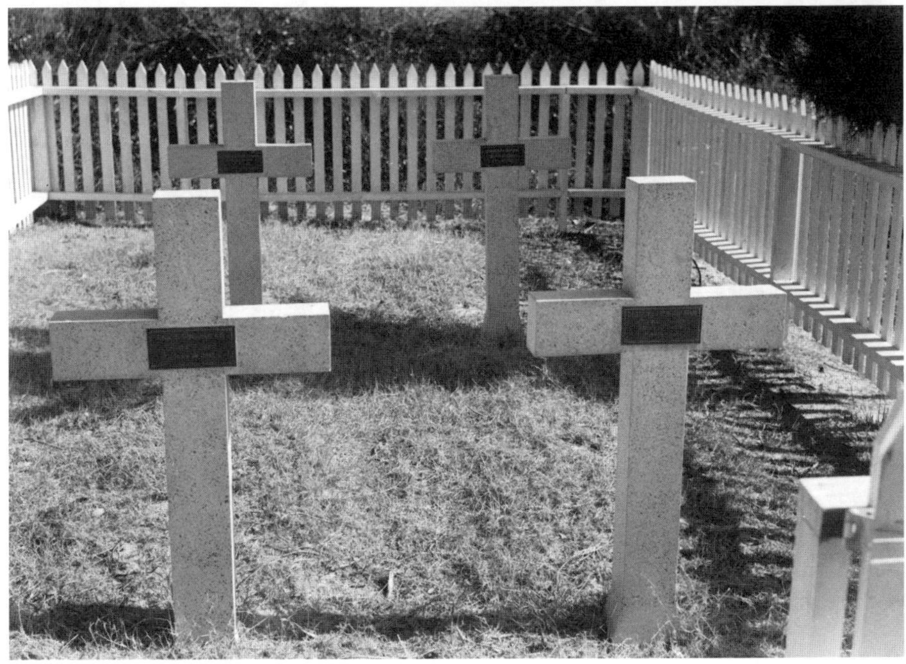

On a military plane flying out from Ocracoke, Aycock wrote in the "Dead Hands" article, he thought it all over:

> *As I sat on the plane, thinking about Cunningham, and regretting that men such as he must die as he did, I knew the man whose fingers I had pickled in my bourbon would not be so easy to identify.... When I'd slipped the skin casings off those talon-like fingers, I'd really only had a glimmering—not a cogently formed plan—of what I'd do with them. Pickled in the bourbon, however, they haunted me....*
>
> *I strode into the sick bay of the Naval establishment at Morehead City, holding my bottle aloft with its freight of fingers, and shouting loudly for a pair of surgical rubber gloves. I'd decided upon a plan; resolved to take the plan in stride; and although the thing was, I confess, ghoulish beyond normal circumstance, I was determined to carry it off as if it was routine.*
>
> *A pair of rubber gloves was forthcoming at once, and a little knot of Navy corpsmen clustered about. But as I fished the finger casings from the*

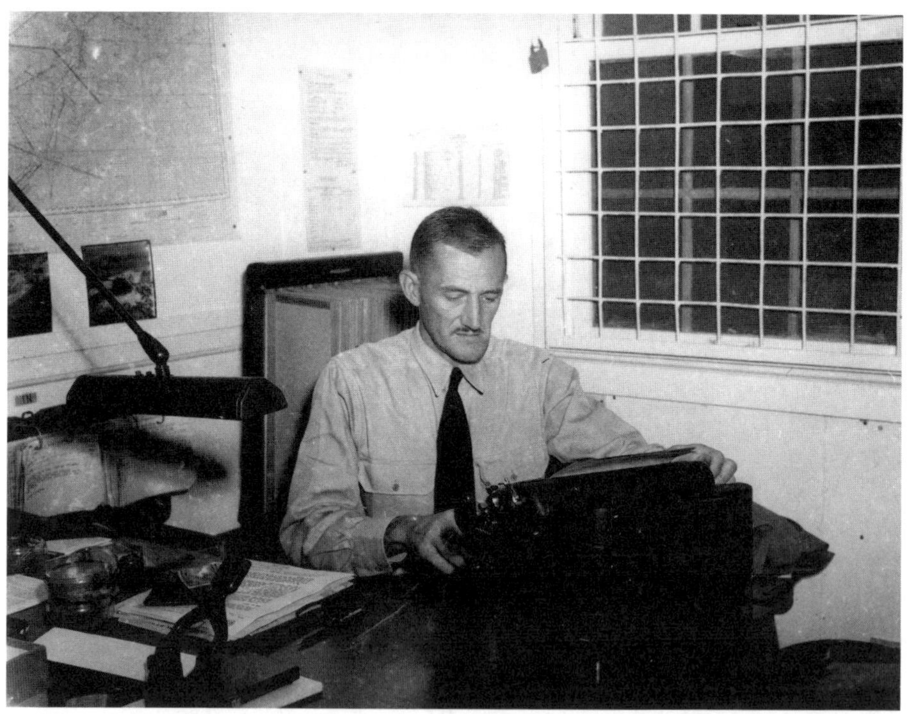

Aycock once told author, historian, and friend David Stick that Ocracoke locals "used to think I was a great guy because I had a typewriter." He employed his typewriter to record World War II history and tell the world about the Outer Banks. *ABC, OBHC, SANC.*

bourbon, one by one, and placed them on a pad of raw cotton to dry, a sudden lack of enthusiasm swept the gathering. Only two corpsmen were left when I was ready for the second step in the experiment, and that pair didn't look any too healthy.

Donning the gloves, I carefully slipped the finger casings over the rubber-protected gloves of my own hand. It was slow, delicate work, for the skin of the dead man's fingers was extremely fragile. When the casings were thoroughly dry, I inked each fingertip and pressed it gently upon the fingerprint blank I'd previously set out. The result was as perfect a set of prints as I've ever made.

The fingerprints were forwarded to the Office of Naval Intelligence, Fifth Naval District, and then in turn to the FBI in Washington. In due time, through channels from London, came the name of our man. From the San Delfino*....He shall remain anonymous, however, out of respect for the feelings and comfort of his family. They would, I am sure, rather not know what he had to do to identify him. But if they did, I'm also sure they'd admit it was worth it.*

Aycock named the man in his war diary. But we will defer to Aycock's wise judgment in not naming him here. Coast Guardsmen from Cape Hatteras buried his body near their station.

Aycock continued his war diary:

5 June: Conduct investigation of ——, master of fishing trawler Sea Queen. [This man] *of Scandinavian descent was in the rum-running racket during 1928, had been arrested on at least one occasion, tried in federal court, found guilty and paid a fine instead of receiving a prison sentence. (This was probably because he was on the verge of implicating a number of prominent Eastern Carolina businessmen who were supposed to be mixed up in the rum deals). Investigation revealed that while* [this man] *had been a rumrunner his loyalty to the United States was unquestioned and therefore he was permitted to continue operating the fishing trawler and later was enrolled as a confidential observer to the Navy....*

6 June: Following investigation of security measures or lack of security measures for Ocracoke Island mail carriers...it is recommended that they be supplied with small arms by Post Office Department for protection. The recommendation was complied with and as a result the mail, much of which was highly classified going to and from Naval activities, was given more protection.

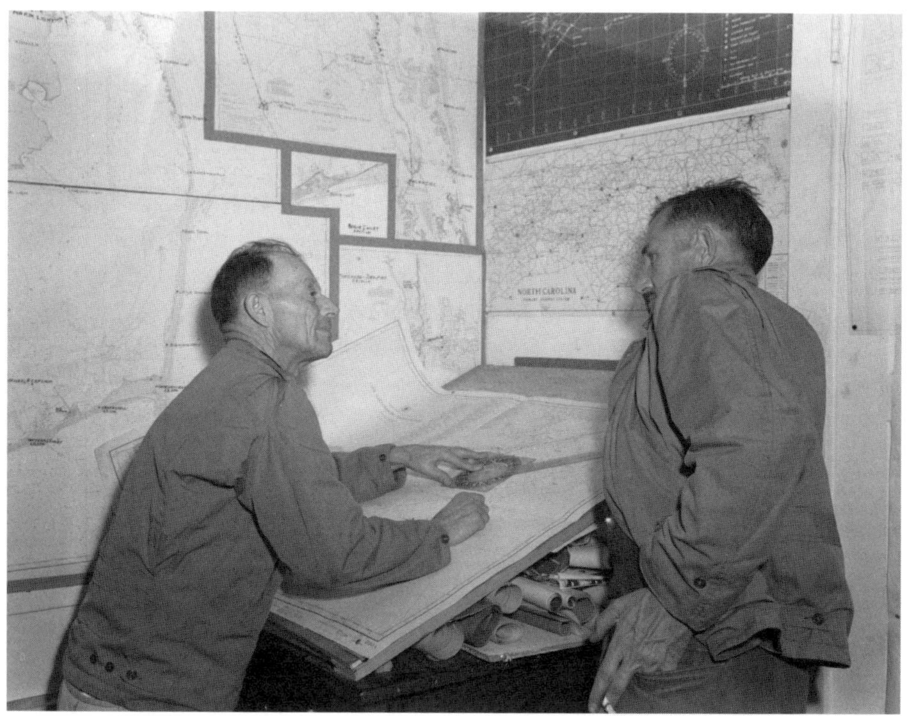

Aycock (*right*) consults with an engineer named Rose over maps at the Ocracoke Naval Station Base. In his position as civilian intelligence officer, Aycock identified bodies, interviewed survivors, and imparted his knowledge of coastal North Carolina. *ABC, OBHC, SANC.*

The characters, the inside deals, and the wild stories abounded, and Aycock was part of it all.

> *24 June: On this date three freighters were torpedoed.... They were S.S.* Nordal, *S.S.* Manuela *and the S.S.* Ljubica Matkovic. *A total of 94 survivors were brought to Morehead City Section Base and briefed by this agent and* [others]. *On the following day, Antonio Figarre, a Puerto Rican, first reported dead aboard* Manuela, *was discovered still alive by a salvage vessel which had gone to two crippled ships into port. Just before the ship went down, Figarre was rescued and brought to Morehead City Hospital in a dying condition. He lived, after remaining in the hospital for several months.*

By July 1942, the U.S. military was finally kicking back the German subs. David Stick wrote:

The amazing thing is that we were able, during that otherwise disastrous six-month period, to so perfect our antisubmarine devices as to almost completely thwart the underseas raiders throughout the remainder of the war.

R. Wayne Gray eloquently summed up Aycock's work:

Aycock Brown's wartime job was not a desirable one, but he took what he could get and performed his duties to the best of his ability....German submarine crews hunted off the North Carolina coast without any great risk to themselves. From Outer Banks villages, ships could be seen from the shore burning nightly at the beginning of the war. Aycock once said, "There were hundreds of people arriving in lifeboats at Ocracoke burned and scarred when their ships were torpedoed. I don't think I'll ever forget the horror in their eyes."

The photos Aycock shot of burning ships will stand for the ages. "Just that set of wartime images of shipping activity is an incredible record by itself," said Drew Wilson, a fine Outer Banks photographer in his own right who came along after Aycock.

The German torpedoes weren't the only threat. In 1944, a hurricane hit Ocracoke hard.

"In that storm, water rose swiftly and engulfed the Brown home," *The State* magazine reported in a February 1967 profile of Aycock. "Aycock fled to higher ground, wading in water up to his armpits. On his shoulders was his 4-year-old son [Billy]. Esther, his wife, clung to one arm, and Brantley, about 11, swam alongside the family."

Aycock's courageous work during the war hardened him to a certain extent. He'd lost Jim Gaskill, the son of the couple who had given him his start on Ocracoke. He'd lost his new British friend Tom Cunningham. And he identified numerous war-torn bodies, those of men younger and older than him. Never again could he look on the paradise he'd discovered as one immune to the horrors of the outside world. In sharp contrast, he never lost his sense of humor and his core optimism that he and his neighbors on the Banks would survive and excel. He never lost his boyish wonder at the characters and natural wonders he met daily. But the war haunted him.

Aycock drank hard through the war and in the time right after it, perhaps self-medicating his experiences, trying to blur them away, like many of his fellows who served in the war. A North Carolina journalist reported:

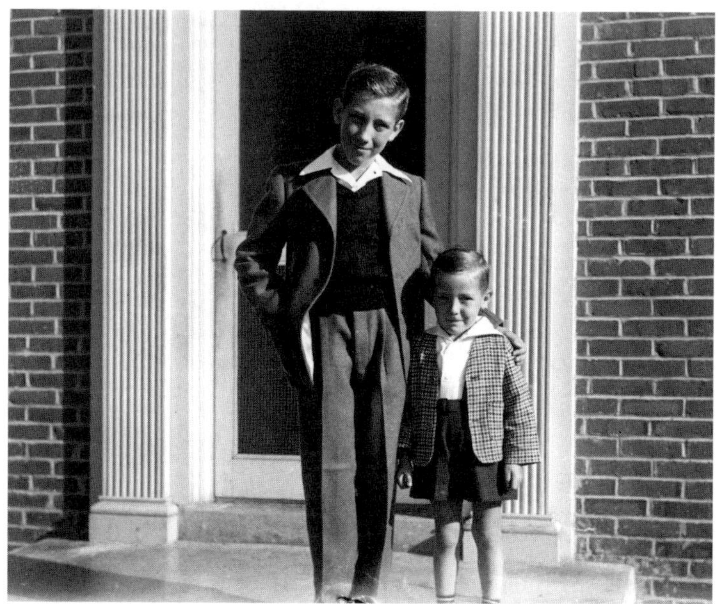

Brantley (*left*) and Billy Brown are dressed in their finest on a day off-island. In September, they experienced the Great Atlantic Hurricane of 1944 that wrecked Ocracoke and caused the Red Cross to come to its aid with food and water. *ABC, OBHC, SANC.*

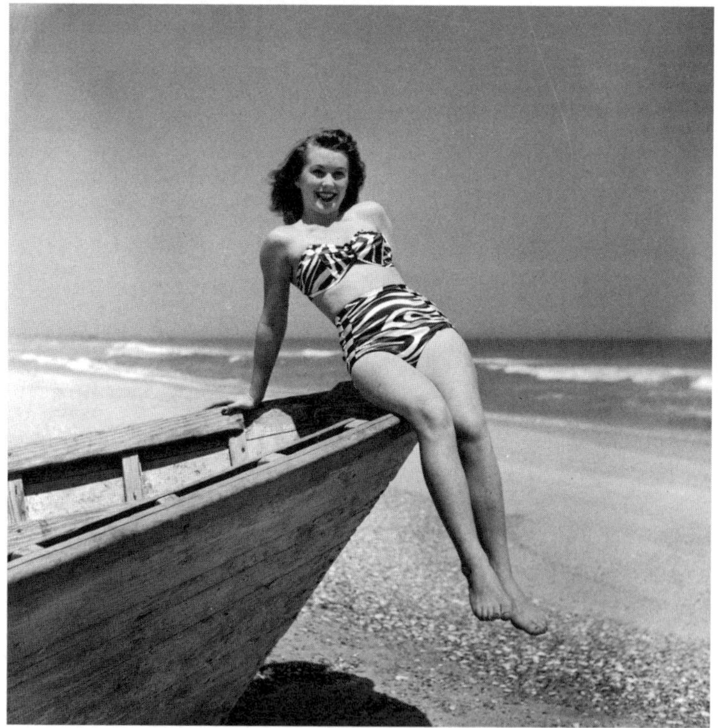

Stepping back into nonmilitary life, Aycock resumed his quest to promote coastal North Carolina. He photographed Lila Willis, who reigned as Miss Dare County 1950–51, on the bow of an old surfboat. *ABC, OBHC, SANC.*

Aycock had reached the point where he was "blacking out." He would wake in the morning, size up his hangover and wonder what had happened to him the night before. Some of it he could remember, but not all. There were big blank spots and they worried him.

Aycock moderated his drinking in the years ahead as he set himself to promoting the North Carolina coast. "I want to help to make coastal North Carolina the best-known coast in the world—like the Riviera, Palm Beach or Miami Beach, Cape Cod or Waikiki," he told *The News & Observer*. He worked out of Morehead City.

He was sleeping little, working late into the night to send out his photos, and heading out early every morning, bidding farewell to his family. Aycock was Huck Finn in his element, going to shoot photos, his job that felt like play to him. He'd head out with two cameras, filters, and a light meter all strung around his crane-like neck. "Brown is happy only when his finger is flicking the shutter of his cameras and each day he shoots upwards of 50 shots [probably much more]," a *News & Observer* writer reported around that time. "As his wife puts it: 'I sometimes wonder why he doesn't carry a desk along on his back, he carries everything else.'"

Esther always had Aycock's back, and he always had hers. "They were the salt and pepper," remembered family friend Kathy Spencer of Manteo.

In 1948, Aycock began doing PR work for *The Lost Colony* outdoor drama on Roanoke Island, a drive of several hours north of Morehead City. Aycock built on the work of Ben Dixon MacNeill, the first publicity director for the outdoor drama. Like Aycock, MacNeill was a newspaperman who had rediscovered himself on the Outer Banks.

By 1948, *The Lost Colony*, which had started in 1937, was struggling. "*The Lost Colony* was about to fold because there weren't enough people [coming]," David Stick later said.

Aycock knew the potential in the drama, its ability to lure in the masses with the right publicity, *his* kind of publicity. Night after night, right there on the Sound, the play was hanging on with its tightly choreographed scenes of Native Americans fighting the colonists, broken by the humorous exchanges between the Englishman Old Tom and the Indian maiden Agona, all culminating in the colonists of 1587 exiting the stage to the great unknown. The writer of the play, Paul Green, a legendary progressive out of Chapel Hill, had some hits and misses with his outdoor plays, but *The Lost Colony* was a major hit, boosted by President Franklin Roosevelt's

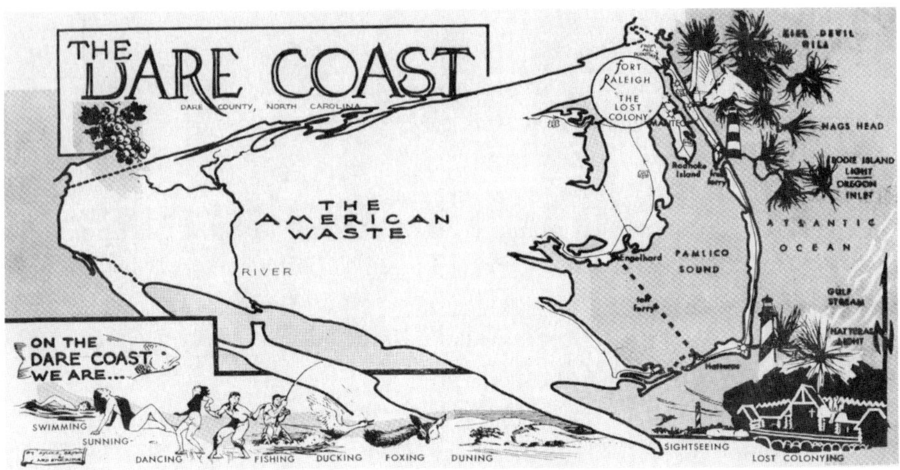

Above: Aycock and Ned Etheridge designed this postcard depicting "The American Waste" to the west and all things wonderful ending in "-ing" along the Dare Coast, the name used before the term Outer Banks was coined. *John Havel.*

Opposite, top left: Aycock kept his senses of wonder and humor throughout his life. Like many of the men of the Greatest Generation, he tamped down the horrors of the war and pushed forward with the business of living life. *Sarah Owens, RV Owens.*

Opposite, top right: From its inception, *The Lost Colony* was to be "theater for the people." Indeed, many local people have held front and backstage roles. The original dance of the milkmaids used island girls who executed steps of their own invention. *ABC, OBHC, SANC.*

Opposite, bottom: In 1949, Aycock photographed Georgia Carroll, a visiting celebrity actress to *The Lost Colony*. Holding the fishing net is her husband and big band leader Kay Kyser, who also performed at the Nags Head Casino while they were in town. *ABC, OBHC, SANC.*

much-ballyhooed visit in the first season. Aycock just needed to find a way to reignite the buzz around the play.

He fell in love with the play's setting. It was lush, with dense pines and live oak trees more than four hundred years old, their widespread, hurricane-forged branches stretching toward the Sound, thick forearms from another time keeping guard and carrying stories of old. You could stand on the theater grounds and know that colony was still somewhere close. Aycock watched rehearsals and nightly performances. Locals and theater hands from the island and nationwide were trying out dialects and dances, transforming themselves into colonists and American Indians, beautiful Native women and men brawny in breechclouts.

Kathy Spencer, who grew up with Aycock's daughter, Stormy Gale, remembered going, a few years later, to the nightly shows with the father

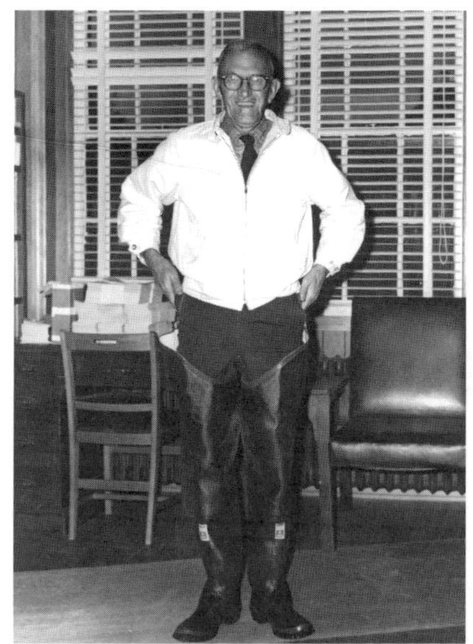

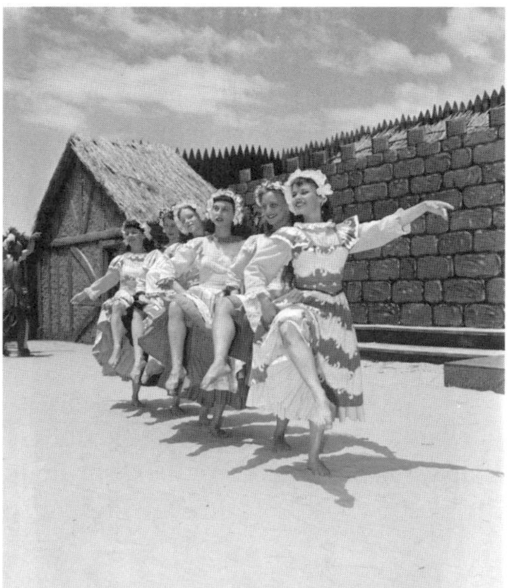

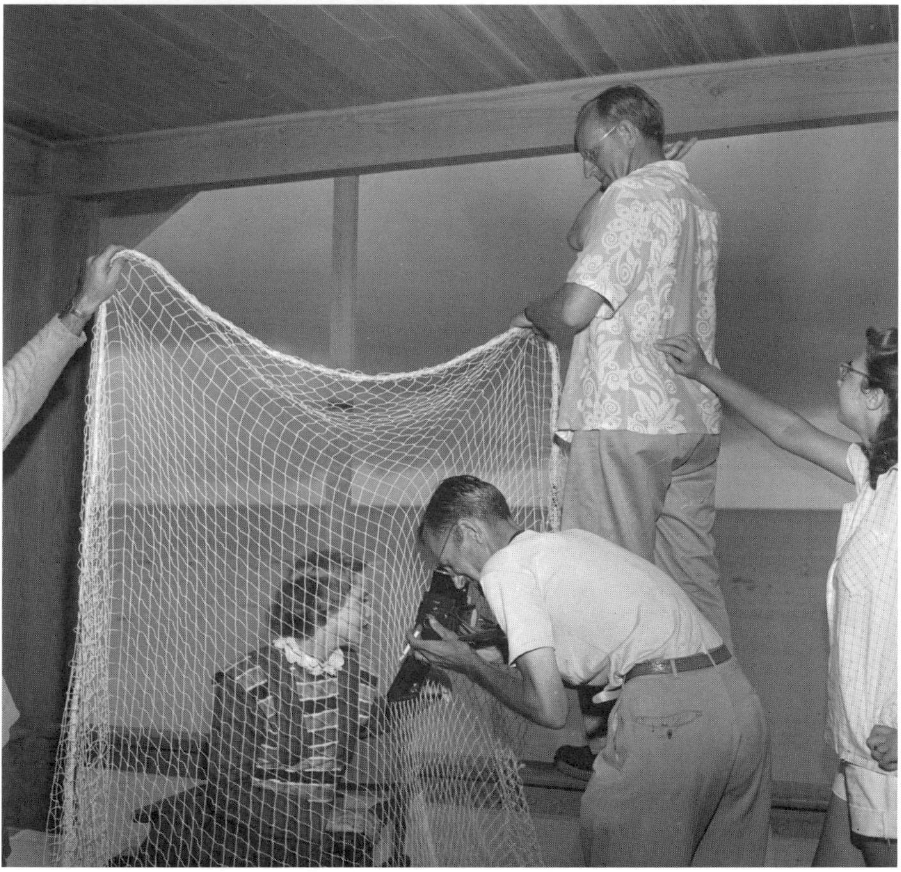

and daughter. "Every night that Gale and I went with him to the colony, he could find something to make a story out of. A senator or a star in the crowd. A beautiful girl by a magnolia tree. He found a picture and a story and that's what he did with everything. He could see a story in somebody and he knew how to bring it out. It was a gift."

Aycock launched a successful media blitz, using promotional celebrity nights and widespread press releases and photos. "I tried for years to get playwright Paul Green to put J. Fred Muggs, a popular movie ape, in a cameo role but he put he put his foot down," Brown later joked.

He was literally working his meager rear off, still promoting the Morehead City area, traveling hundreds of miles a week between there and the Outer Banks, sleeping no more than four hours a night in the summer, starting off the season at 136 pounds and ending it about 122.

3

PROMOTING *THE LOST COLONY* AND ALL THE REST

Sarah Owens' "assistant" title became irrelevant because she rose above it, becoming Aycock's equal, running the office as he raced up and down the Outer Banks.

Aycock's work for *The Lost Colony* went so well that, in 1952, Dare County established the Dare County Tourist Bureau just for Aycock, with him as the director. The bureau kept him on his *Lost Colony* work but expanded the job to promoting all of Dare County. Before the bureau, Dare County's towns had basically competed for tourism business in unorganized efforts. The county officials recognized that Aycock had done solid work in the Morehead City area and on Ocracoke. They also knew his organizational skills weren't the best but recognized that his visionary risk-taking, and his growing network of national contacts, might outweigh his organizational weakness. David Stick, one of the founders of the bureau, became one of Aycock's biggest supporters and friends.

Aycock worked hard, and he was lucky, especially in his choice of his assistant, Sarah Owens. She was from an old-line Manteo family and helped secure his local contacts. She also had a knack for organization that Aycock lacked. She beautifully complemented Aycock's vision.

Aycock and Esther settled into a modest frame house in downtown Manteo and continued to raise their children. For a while, Esther made women's hats, most notably, in the early 1960s, pillbox hats like those worn by First Lady Jackie Kennedy. Esther's pillbox hats became all the rage in Manteo

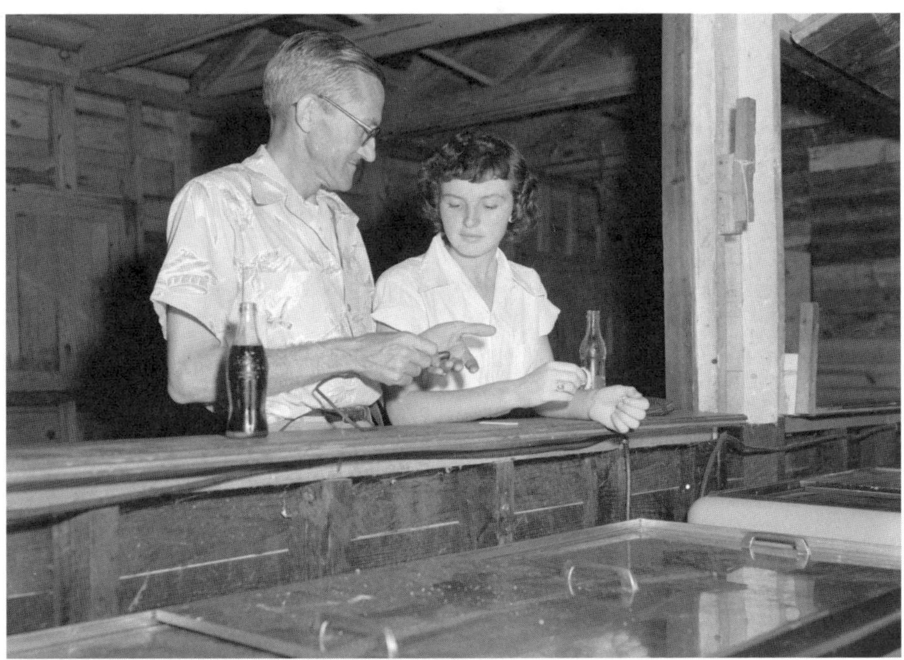

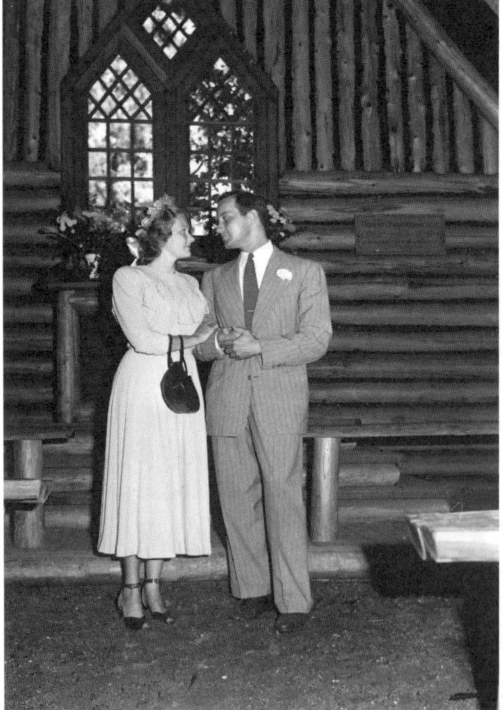

Above: Aycock takes a Coke break in the concession stand area of the Waterside Theatre on Roanoke Island in 1950. His promotional photographs renewed interest in *The Lost Colony* and kept the outdoor drama viable for another generation. *ABC, OBHC SANC.*

Left: David and Phyllis Stick were married in the Fort Raleigh Chapel on Roanoke Island in 1949. The Works Progress Administration built the Cittie of Raleigh, a re-creation of what artist Frank Stick, David's father, thought the settlement might look like. *ABC, OBHC, SANC.*

Opposite: Billy, Gale, and Brantley pose yet again for their dad in the early 1960s. With a span of almost fifteen years between Gale and Brantley, Gale was still young enough to play with Brantley's children, her nieces and nephews, as they grew up together. *ABC, Patrick Byrd.*

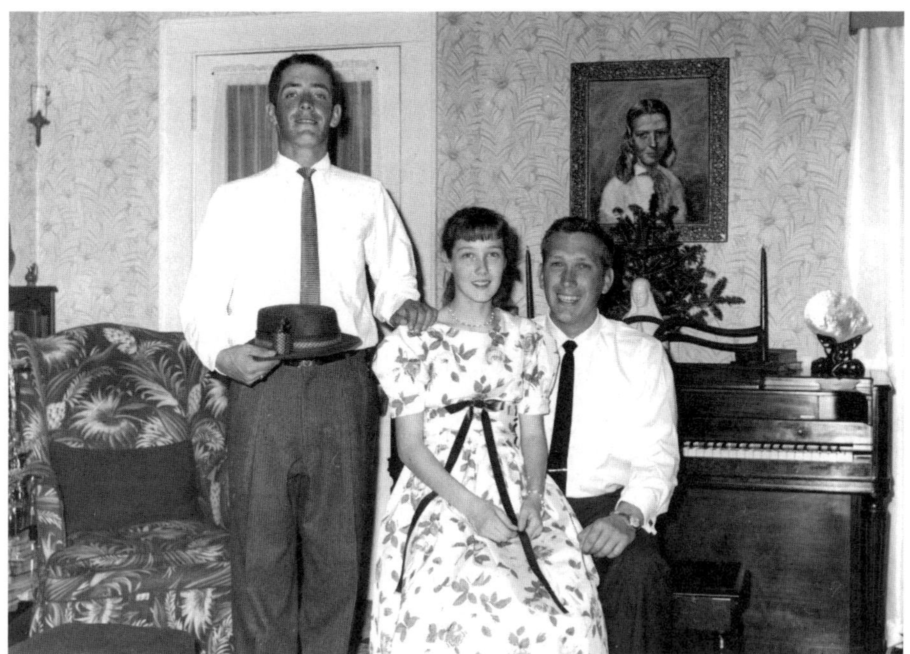

remembered Kathy Spencer, who grew up with Stormy Gale. On trips to Norfolk, she said, her mother and Esther would tell the children, "It's dime, not doime"—in other words, to curb their brogue in the big city.

Aycock had many friends but few close ones, as he was constantly working. His best friend was his wife. He and Esther drank some, but nothing like their contemporaries on Roanoke Island. The island had always been free-spirited, with many locals feeling that marriage wasn't necessarily sacred and freely accepting gay and bisexual couples, a spirit *The Lost Colony* crew enhanced. For his part, Aycock never judged.

His tiny office was in downtown Manteo near the corner of Budleigh Street and US 64 and next to *The Coastland Times*. His desk was shaded by old-school venetian blinds, cluttered with hundreds of files bulging with negatives and a sign saying "A neat desk is a sign of a sick mind," Aycock would sit at his typewriter every day, pounding out press releases, ashes dropping from chain-smoked cigarettes. Sarah Owens, thirty years younger, was always nearby, matching him cigarette for cigarette. Her well-organized desk was at the entrance to the office, in sharp contrast to Aycock's bulging desk just behind hers. Her son, RV, later remembered that his mother was "the glue that held everything together" while Aycock became the eyes on the Outer Banks for the world at large through his photography.

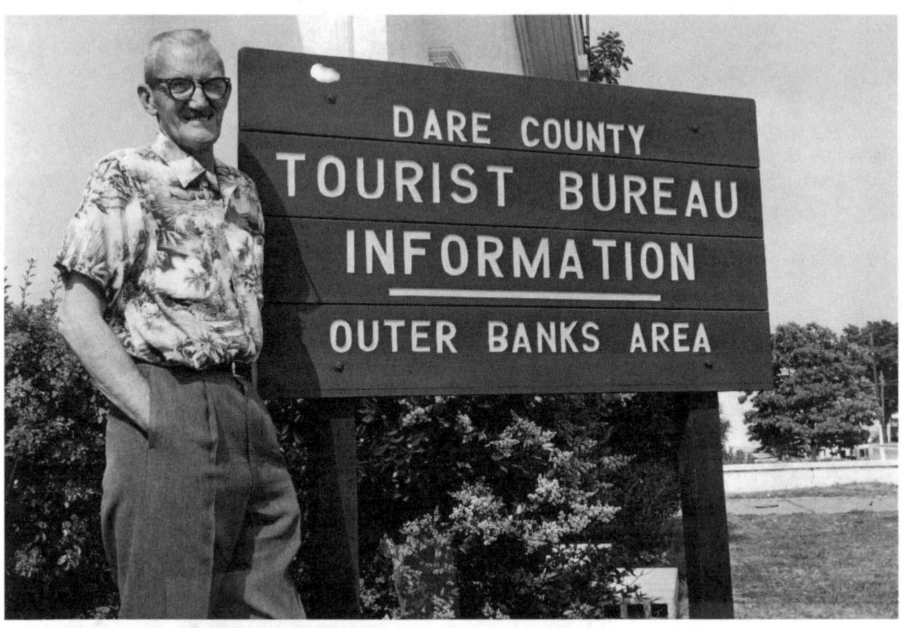

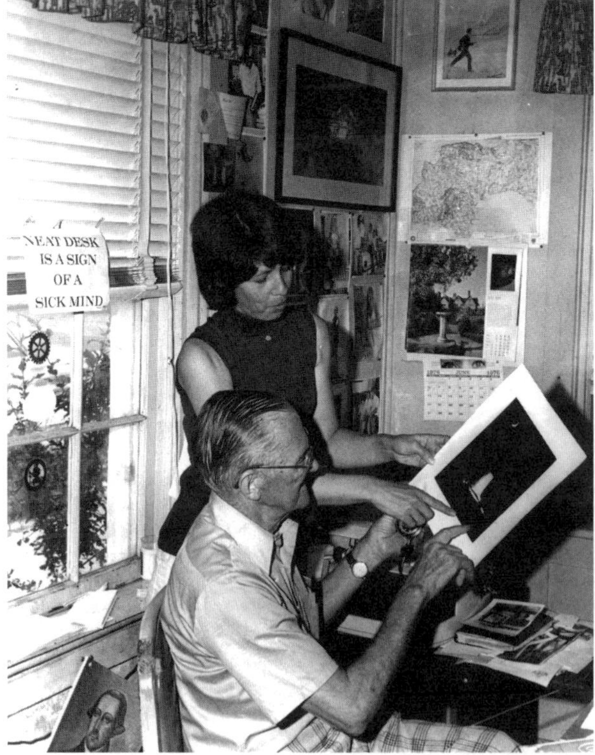

Above: Sporting a trademark Hawaiian shirt, Aycock poses by the sign marking the newly formed Dare County Tourist Bureau in an office building on the corner of US Highway 64 and Budleigh Street in Manteo. *Dare County Tourist Bureau Records, OBHC, SANC.*

Left: In 1976, well into their decades together, neither Aycock's office nor his beneficial relationship with Sarah Owens had changed much. In this instance, they are pointing to his most famous photograph of the Wright Memorial. *Dare County Tourist Bureau, RV Owens.*

Sarah kept the restless Aycock on track, day after day. Her "assistant" title became irrelevant because she rose above it, becoming Aycock's equal, running the office as he raced up and down the Outer Banks.

Pam Jones, who worked for *The Lost Colony* in an office next to the Tourist Bureau, remembered this:

> *In the days before looking things up on the computer, we would get stacks of letters daily from people asking about where to stay and what to do when they came on vacation here. Each office had their own brochures, and we'd mail out the appropriate brochure for their questions. Depending on who was the busiest, we would jump in and help each other. Aycock was a good person—kind, sensitive, family-oriented, and loved people. He was a great storyteller, and would tell Sarah and I stories about growing up in the mountains while we worked. He also would tell stories about finding bodies during World War II. We would protest because we didn't want to hear gory details, so he would leave out the worst parts and tell the stories anyway. He would often bring flowers and candy to the office for us to enjoy.*
>
> *People from Ohio, Pennsylvania, and all over would stop in the Tourist Bureau when they came on vacation specifically to see Aycock. He had quite a following because of the stories he told with his pictures.*
>
> *One time, Aycock and Esther witnessed a head-on collision on the old Manns Harbor bridge in which some people were killed. A piece of metal from the accident hit the Browns' car. Aycock said, "Esther, are you okay?" When she said she was, he jumped out and started taking pictures.*

Aycock taught himself photography. "Aycock Brown was known for taking a photo of something ordinary and turning it into something extraordinary. Having no real training in the art of photography, he used the people around him and his own determination to learn how to work a camera and develop the film in a darkroom," Shawna Hubbard wrote in her COA paper. "He also had a knack of knowing what people wanted to see."

Aycock also had a talent for branding his skinny self, as Jack Aulis, a columnist for *The News & Observer*, noted:

> *To find Aycock, you look for a floppy straw hat who has cameras and camera equipment draped over him the way pistols and bandoleers would be draped over a Mexican revolutionary. And if under all that equipment, the man is wearing a peacock-bright, open-collared shirt, that's Aycock....*

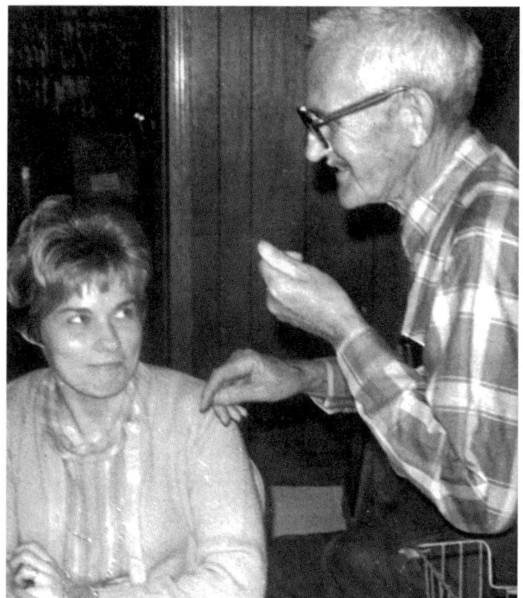

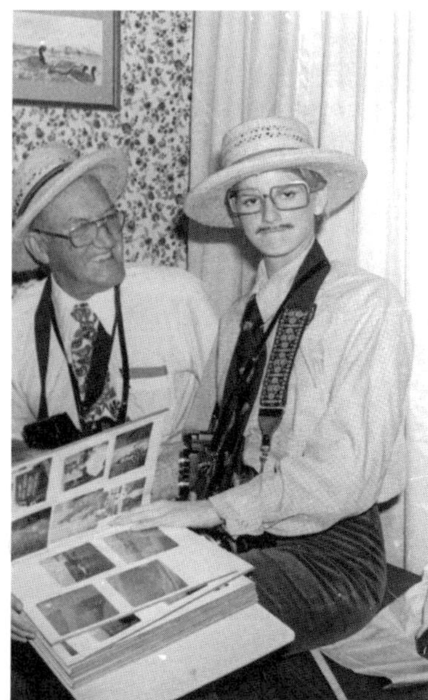

Left: Pam Daniels Jones, an employee of *The Lost Colony*, gives Aycock the side-eye as he regales her with his latest tale. Offices for the Tourist Bureau, Dare County Social Services, Veterans' Affairs, and *The Lost Colony* were all located in the same building. *ABC, RV Owens.*

Right: It was easy to mimic Aycock by copying his predictable look. Vanessa Foreman dressed as her beloved mentor on Halloween in the early 1980s. She still has one of his Italian-made straw hats and a camera as mementos of their time together. *Brantley A. Brown, Vanessa Foreman.*

> *He has about 50 sports shirts now, many given to him by people who have noticed that he will wear them in public.*
>
> *Aycock said: "Most of them are what I guess you'd have to call gaudy. They've got trees and flowers and things like that on them."*

That was Aycock, with his stamps on the back of each of his photos: "Aycock Brown: Covering the Waterfront." Aycock would also mix his brand, just for fun, sometimes wearing Ivy League seersucker pants, like his buddies at St. Andrew's Episcopal Church in Nags Head got from the Galleon.

And always, there was his pencil-thin mustache, anticipating the song of the same name by Jimmy Buffett, who could have been a kindred spirit to Aycock if they had ever met. *Virginian-Pilot* columnist Lawrence Maddry wrote:

> *Before leaving Ocracoke, Aycock had all his teeth pulled by an itinerant dentist who performed his services free. Unable to afford an upper plate, he grew the slim bristling mustache which has become his trademark, so his mouth wouldn't look funny. Today he wears an upper plate, but friends say his mouth still looks irregular. That is because he is always talking.*

Outer Banks author R. Wayne Gray wrote of Aycock: "He sent out press releases nationwide, always accompanied with his signature photographs of grinning anglers, bathing beauties, and happy families at play." Maddry wrote, "An editor would look at a photo with Aycock Brown's name on it and tell the desk man to run it. 'It's not that good,' he'd say, 'but Aycock's going to raise hell if I don't print it or else fill my mailbox with shipments of those Dare County figs. I don't know which is worse.'"

In September 1965, Aycock told a reporter for *The News & Observer* that he wrote about "anything that's tourist bait":

> *The place is drenched with history and I write lots of historical items that I send out with pictures. History is good copy; the newspapers will use it. And it draws tourists, too. People will come in the middle of the winter to see a historic site. History draws people from far away. I don't know why but it does....*
>
> *When a man comes down here and catches a big fish, I take a picture of it and send it along, with proper information, to his hometown paper. This morning I went out and got some pictures of a group of young girls from Greensboro who are going to ride bikes down the Outer Banks, down to Ocracoke, they said. I'll do that one for the Greensboro papers. Since they're wearing bathing suits, I'll probably take an extra picture or two and send them to other papers. I think they'll use 'em.*

Aycock unabashedly used shots of women on the beach, tourists, and favorite models of his, including Dotty Fry, to publicize the Outer Banks. He was a natural flirt, but he was always professional, his first and only love being his Esther.

Aycock continued his chat with the Raleigh paper, talking about going out on fishing boats to take shots, even though he didn't fish himself. "There's something romantic about fishing boats," he said, "In fact, there's something romantic about just about everything. Why, I believe I could fill up the hotels here with people who want to be in a hurricane."

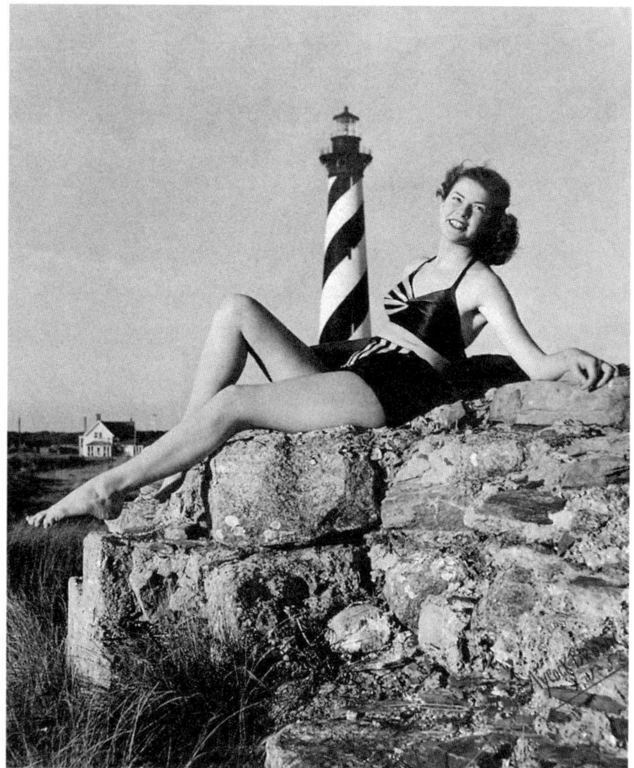

Reclining on old foundation blocks from an earlier lighthouse, Barbara Lee Barnett of Buxton manifests the beauty that could be found on Hatteras Island. Aycock played off her striped bathing suit when composing the photo in 1952. *ABC, John Havel.*

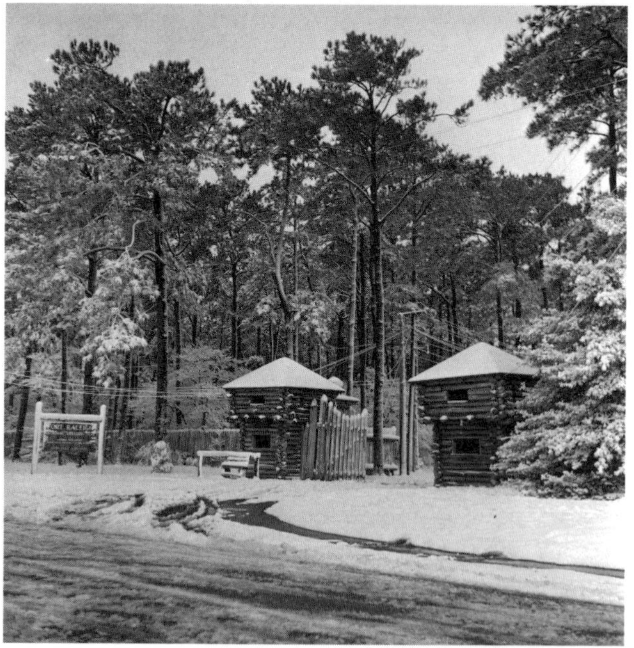

Aycock captured the entrance to Fort Raleigh on a rare Roanoke Island snow day. When the National Park Service took control of the site in 1941, it began tearing down the log buildings that the Works Progress Administration constructed, citing that they belonged on the Western frontier. *ABC, OBHC, SANC.*

Aycock kept casting his PR lines far and wide. One of the many caught on his hook was Chester Davis of *The Winston-Salem Journal*:

> *Aycock is not a sensational literary light. He is a man of unbelievable enthusiasm…that heats his thinking to a point where words steam out of his mouth with a hiss and a sizzle. In writing, Aycock has a tendency to fire words so fast that they climb up on one another's back and ride piggy-back.*
>
> *Give Aycock Brown sand and sea and water and he will make something newsworthy of it…whether it be a two-headed turtle, a hurricane, a bathing beauty, or a bit of lore from the Outer Banks, it takes on freshness when Aycock tells a story and fires it out to editors.*

Aycock's lines were also hooking pundits nationwide. Gilbert Love, the travel columnist for *The Pittsburgh Press*, wrote about an Outer Banks visit in the 1950s:

> *Rain had lashed the Outer Banks all night. At dawn I was awakened by the telephone in my room at the Carolinian hotel, Nags Head.*
>
> *The caller was Aycock Brown. "If you still want to go to Hatteras today, I'll take you," he said. "You might get stuck. Anyway, there are some things I want to show you."*
>
> *He picked me up and we went splashing southward over often-flooded roads, hurrying to make the Oregon Inlet ferry, as one often did in the days before the big bridge. As we rocked across the inlet, Aycock recited tales of sports events that had to be cancelled, with audiences in their seats, because one team got hung up on a shifting sand bar.*
>
> *The weather cleared somewhat while we were driving the long, lonely road through the Pea Island National Wildlife Refuge. We stopped to inspect the remains of a wrecked ship….At Rodanthe, Aycock chuckled over tales of the Old Christmas celebration held there each January 5. He was much more serious in telling about the lifesaving stations on this coast and the crewmen they had rescued after ships were torpedoed, often within sight of persons on shore.*
>
> *In Buxton we listened for a time to an elderly gentleman who told some fairly wild stories about his adventures at sea. In Hatteras, Aycock steered me to backyards where grapefruit and orange trees were growing.*
>
> *Somewhere along that area we walked through a big house whose first floor was almost entirely devoted to pieces of driftwood picked up by the lady of the house because of some resemblance to Bible characters or situations.*

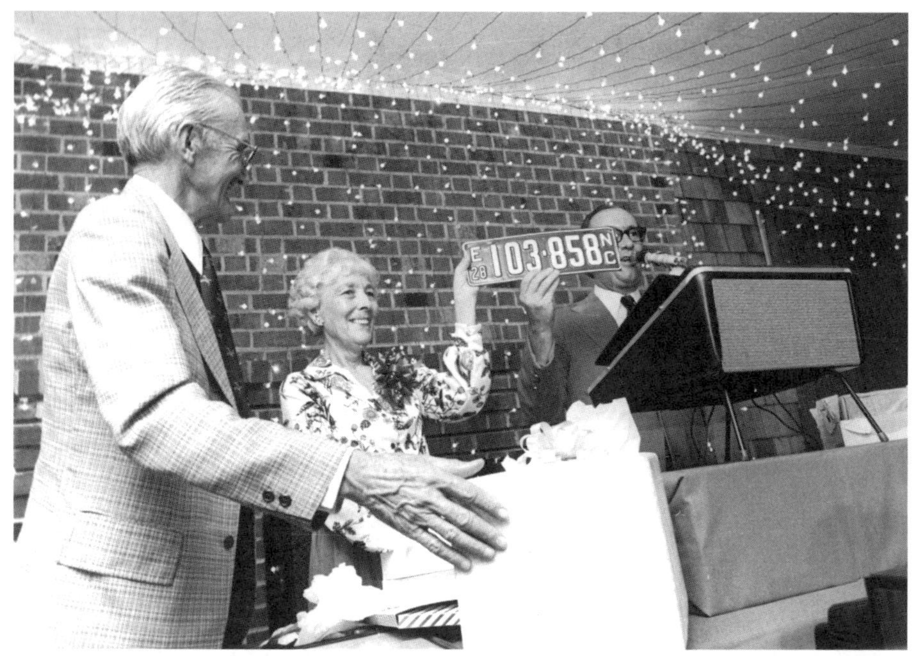
E 28 103·858 NC

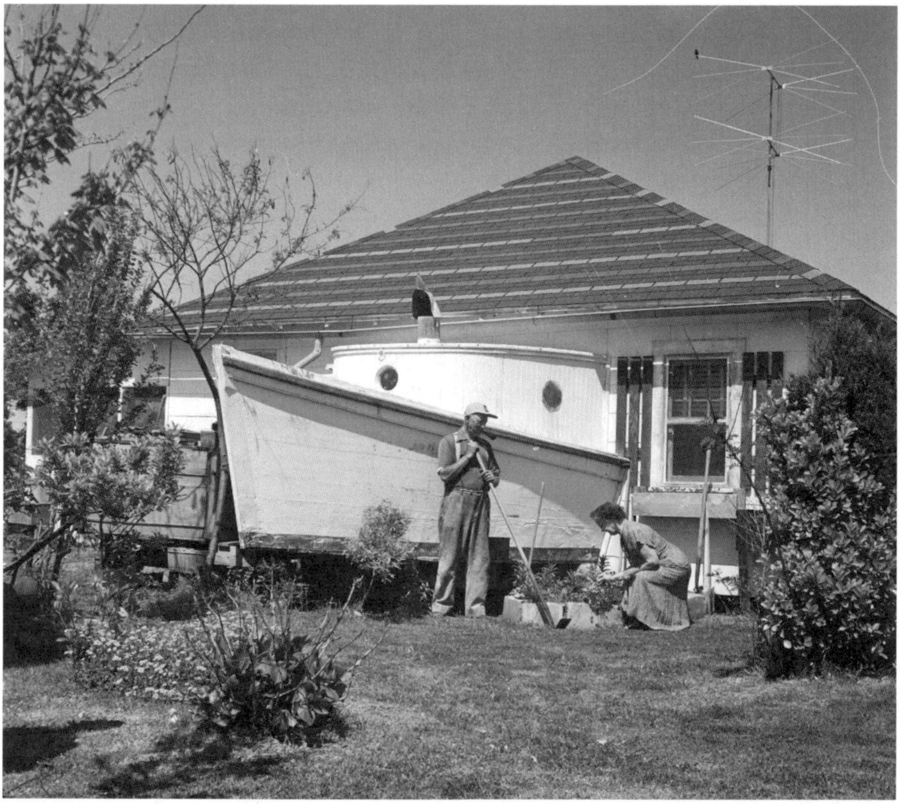

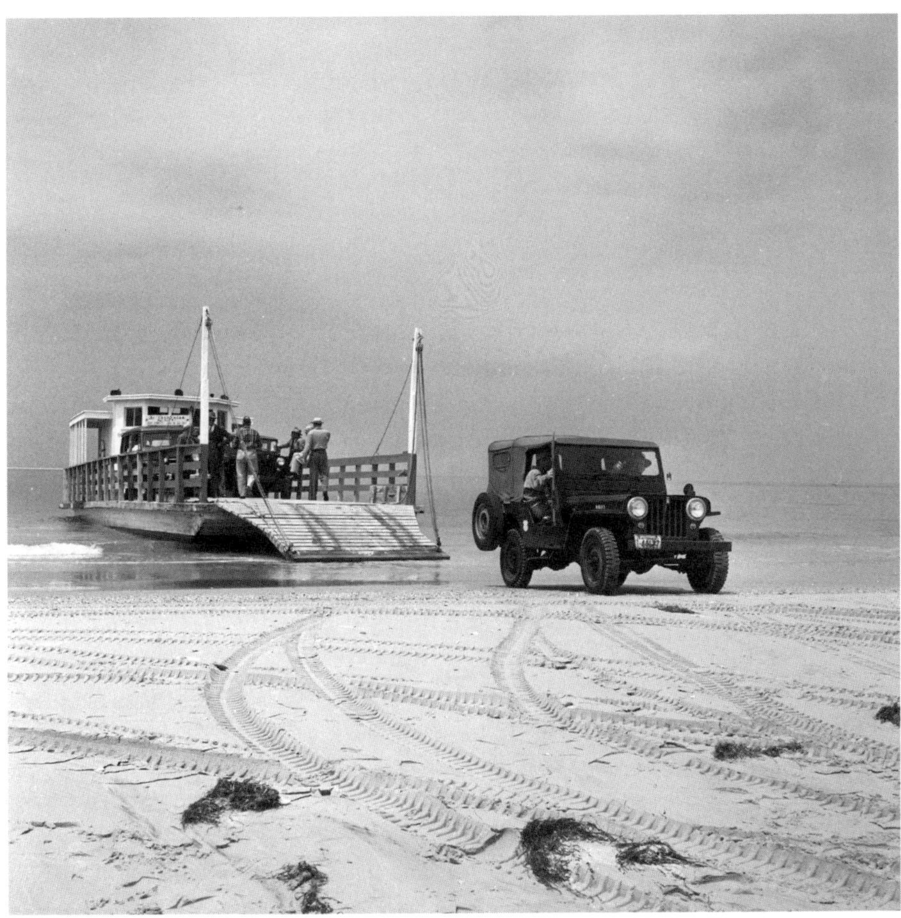

Opposite, top: At an event celebrating Aycock's life at the Seafare Restaurant in 1972, Esther was also honored and given a vintage license plate. Aycock and Esther were a solid couple and a loving example for their family. *Mike Williams, RV Owens.*

Opposite, bottom: Aycock's photo of Jerry Turner and his wife at their home in Wanchese caused the site to become an unofficial tourist attraction. This house built around an old boat was originally cobbled together by Colonel George Gillette in 1950. *ABC, OBHC, SANC.*

Above: As one of the vehicles advertised, The Carolinian hotel sponsored Jeep junkets along the Outer Banks. Aycock took a travel columnist on a similar lark and photographed a Jeep disembarking the Hatteras ferry in 1954. *ABC, OBHC, SANC.*

> *When we got back to Nags Head I had material for half-a-dozen columns in* The Pittsburgh Press. *I'm sure they did no harm to the cause of tourism on the Outer Banks.*

Indeed. To this day, visitors from Pennsylvania make up a large part of Outer Banks visitors.

~

Aycock began using Yashica twin-lens reflex cameras when they first came out in the early 1950s and stuck with them for most of his life. He did all his own developing and printing, not at his office but in a darkroom at his house, carefully developing his negatives and hanging them out on a short clothesline to dry and transform to finished photos. "Pictures help to sell the area better than anything else," Aycock once said. "They'll cut your stories [press releases] but if the picture is good, they'll use it. All told, I have about 500 outlets, including newspapers, both daily and weekly; outdoor editors; drama editors; metropolitan editors in other states; and radio and television stations. There is one thing about it: If you don't have publicity, you don't get people to come, and if people don't come, nothing happens."

Photographer Drew Wilson said:

> *Aycock was remarkable in that he not only got out to make the pictures, but he had to return to Manteo to develop and print them. Aycock wasn't making just one print. He would make dozens and dozens of copies of a particular picture to send in the mail to newspapers across the state and to some of the larger papers out of state. He wrote captions for every batch of photos. He would write a short release and a personalized note to the newspaper editors he knew. Then he would put each batch in its own envelope, address it and cart it off to the post office in tall stacks to be mailed up and down the east coast. With every envelope, Aycock was "selling" the idea of the Outer Banks, from happenings at* The Lost Colony, *shipwrecks, pretty girls on shipwrecks, big fish, big fish with pretty girls, Wright Brothers commemorations, lighthouses, all of the magnificent aspects of the great "Sir Walter Raleigh Coastland."*

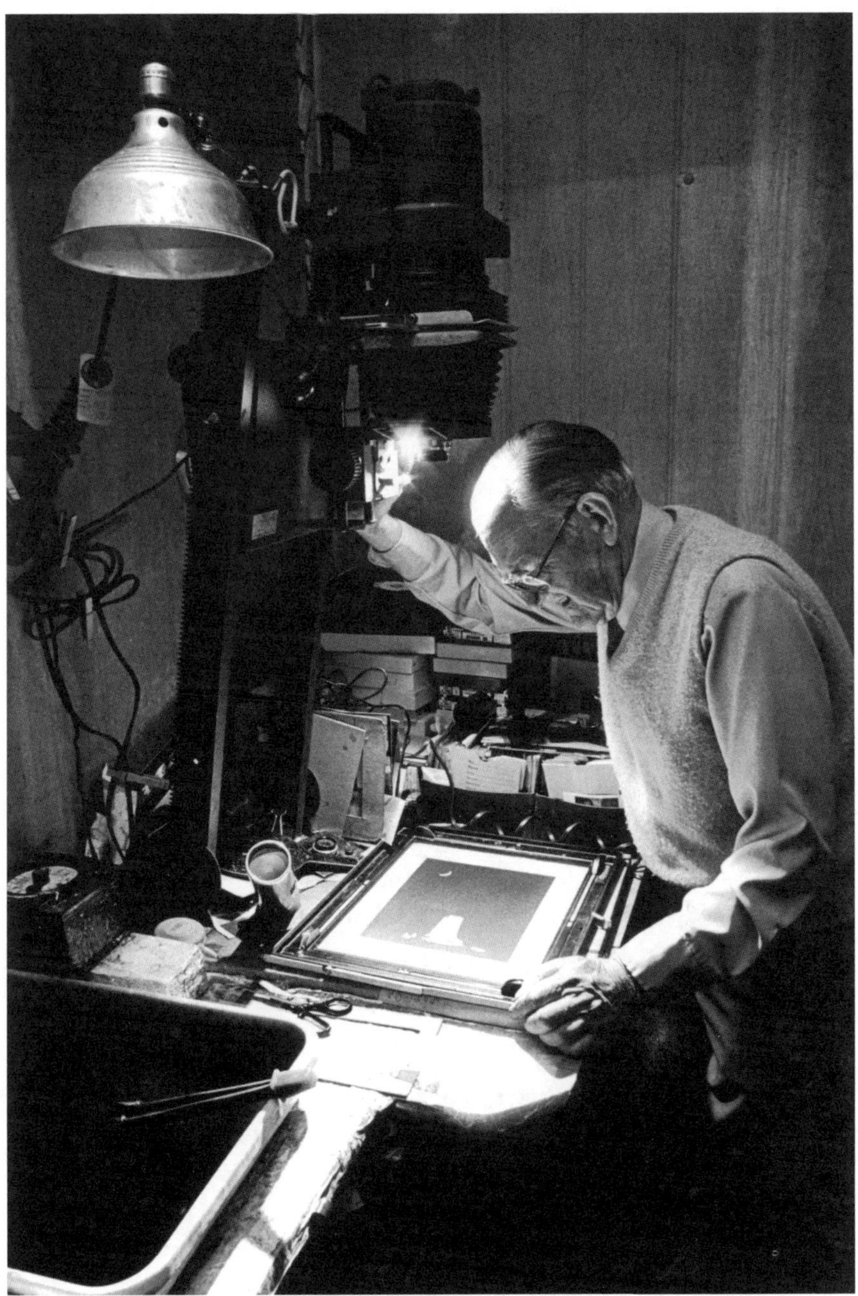

The end of every day found Aycock in the darkroom at his home processing the day's film. He re-created those moments with his most famous picture for photographer J. Foster Scott toward the end of his life. *J. Foster Scott, Vanessa Foreman.*

David Stick wrote, "Though Aycock won several awards for news photography, his effectiveness was not in the quality of his work but rather in the fact that his pictures appear in print, day after day and year after year."

Aycock knew he had to do the office work, but he was most comfortable cruising the Outer Banks coastline, stopping often to talk to his many friends and snap photos. The North Carolina coast runs for about three hundred miles, the largest segment being the two hundred miles of the Outer Banks, from the Virginia border north through Hatteras and Ocracoke, before the southern coast of the state begins. NC 12 closely parallels the Outer Banks beach line, the closest thing North Carolina has to an oceanfront highway. Aycock, who began his work on the southern coast, was determined to make the Outer Banks the most sought-after part of his state's coast. He fell in love with that region and the people who lived and worked on it. They were hurting, with fishing and Coast Guard jobs being their main line of work. Aycock knew that tourism could save them.

Up and down the East Coast there were better shooters and better writers than Aycock. He wasn't an artist and never claimed to be. But he was tireless, fast, creative, and, yes, gimmicky with his shots, charming newspaper and magazine friends to take his photos and stories nationwide. "He thought quickly, he moved quickly, and he was very loyal to his county," Kathy Spencer said. Aycock's work was paying off. By the 1960s, the Dare County population of 7,500 year-round residents was swelling to 50,000 in the summer, bringing in tens of thousands of dollars.

Aycock's heart for the Outer Banks was as big as the ocean.

He gave back through his work and through constant small ways, including holiday gifts to widows and bank tellers, as *Virginian-Pilot* reporter Lorraine Eaton later wrote. Strangers in need also found an easy touch with Aycock. *Virginian-Pilot* columnist Larry Maddry once watched Aycock give fifty dollars to a stranger:

> *"How do you know you'll ever get that money back?" I asked Aycock.*
> *"Oh, I always do," he replied. "I have a theory that if you do something for somebody, it comes back to you tenfold."*

Aycock's son Billy gave a fine example of his father's giving nature in his 2006 memoir *Mullet Roar and Other Stories by an Outer Banker.* Billy, who has since died, wrote about a December afternoon in 1950 when he was ten, riding through Manteo with his father, who went to work before daylight and came home after dark:

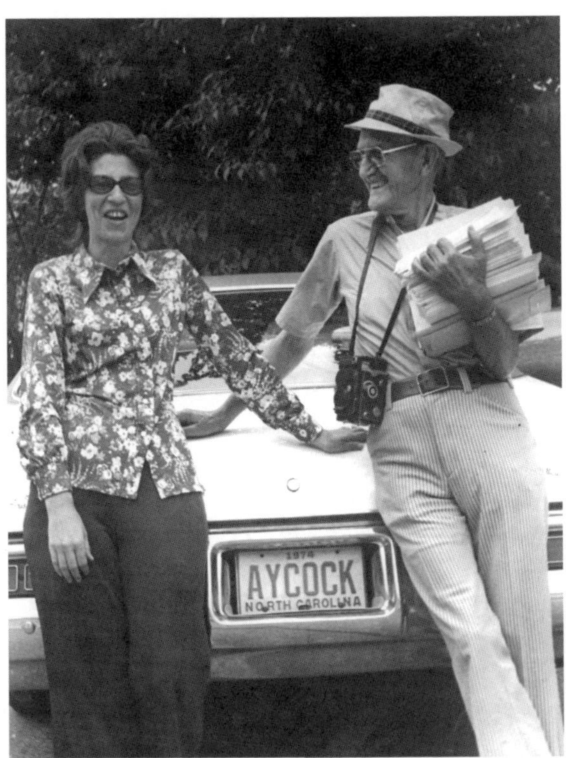

Right: Sharing a laugh, Aycock poses with longtime friend and coworker Sarah Owens at the rear of his car. He was on his way to the post office to mail a stack of press releases and accompanying photos. *Ray Couch, RV Owens.*

Below: Returning from his daily trip to the post office, Aycock showed Sarah Owens all the letters she would read and answer. As his associate at the Dare County Tourist Bureau, she would send brochures in response to vacationers' inquiries. *J. Foster Scott, RV Owens.*

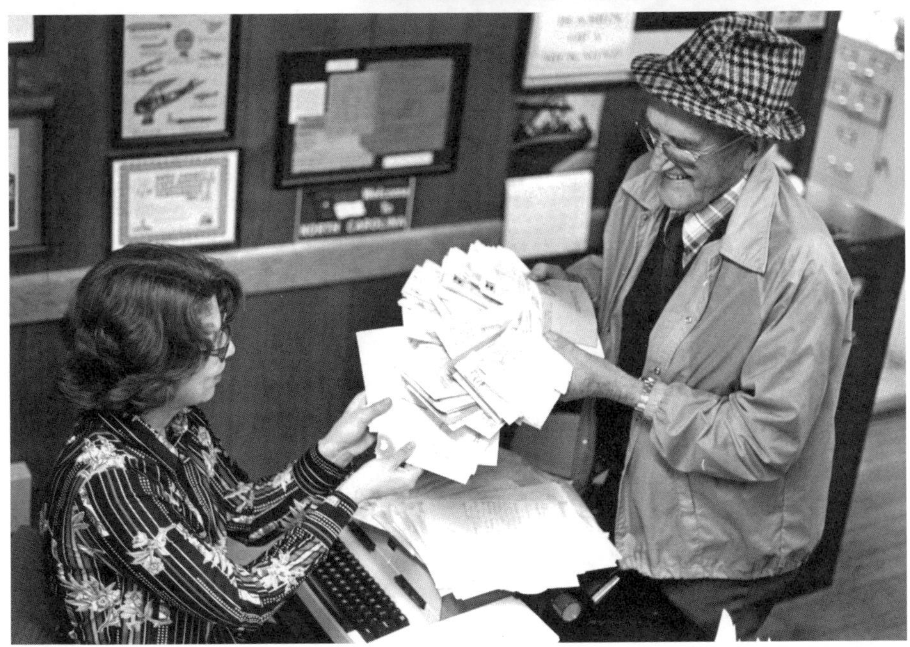

We were not a rich family. My father and mother didn't talk about money in front of me or my brother and my sister. To tell the truth, not many people earned very large salaries in 1950 along the Outer Banks. Still, we knew that we were not rich. It seems like we had everything except money. My dad had a very respectable job, and his efforts earned him the confidence and respect of almost everybody in our little community....I remember that school was out for the Christmas holidays and that it was getting late on a cold December afternoon when I dropped by my dad's office to see if he would give me money for the movie that night. As I walked in, I met him on his way out. He was heading to the post office to get a news story out in the late mail. At first I just stood there making small talk and trying to get the nerve to ask for some money. He knew I was after something, and he interrupted me, saying, I'm in a hurry to make the mail, so come on and we'll talk in the car....

It was starting to get dark. Twilight was creeping in. Christmas lights hung from pole to pole across Main Street all the way up town. I can shut my eyes now and see those bright colors of red, blue, green and white against a dark bank of clouds hanging out over the water....I noticed an old Black man coming along the sidewalk on the right-hand side of the street. From his outward appearance, the old man looked like had endured many years of poverty and hard living. He was steadying himself with a walking cane as he limped along, his right hand holding an old hunting jacket together as he tried to defend himself against the wind. He had on a hunting cap with the earflaps pulled down. His white whiskers stood out against the dark tone of his skin, he wore brown corduroy pants and an old pair of cutoff rubber boots with a slit cut for the little toe on his right foot.

As we passed this man, my dad pulled his car over on the right. He stepped out on the driver's side saying, "Come with me, son." I slid across the seat and followed him toward the back of the car. Using his key to open the trunk, he reached into a cardboard box and pulled out a bottle of wine. Next, he reached into a paper bag and pulled out a roll of aluminum wrap. He quickly wrapped the bottle and then reached back into the bag for a stick-on bow. I didn't know why he wanted me to watch him wrap a bottle of wine. As I looked around, I noticed the newspaper office was right across the street from where we were standing, so I figured he was going inside to give a Christmas present to the editor of The Coastland Times.

Instead, he walked over and handed the present to the Black man, who was now approaching our car. The man's face lit up from ear to ear. I hope I never forget that smile. They talked for a moment or two and then parted.

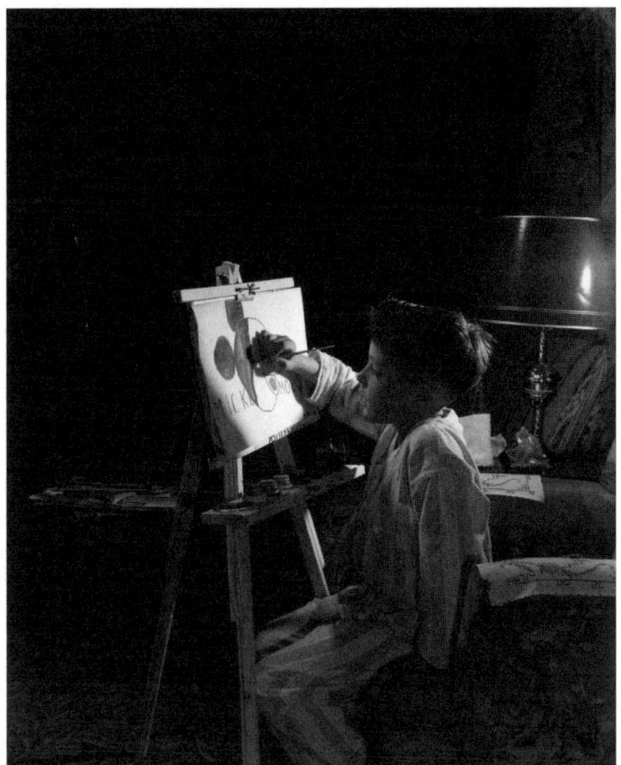

Nine-year-old Billy Brown showed artistic talent at an early age. He became an accomplished part-time artist who sold paintings out of his backyard barn. He eventually published a 2006 book containing his short stories and art, *Mullet Roar and Other Stories by an Outer Banker. ABC, OBHC, SANC.*

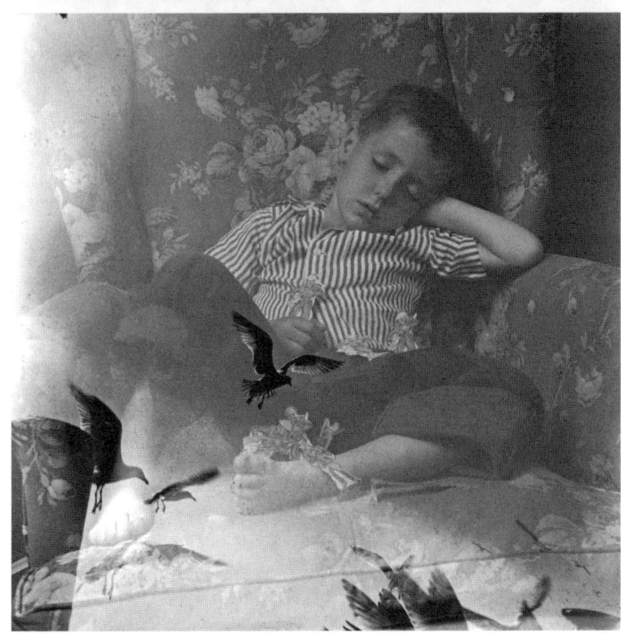

Flying seagulls over a sleeping boy tell a story of sweet dreams. This experimental photo was actually a double exposure with serendipitous results. The boy is Aycock's son Billy, who was playing with paper soldiers before falling asleep. *ABC, OBHC, SANC.*

> *By then I was back inside the car with the window rolled up. I heard them both say, "Merry Christmas" as my dad opened his door to get in. The old man was still standing there tipping his hat as we drove off….*
>
> *I asked, "Why did you give that man, a complete stranger, a present?" Daddy slowed the car to a stop right in the middle of the street and turned to me and said, "Because it made me feel good, and someday you'll understand." It took me a few years for me to understand, but he was right.*

It could have been an episode of the show Aycock's Manteo friend Andy Griffith would launch ten years later. Perhaps Aycock had told Andy the story, or similar ones, about Manteo, the real Mayberry.

4

AMERICA, MEET ANDY GRIFFITH

I found your letter perceptive, informative and enormously helpful. You may find that you have been saddled with a correspondent who will frequently draw upon your knowledge and seek your advice.
—Sheldon Leonard, producer of The Andy Griffith Show, *in a March 22, 1960 letter to Aycock, before the show premiered the following October*

In the summer of 1948, as Aycock began promoting *The Lost Colony*, he noticed a young actor relatively new to the play. Andy Griffith, a student at the University of North Carolina at Chapel Hill, had a bit part, that of a soldier. But his girlfriend, Barbara, had a big role, that of Eleanor Dare, the mother of Virginia, the first English child born in what would become the United States. Andy's good friend R.G. "Bob" Armstrong also had a starring part, that of John Borden. Toward the end of the play, after Eleanor's husband is killed by Native Americans, Eleanor and John Borden all but flirt. Andy, always competitive, must have been seething backstage. Not only did his two friends and Carolina classmates have bigger roles than he did, but Armstrong had, by some accounts, also dated Barbara before Andy.

Aycock, who relished always having the inside scoop, probably noticed that triangle and got a kick out of it. But what he really enjoyed was watching Andy's talent grow. Within a summer or two, Andy worked himself up to a starring role in the play, that of Sir Walter Raleigh. He was good in the role but could get distracted, as when Aycock once caught him on stage messing with his hair—and snapped a photo of it.

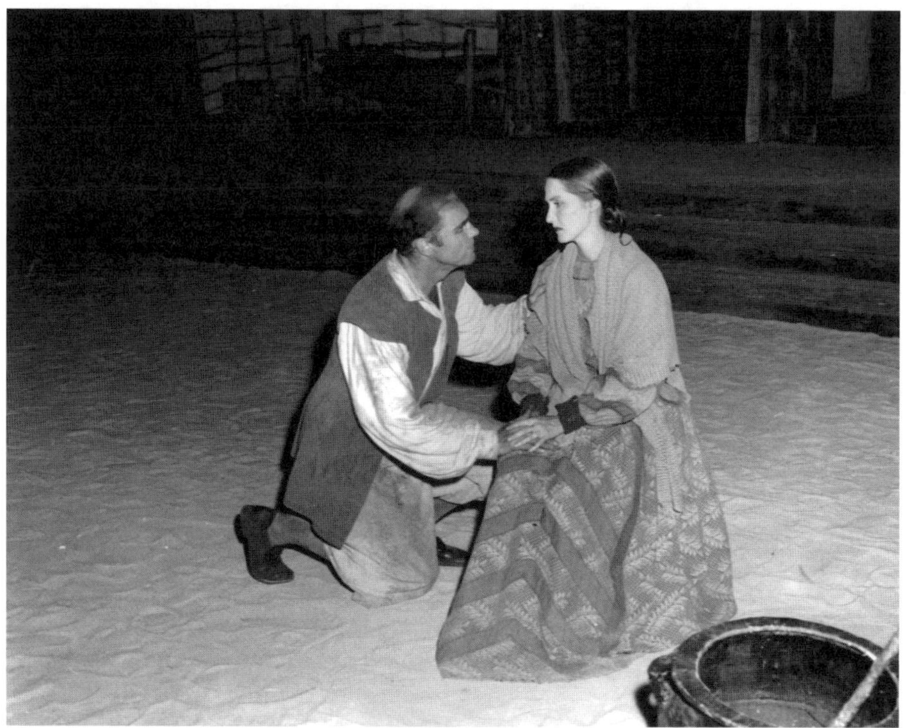

Maybe Andy was thinking about Elizabethan England and dreaming of the comedy acts he was starting to do at local nightclubs, riffing off Shakespeare's *Hamlet* and doing other routines. Aycock photographed Andy working the clubs. Aycock might have sensed the star power developing in the young entertainer. Andy learned to know the camera and meet it, on *The Lost Colony* stage and in clubs. He was charismatic and endearing with his piercing eyes. Aycock's photos captured that. Among the many photos of Outer Banks scenes Aycock was sending to his friends across the country, pressing his buddies to run them in their newspapers, were ones of Andy, his first introduction to the nation.

And just as important, Aycock may have recognized that he and Andy were kindred spirits, "wash-ins," to use the local term for outsiders on insular Roanoke Island. Few wash-ins are fully accepted by the islanders. Aycock and Andy were quickly becoming the exceptions. Aycock would have noted that Andy was becoming close with mutual island friends, the Basnights, the Wilsons, the Owens, the Daniels, the Harveys, the Bells, and others. Andy, known to party hard one night and be in church the next day, was choir director one year at Mount Olivet United Methodist Church in Manteo.

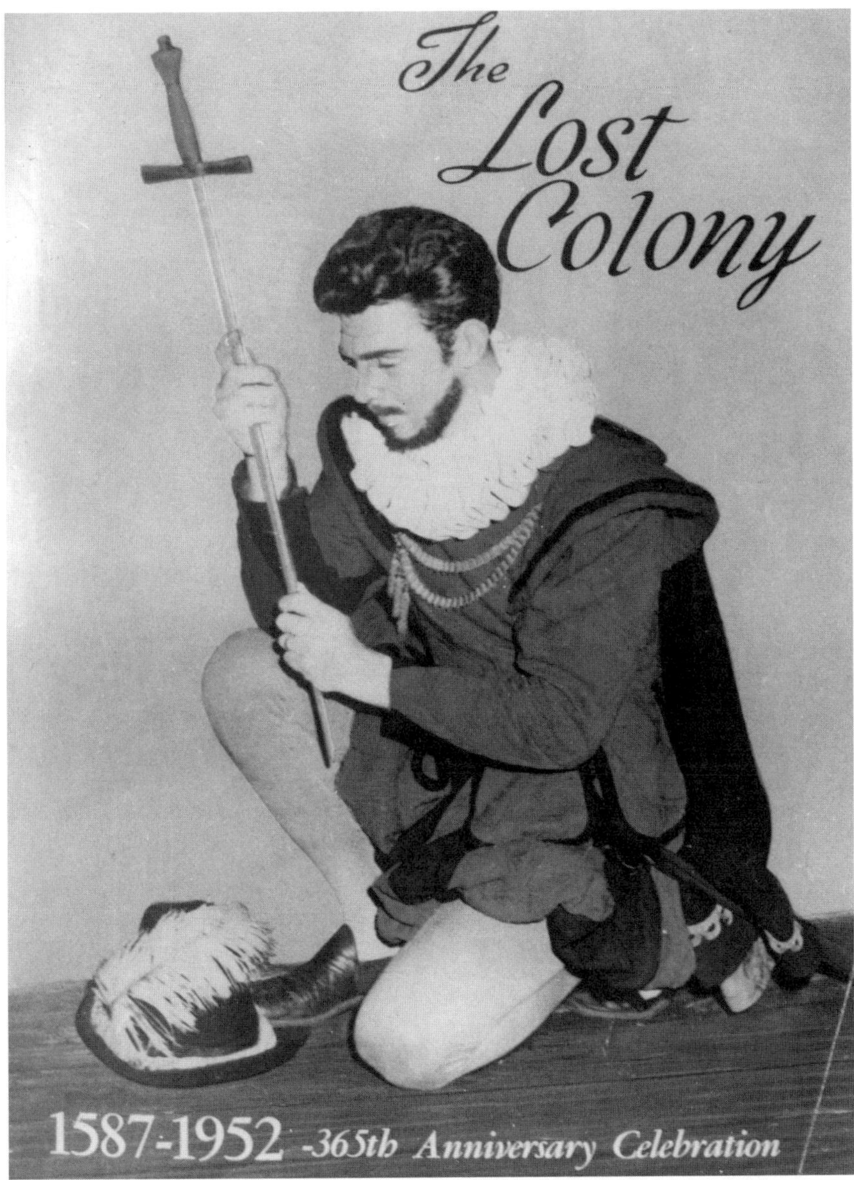

Opposite: In *The Lost Colony* drama, colonist John Borden, played by R.G. "Bob" Armstrong, appeals to a distressed Eleanor Dare, portrayed by Barbara Griffith. Bob, Barbara, and Andy Griffith met in college where they were part of the UNC–Chapel Hill acting troupe the Carolina Playmakers. *ABC, OBHC, SANC.*

Above: Sir Walter Raleigh, as portrayed by Andy Griffith, appeared on the cover of *The Lost Colony* program in 1952. Aycock recognized Andy's charismatic star power when Aycock was promoting the outdoor drama. *Manteo, A Roanoke Island Town, OBHC, SANC.*

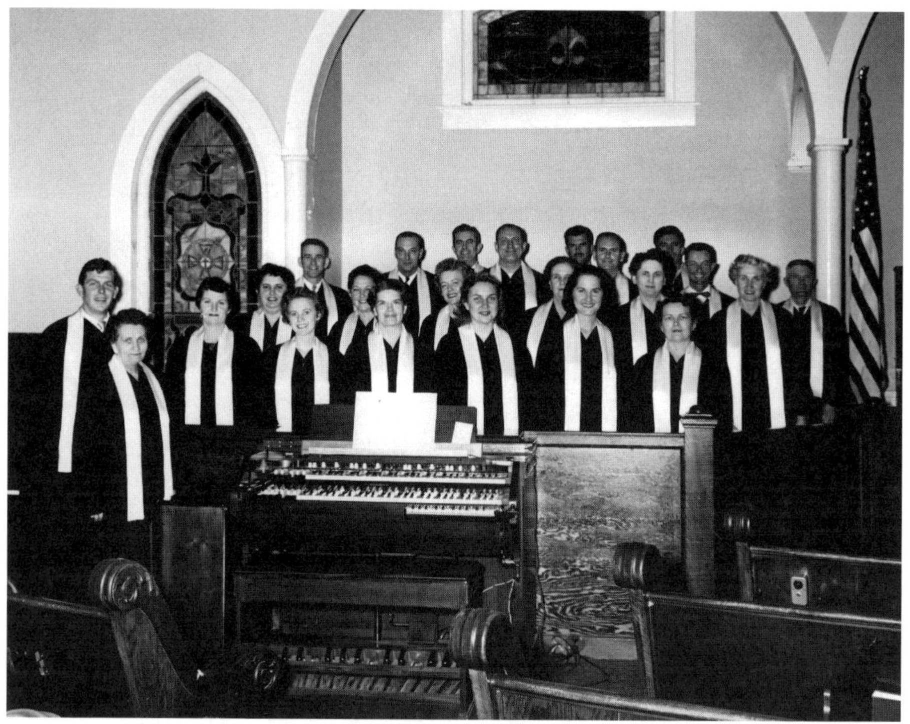

The Griffiths were part of the Mount Olivet Methodist Church choir in Manteo in the early 1950s. Andy stands to the far left, and Barbara is on the first row, the second from the right. Two episodes of *The Andy Griffith Show* revolve around Mayberry's choir. *ABC, OBHC, SANC.*

Over the next several years, Aycock watched Andy rise on Broadway and in his early movies *A Face in the Crowd* and *No Time for Sergeants.* Aycock shot an iconic photo of a wildly grinning Andy by the marquee of Manteo's Pioneer Theater for the local premiere of *A Face in the Crowd* in 1957. By then, Aycock and Andy were friends, sharing stories and gossip about their adopted hometown of Manteo.

In 1960, as Andy planned his breakthrough, his namesake show, he introduced his iconic producer, Sheldon Leonard, to Aycock by mail, apparently so that Aycock might advise Leonard on how Mayberry could look. In the years ahead, Andy would always be clear: "If Mayberry is anywhere, it is Manteo," as he once told Manteo author Angel Khoury.

In a March 17, 1960 letter to Leonard, Aycock enclosed some photos of Manteo sights and scenes and Andy on the island. "If I had a written synopsis of the plans for the show, I perhaps could think of other pictures in this general area which would tie in with Andy," he wrote.

Leonard quickly wrote back to Aycock, in a letter dated March 22, 1960.

> *I found your letter perceptive, informative and enormously helpful. You may find that you have been saddled with a correspondent who will frequently draw upon your knowledge and seek your advice.…The background material you sent me is very valuable.*

As *The Andy Griffith Show* premiered on October 3, 1960, Aycock might have gotten a kick out of the fact that the starting date was famed North Carolina novelist Thomas Wolfe's birthday—and four days before Aycock's

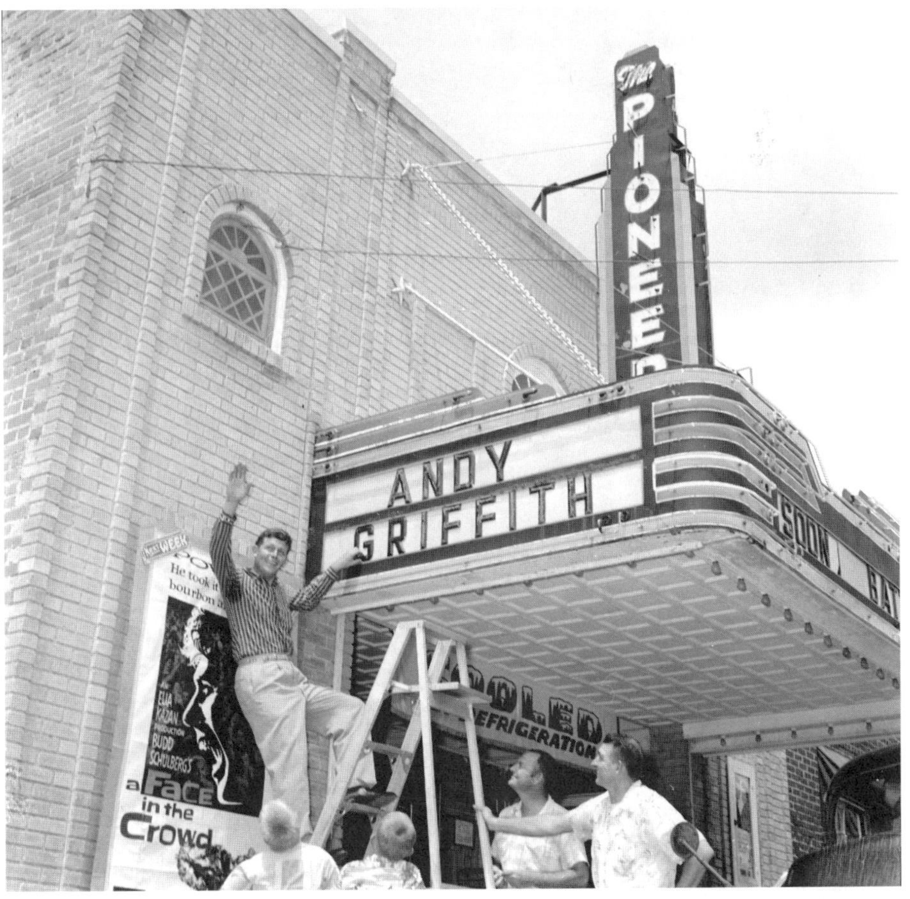

Aycock's 1957 shot of Andy Griffith announcing the opening of his movie *A Face in the Crowd* in Manteo lives on in perpetuity. Today's musical artists who play the Pioneer often "do the Andy" by waving and standing on a stepladder next to their names on the marquee. *ABC, OBHC, SANC.*

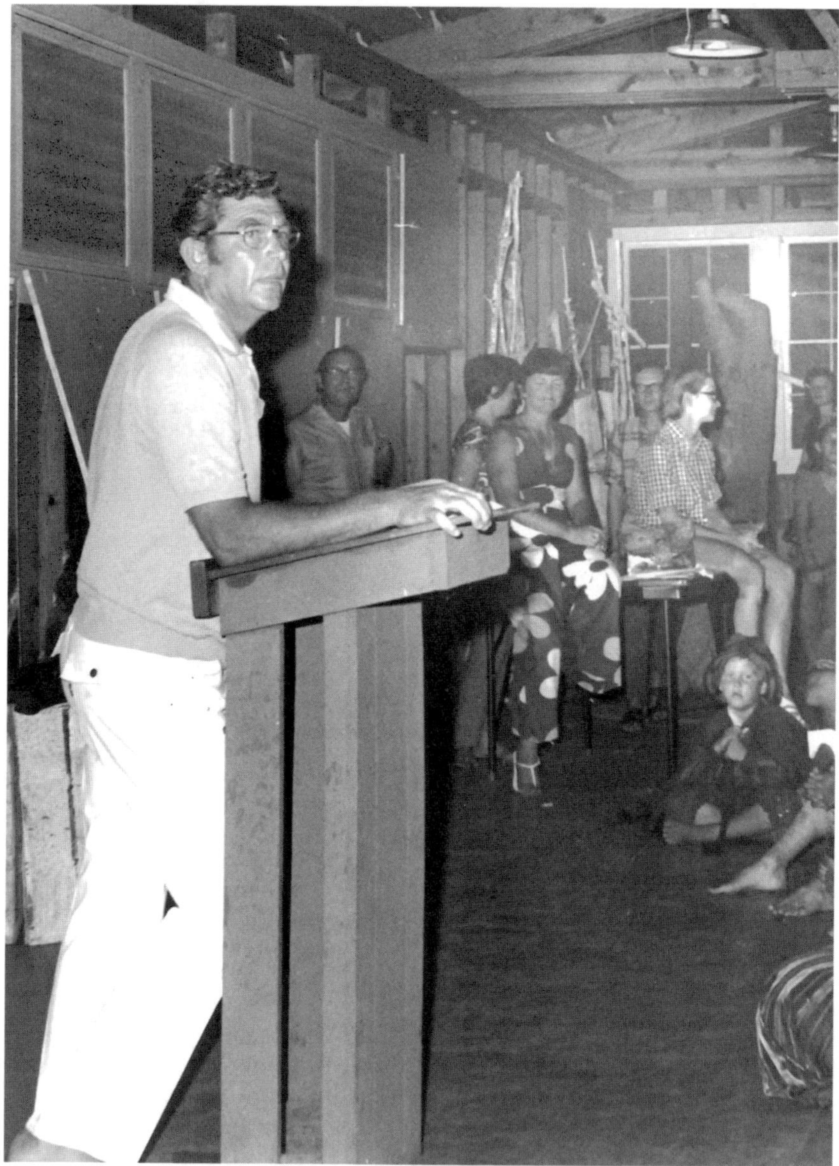

Above: Barefoot and comfortable, Andy shares some of his experiential wisdom with student actors backstage at *The Lost Colony.* His show business success allowed him to purchase a house and sixty acres on the north end of Roanoke Island near Waterside Theatre. *ABC, OBHC, SANC.*

Opposite: Irene "Renie" Smart Rains, who was often no-nonsense, affectionately gazes at Andy Griffith holding the prop sword he used playing Sir Walter Raleigh. As *The Lost Colony* head costumer and a theater arts professor at UNC–Chapel Hill, island native Rains had a long friendship with Griffith. *ABC, OBHC, SANC.*

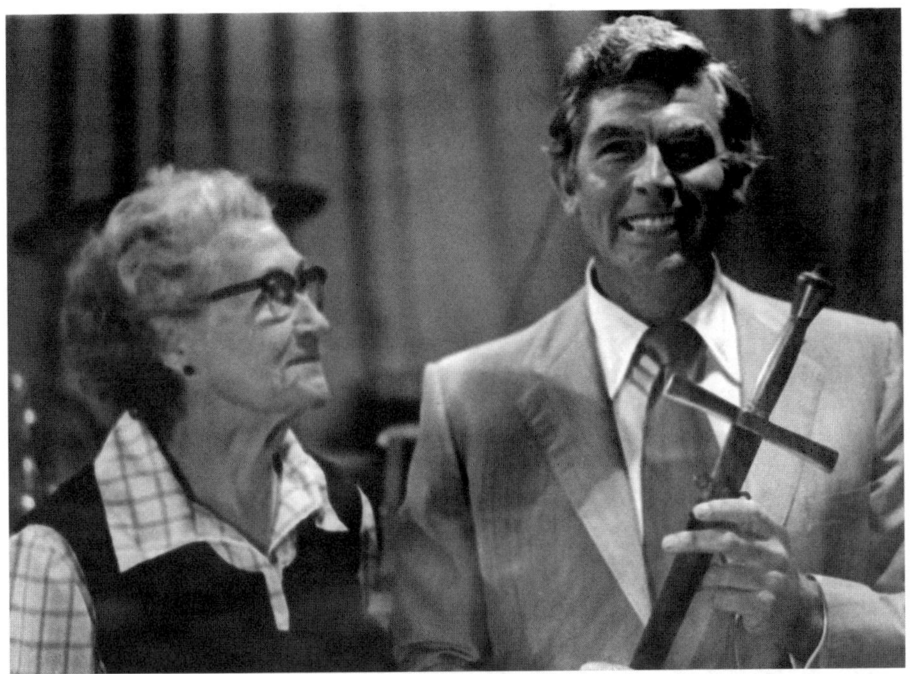

birthday. Aycock watched as the show took off. In one of the first episodes, "The Stranger," Andy's Sheriff Taylor berates his fellow residents for their cruel treatment of a newcomer to town, a lesson that could have come right out of Aycock's Manteo playbook: Welcome all.

Andy was always clear: His hometown of Mount Airy in the North Carolina foothills, where he'd been called "white trash" growing up, was not Mayberry. Andy once said, "I struggled all my young life to get out of Mount Airy. When I first came here [to the Outer Banks] in '47, I had been 'second class' all my life in Mount Airy, and Chapel Hill was a class-conscious place. I came here [to *The Lost Colony*] and Manteo—all of us lived in this solitary place—and it was classless. All of us who were colonists and singers and all that—it didn't matter where we came from—we were classless. And that was the first thing that drew me to this place. We all had an equal opportunity; we all started from the same place," Angel Khoury wrote in *Manteo: A Roanoke Island Town.*

Aycock, whose father had known a governor but grew up in modest means, could have identified. Aycock was straddling the line on the Outer Banks, hanging out with friends of all economic classes but worshiping on Sunday mornings with the landed, or sanded, gentry at St. Andrew's Episcopal Church in Nags Head.

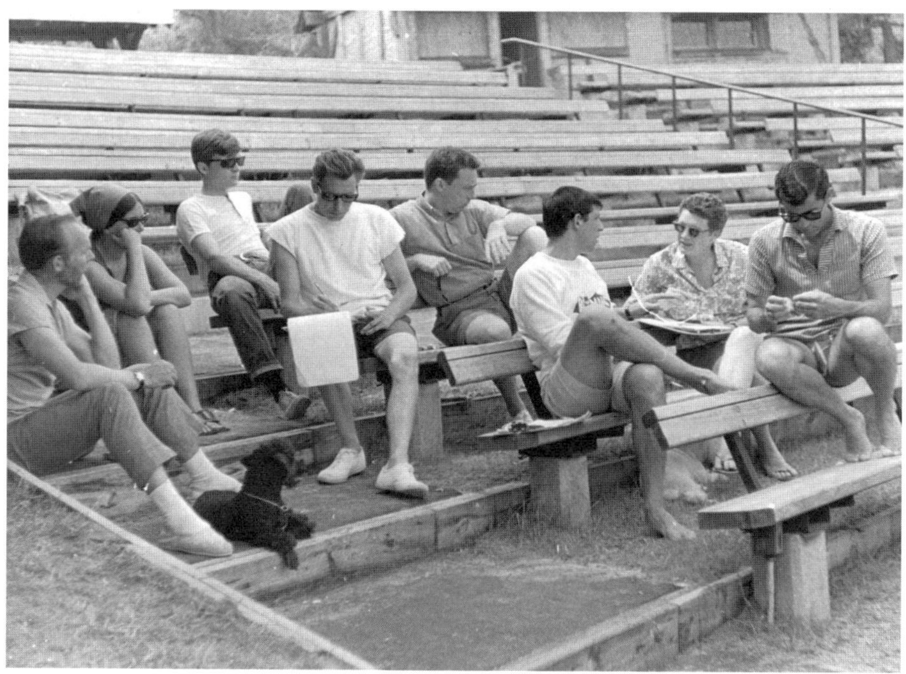

Producer and director Joe Layton (*second row from bottom, on left*) brought new life to *The Lost Colony* from 1964 to 1984. His involvement in all aspects of the show was illustrated by this collaborative meeting in the 1970s. *ABC, OBHC, SANC.*

Andy was famously private, but he let a few friends in, including Aycock and his cameras, the only shooter so trusted. Aycock shot numerous photos of the real Andy, most often when the actor was visiting backstage at *The Lost Colony*, wearing glasses and all tousle-haired with longtime friends, including Renie Rains, the play's costume designer, and Cora Mae Basnight, who played the Native American maiden Agona and was the mother of Marc Basnight. Andy watched Marc grow up and promoted his start in the state legislature. Basnight became the most powerful leader of the state senate in modern history as he pushed causes such as improving public education, one of his shared interests with Andy.

Aycock also shot numerous photos of Joe Layton, the director and choreographer of *The Lost Colony* from the mid-1960s through the early 1980s, towering, flamboyant, and handsome with angular features and dark swept-back hair, given to calling women "dahling" with a borrowed Southern accent. He was born Joseph Litchman and grew up in Brooklyn, embracing theater from early on. He worked in choreography and directed musicals in an Army Special Services unit before making his way on Broadway and in TV, working with Julie Andrews, Carol Channing, Mary Tyler Moore, Carol Burnett, and Barbra Streisand and winning Tony and Emmy Awards. Layton, brought in to rejuvenate the play, delivered a Broadway shimmer to it.

Layton was brilliant and charismatic, bringing out the best in his cast, pacing, and coaching, occasionally nipping a bit at vodka. He could live and work anywhere in the world he chose, but he loved Manteo. He was as fun-loving as a pirate, meeting his local buddies, mostly men, for breakfast at the Dutchess of Dare restaurant, where Aycock also hung out, joking and swapping island gossip. Layton was happily married to a woman but actively bisexual. He didn't tout the latter part, but the islanders, including Aycock, knew all. Their acceptance of Layton spoke volumes about their nonjudgmental way of life. The islanders had long accepted that marriage

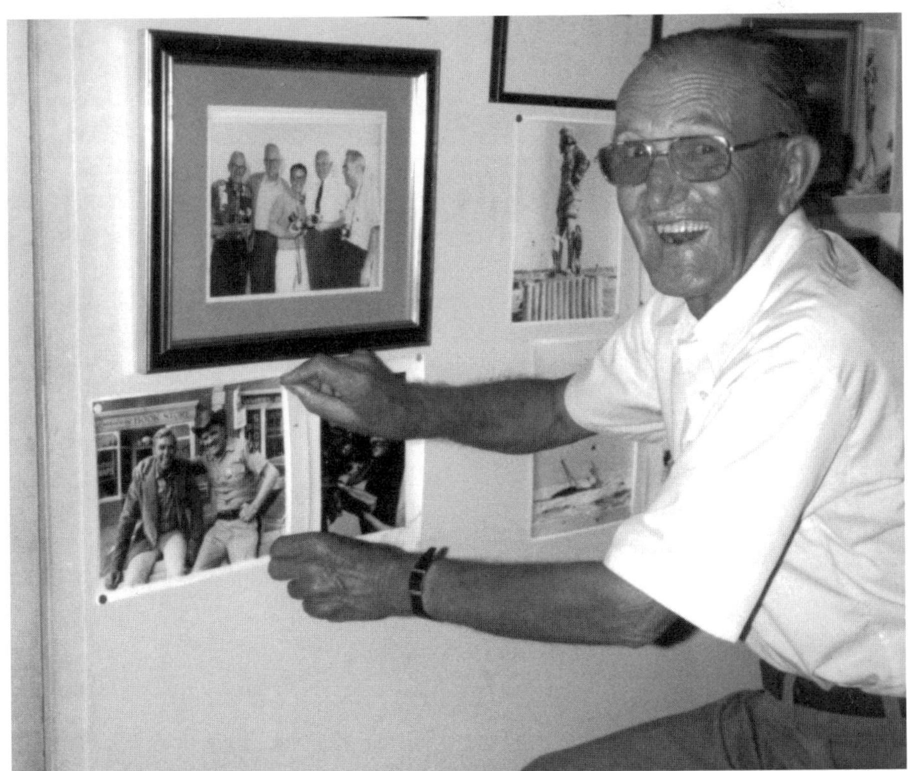

Susan Lowrance, a *Lost Colony* alumnus, took this picture of Aycock showing a photo of Andy Griffith and R.G. "Bob" Armstrong taken during a *Salvage* taping. She remembered Aycock as "an amazing person and so warm and friendly." *Susan Guthrie Lowrance.*

was not necessarily sacred and that there would be gay and bisexual relationships. The *Lost Colony* company, with its free-living members, enhanced that mindset.

The locals came to welcome Joe Layton as one of their own, just as they'd done for Aycock and Andy.

5

ALWAYS WITH THE FISH—AND A BIG EVENT

Aycock was laying the seeds for the Outer Banks, eventually Oregon Inlet in southern Dare County, to become a popular launching point for the Gulf Stream, building on the strong work of charter boat Captain Ernal Foster of Hatteras and others.

Commercial fishermen on Hatteras Island knew there were large gamefish in the Gulf Stream thirty-five miles off their shores. Occasionally, a tuna or marlin carcass would wash up on the beach. It wasn't until World War II concluded, however, that they had the know-how, technology, and better boats to get out there. Aycock was on the scene at the beginning, envisioning the tourism dollars this enterprise could reap.

Fishermen on both Roanoke and Hatteras Islands heard about the big money tourists were paying in other states, and in the Bahamas, to get out to warmer Gulf Stream waters to try to catch the monster tuna, swordfish, and marlin that swam there. Big-game fishing was gaining popularity on the East Coast as books and articles by Ernest Hemingway and other adventure writers piqued the imaginations of sportfishermen. Commercial fishermen turned charter fishermen began to buy World War II surplus items such as military ocean charts, LORAN navigational systems, and marine motors that could help them make the trip to deeper waters. They also used their skills, intuition, and the ability "to think like a fish" to learn the behaviors and probable location of trophy fish. Finally, they banded together, always going out in groups of charter boats so that they could help each other in the event of breakdown or unexpected foul weather.

During this postwar era, captains made trips to fishing meccas like Ocean City, Maryland, to pick the brains of charter sportfishermen about

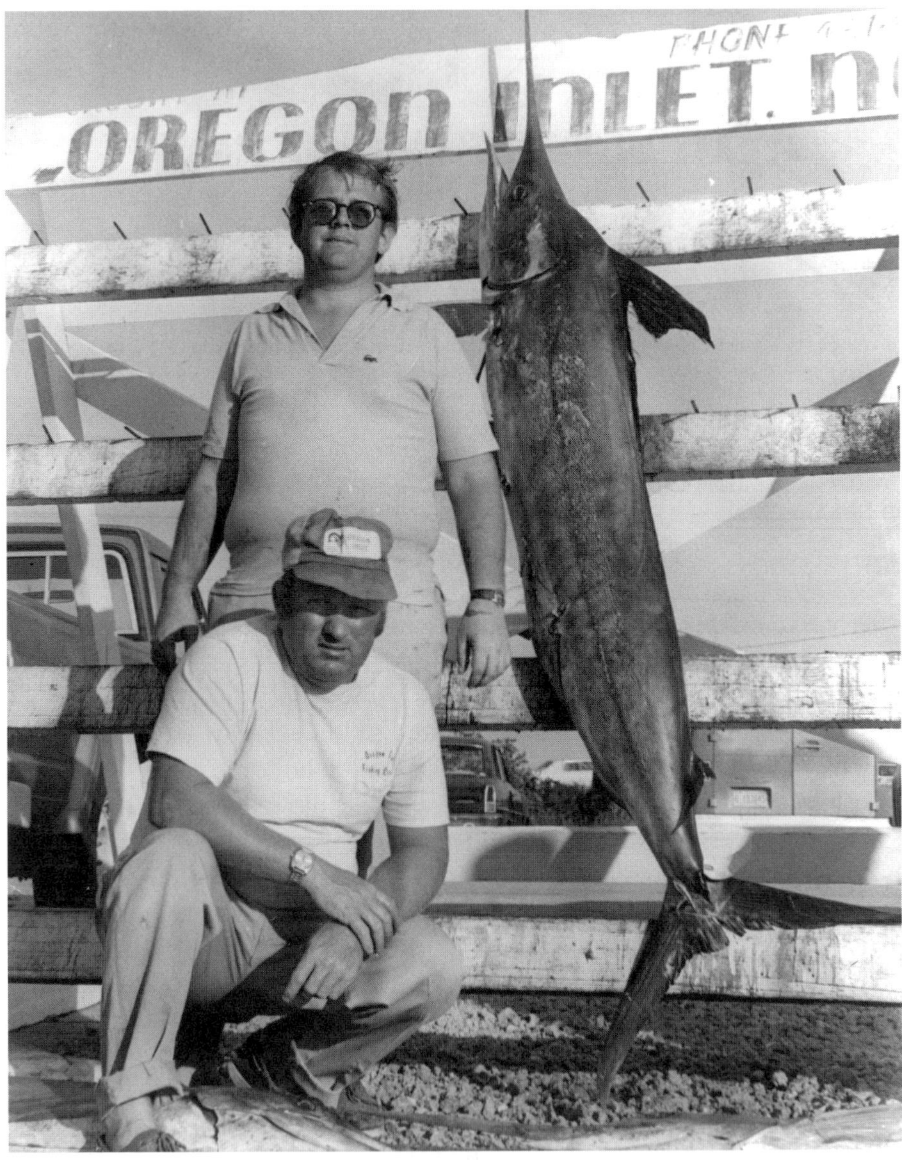

Aycock snapped thousands of fishing photos like this one of Richard E. Railey Jr. (*standing*), a lawyer from Courtland, Virginia, and the brother of coauthor John Railey. Captain Bobby Sullivan (*kneeling*) took Railey out on the *Marlin Fever*. *ABC, Sam & Omie's.*

what tackle and methods to use. Aycock went hunting info, too. In 1959, he flew to Nassau in the Bahamas to mine how those islands did the big-game fishing business. He told a conference there:

> *Unless the Gulf Stream changes its course, there is, in my mind, little likelihood that Hatteras will ever fail to produce big-game fish. Any area where almost 400 billfish can be boated in one season is not likely to see any of its nearby game-fishing communities become ghost towns.*

Upon his return, Aycock noted to the Manteo Rotary Club that the Bahamas are east of the Gulf Stream. "As a matter of fact, Cape Hatteras is much nearer the western edge of the Gulf Stream than Nassau is the eastern edge. And Cape Hatteras, incidentally, is actually farther east than Nassau."

He also traveled to Acapulco, Mexico, to promote big-game fishing on the Outer Banks.

Aycock was planting the seeds for the Outer Banks, eventually Oregon Inlet in southern Dare County, to become a popular entrance to the Gulf Stream, building on the strong work of Captain Ernal Foster of Hatteras and other charter captains.

"I don't know who discovered the Gulf Stream, but I do know that the romantic and mysterious body of water never had a more enthusiastic sponsor than [Aycock]," journalist W.D. Wallace wrote in the late 1950s. "Scores of people tell me that they first heard that the Gulf Stream was off North Carolina's coast through Aycock. It has been a hard struggle against Carolina indifference, and the triumph is not yet....Only in the last three years has his enthusiasm been thoroughly vindicated."

The distance from Oregon Inlet to the Stream is about thirty-five miles, or about two hours for sportfishing boats. In the 1960s and '70s, big-game fishing out of Oregon Inlet, especially for blue marlin, grew exponentially. The charter boats rolled out of Oregon Inlet at dawn throughout the summer season, with Captain Omie Tillett broadcasting a prayer over the maritime radio, and returned to the docks in a grand parade around four o'clock in the afternoon. Aycock was there, snapping photos of the patrons off the charter boats and their catches, weaving his way through small crowds of tourists who'd come to see the boats come in, flying flags that indicated what they'd caught. Four o'clock at Oregon Inlet was a big deal.

Aycock sent his photos of the really big catches, record blue marlins, to newspapers nationwide, and many of those papers ran the photos. He

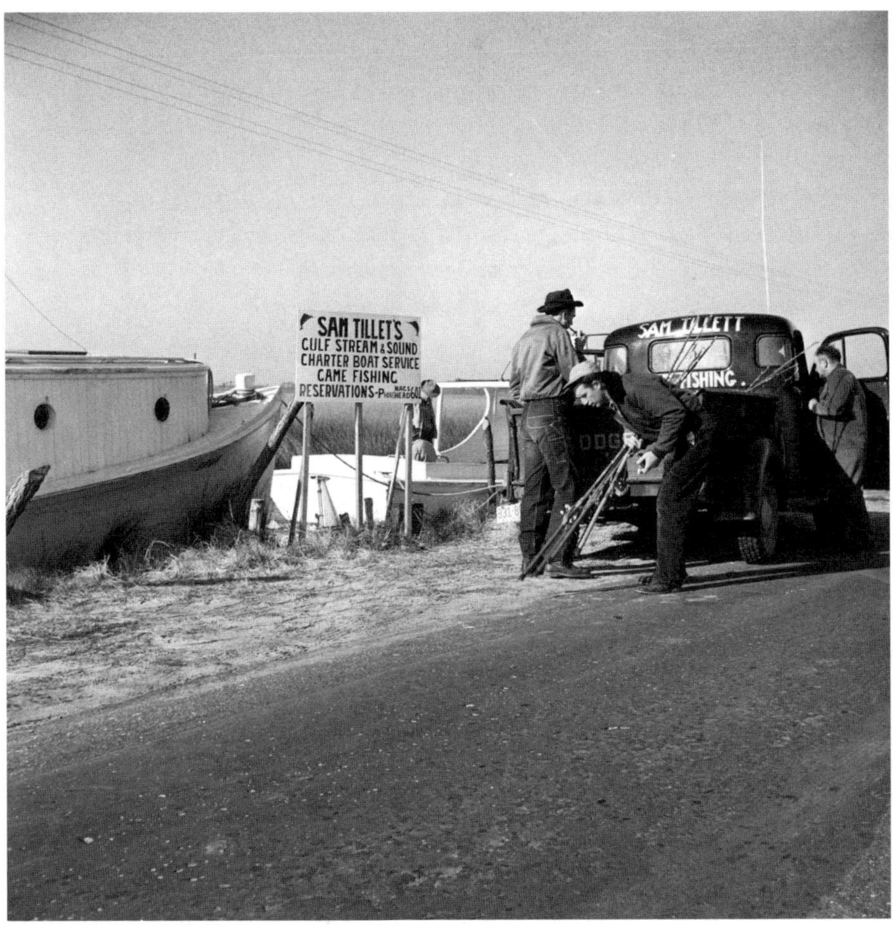

sent his photos of routine catches, a few bluefish and such, to *The Coastland Times*, which would inevitably run the shots with a credit line to Aycock and a couple of lines from him such as "John Jones, pictured here, of Pittsburgh with the fine catch he made on board the *Ava G* with Captain Frank Singer out of Oregon Inlet last week."

Aycock also sold the shots to patrons, often with his trademark wit. "Like the day…he'd posed the happy farmer with a 350-pound blue marlin the farmer had caught that day," Woodrow Price, a Raleigh newspaperman, once wrote. "'How much for one of those pictures?' the angler asked, touching Aycock on the arm.

"'I get three dollars for an eight by ten,' Aycock said.

"A pause, and then the fisherman asked, 'How much for a smaller one?'

"'I don't make 'em any smaller than that,' Aycock replied."

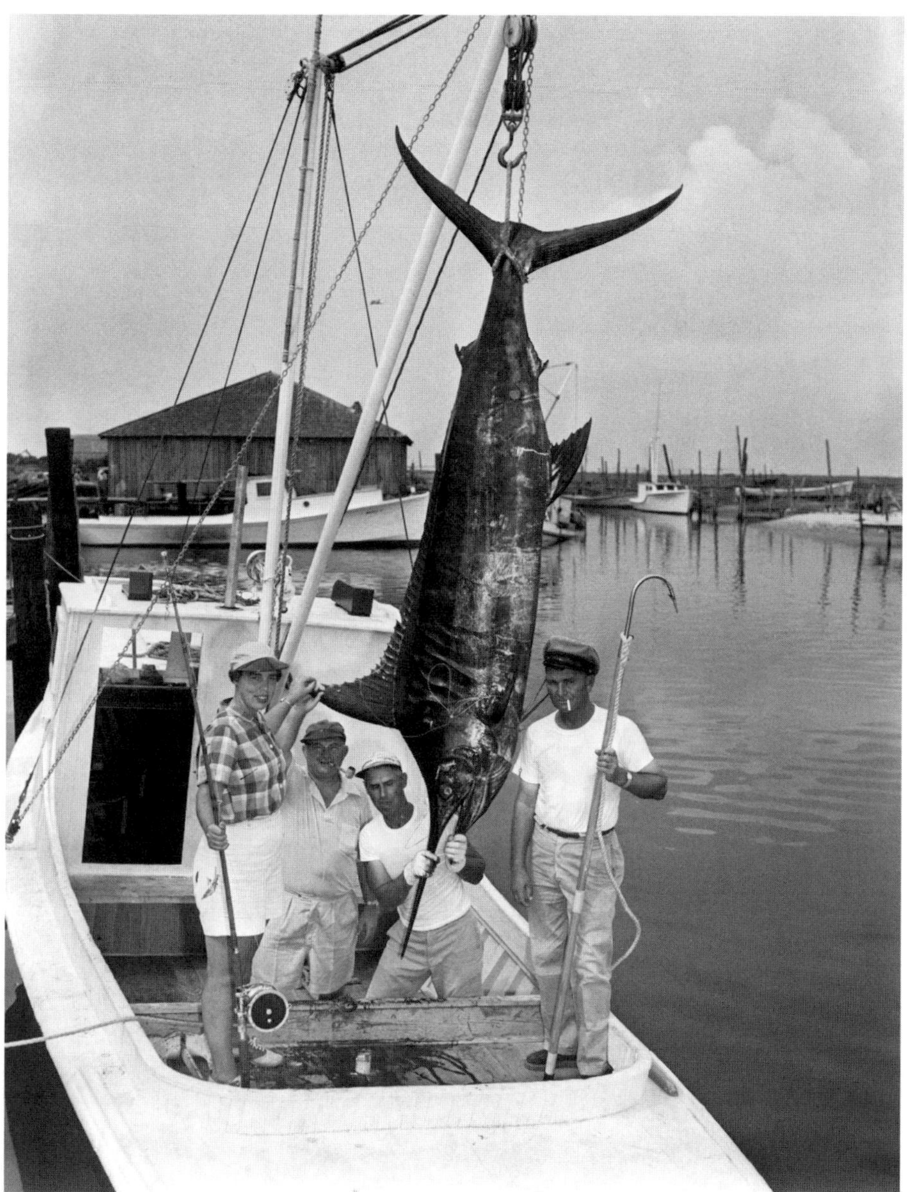

Opposite: The Tilletts, father Sam and sons Omie and Tony, were some of the first charter captains to go to the Gulf Stream. They kept their boats in Roanoke Island's Dykstra's ditch, across the road from present-day Pirate's Cove, and used their restaurant, Sam & Omie's, for booking fishing parties. *ABC, OBHC, SANC.*

Above: Aycock was at the Hatteras docks in 1952 to photograph Betsy Walker, the first woman to land a blue marlin in North Carolina. Ernal Foster (*holding bill*) was one of the pioneering charter captains to study and practice deep-sea fishing locally. *ABC, OBHC, SANC.*

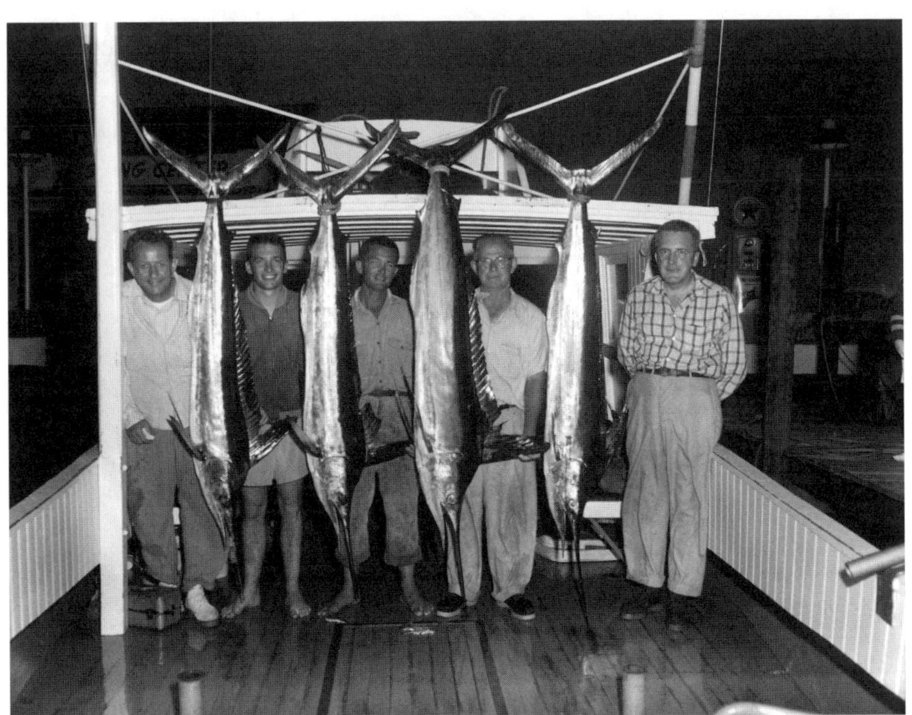

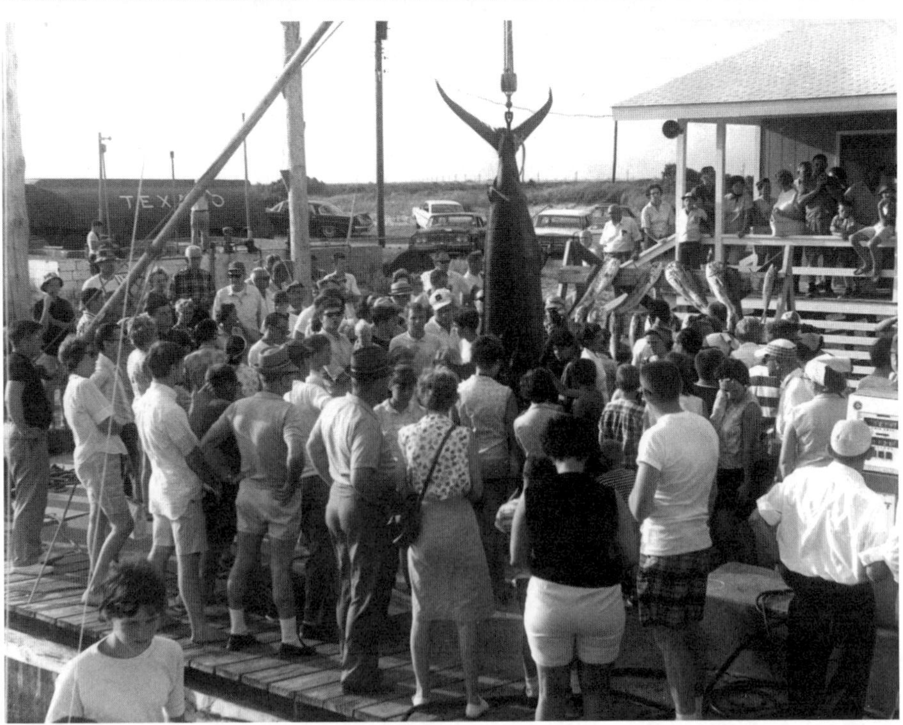

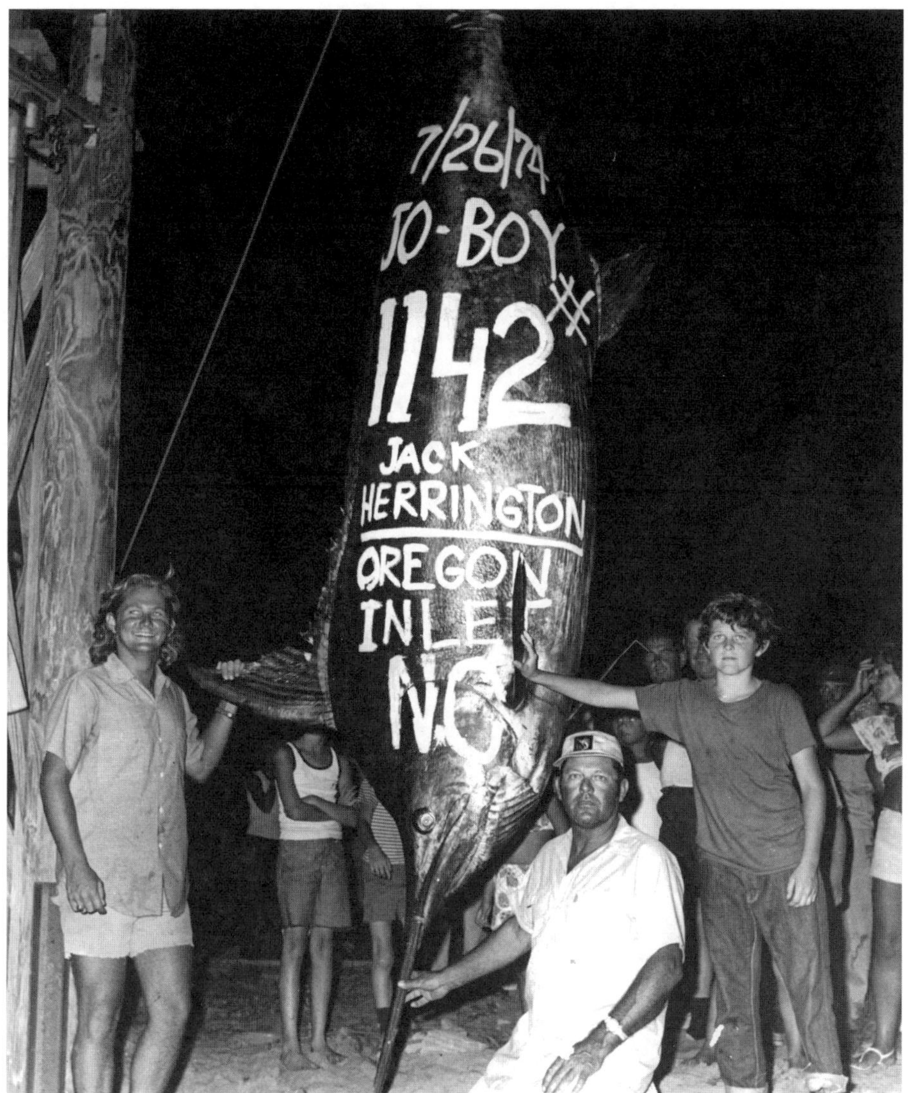

Opposite, top: Aycock kept photos interesting for the fishermen who would receive them by mail and the newspapers that would print them. Captain Omie Tillett (*center*) and his party made a nice pattern of men and white marlins aboard the *Jerry Jr.* in 1956. *ABC, OBHC, SANC.*

Opposite, bottom: The thing to do on a late summer afternoon for tourists and locals alike was to go to the Oregon Inlet Fishing Center and watch the sportfishing fleet return. Aycock was there daily to see and photograph the big catches and the beaming fishermen. *ABC, Lois Midgett Dunnigan.*

Above: Aycock dashed to Hatteras to shoot this monstrous blue marlin. After it was weighed and determined to be the world record, family-oriented Aycock pulled both of Captain Harry Baum's sons into the photograph to memorialize the significant moment. *ABC, Baum Family.*

Angel Ellis Khoury, who worked with Aycock at *The Coastland Times*, remembered editor Francis Meekins being fiercely proud of Aycock:

> *When the first-ever rival to* The Coastland Times *set up shop on the beach in 1980, Mr. Meekins banned it from the office. Marvin Beard, an LA native and once the youngest bureau chief for The Associated Press, was the first editor of the now-defunct* Outer Banks Current. *It wasn't so much the competition but rather Beard's swat at "dead fish pictures" that brought about Mr. Meekins' ire. No upstart was going to make fun of Aycock. And certainly no one who called himself "The King of Timeshare," as Beard billed himself. For Aycock, Beard was just one more person he'd lured here, another character who, thanks to his "dead fish pictures," had found his way to the beach.*

Aycock would generously make copies of his photos for the captains and their mates. Many retired charter captains have a stack of Aycock's quality photos to remember their glory days by. The captains respected Aycock. He was good to them by spreading the word about the great fishing to be had

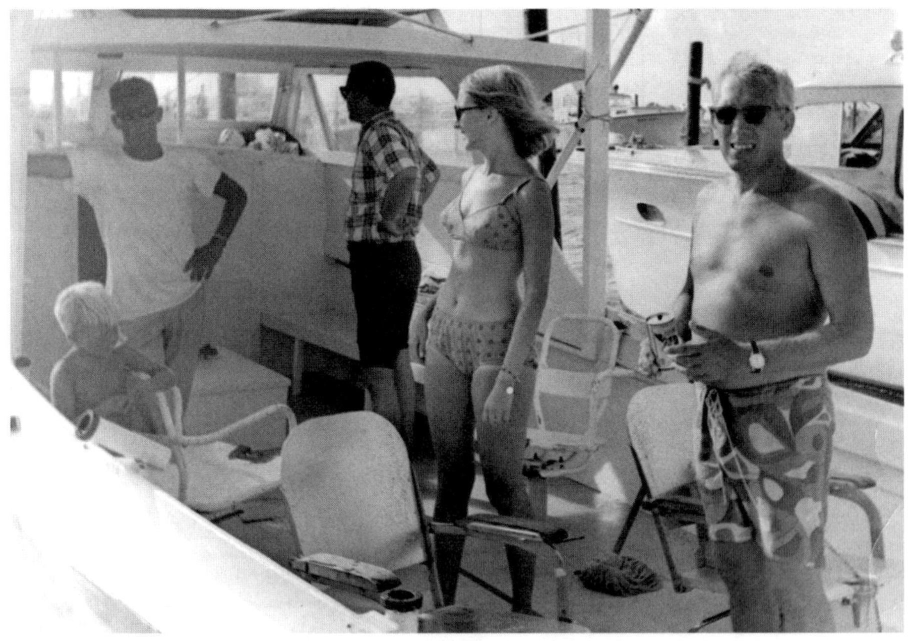

Aycock photographed his sons Billy (*left*) and Brantley (*right*) aboard Billy's charter fishing boat the *Erma Queen.* Billy taught history at Manteo schools during the school year and ran charters during the summer. *ABC, Nettie Brown Tisch.*

on the Outer Banks. He promoted them as individual captains by always printing their name and the names of their mates and boats. In turn, the captains worked with Aycock by encouraging their parties to wait for Aycock to photograph their catches.

Aycock and the captains operated in a hardworking, fun-loving, and close-knit culture. Aycock's son Billy spent his youth at Oregon Inlet, mating for many captains, most often for Joe Berry, the Inlet's first Black captain, on the *Phyllis Mae.* He eventually purchased his own boat, the legendary *Erma Queen*, which was said to have caught more fish than any of the boats in the fleet. All of Aycock's grandsons grew up working as mates on Oregon Inlet boats. Brantley's son Charlie Brown has captained charters and worked on private sportfishing boats, while his brother Mike Brown focused on commercial fishing. Billy's sons, Kenneth and Matthew, mated aboard the *Erma Queen* for their dad. Kenneth Brown went on to be a successful charter captain. Gale's son, Patrick Byrd, is a well-known charter captain. Both Kenneth and Patrick have placed in big gamefish tournaments and have won significant prizes.

Starting in 1954, Aycock promoted a key event to promote the Outer Banks—the Dare County Tourist Bureau's Pirates Jamboree—a three-day spree in which locals, including Aycock and Esther, dressed up like pirates. The event was based at the venerable Carolinian, an iconic oceanfront hotel in Nags Head that Aycock heavily promoted. The jamboree included jalopy races, pony races, fish fries, visits from dignitaries (including at least one governor), demonstrations of how the U.S. Lifesaving Service conducted rescues, and a religious service at the Waterside Theater, home of *The Lost Colony.*

That service was in sharp contrast to much of the rest of the hard-partying jamboree. Participants took off from the Carolinian in cars tricked out like pirate ships, driving south to Cape Hatteras for photos in front of the lighthouse, then came back to Manteo to hop aboard boats rigged like pirate ships for a race around Shallowbag Bay. Men grew beards for the event; even Aycock made a scruffy attempt. Beards and costumes were judged, and a king and queen were crowned at a Pirates Ball at the Casino.

The popular event ended in 1964 when the boat races in Manteo got too rowdy.

The jamboree had all been in good fun—and most important for Aycock, good business—and brought in thousands of tourists. On the streets of New York where he'd once roamed, the hard-drinking, chain-smoking "Mad Men" of Madison Avenue, with huge expense accounts, were brainstorming iconic commercials such as the one for Alka-Seltzer, "Plop plop, fizz fizz, oh what a relief it is." The Outer Banks had its own Mad Man in Aycock.

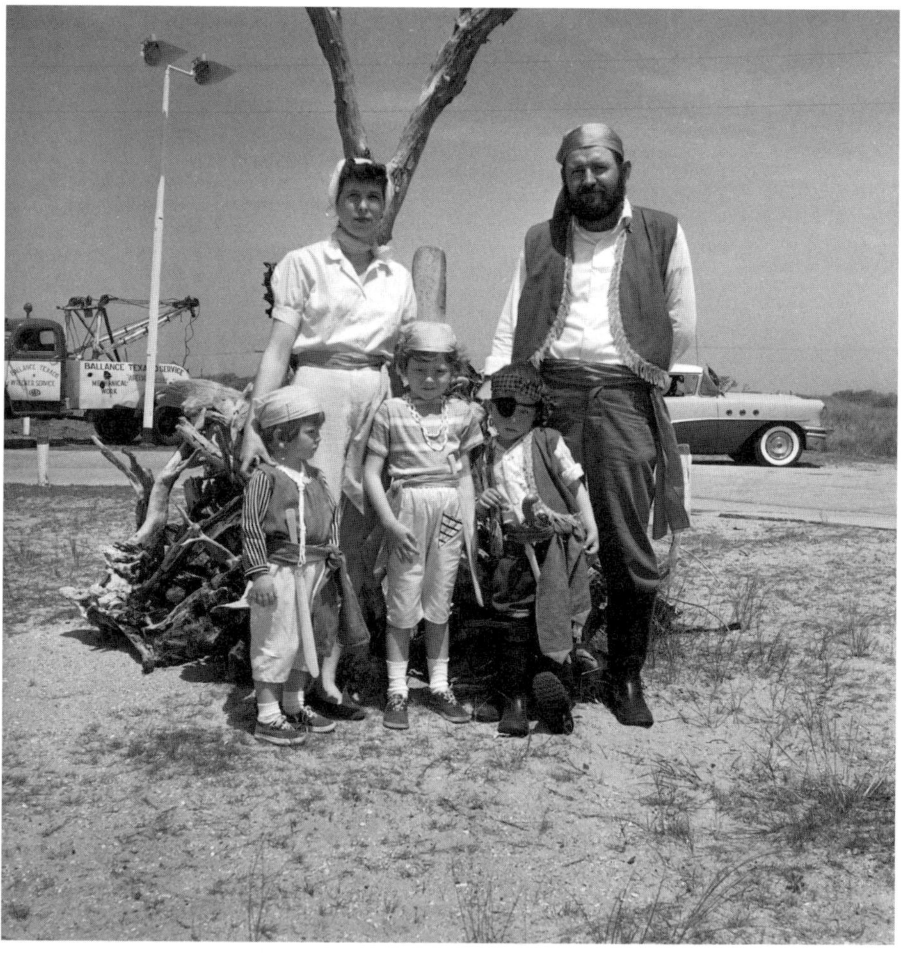

Surely frontrunners in the costume contest, this family on Hatteras Island stopped for a quick photo during the Pirates Jamboree celebration in 1956. The Pirates Jamboree was one of Aycock's most successful promotional ventures. *ABC, OBHC, SANC.*

He loved his strip of sand and its residents. Among them was Billy Tarkington of Manteo, a Navy veteran of the South Pacific in World War II who owned the Ocean House motel in Kill Devil Hills with their mutual friend Sheriff Frank Cahoon. Aycock hung out in the Ocean House lobby with Billy and Billy's beloved clerk Annie Mae Midgett, sharing cigarettes and watching TV out of Norfolk; aluminum-wrapped rabbit-ear antennas sprouted out of the TV set to reduce the fuzzy reception but never by much. They watched shows and commercials from the big cities and concurred that they were doing fine on their own sandy spot of the world. They were even enduring the big storms.

6

THE ASH WEDNESDAY STORM

Few of Aycock's fellow Outer Bankers, even the old-timers, had seen anything like the Ash Wednesday Storm.

When you live on an island, as Aycock did, you get used to the wild changes in weather, Mama Sea and Sister Sounds going from millpond flat to pounding fury within hours. You love it all.

Ernest Hemingway said it well in his novel *Islands in the Stream*:

> *After one has lived in those latitudes long enough the changes of the seasons become as important as anywhere else and Thomas Hudson, who loved the island, did not want to miss any spring, nor summer, nor any fall or winter. Sometimes the summers were too hot when the trade winds sometimes failed in June and July. Hurricanes, too, might come in September and October and even in early November and there could be freak tropical storms any time from June on. But the true hurricane months have fine weather when there are no storms.*

You relish the good weather and you take the bad in stride, the power outages and property damage, neighbors constantly banding to rebound together. But few of Aycock's fellow Outer Bankers, even the old-timers, had seen anything like the Ash Wednesday Storm.

The storm, which Aycock named, was a freak that howled in on March 7, 1962, putting him to the biggest test he'd faced since identifying all those

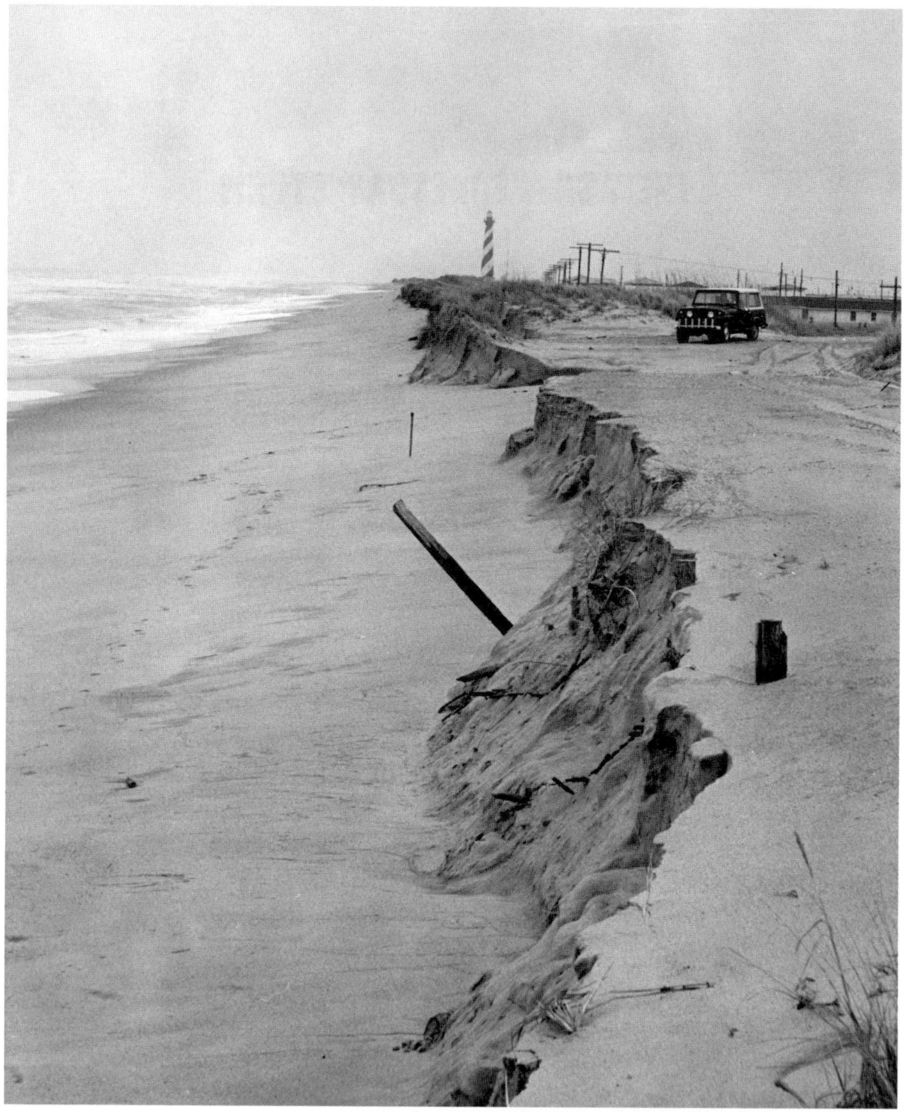

Above: A severely eroded shoreline put the Cape Hatteras Lighthouse even closer to the pounding waves of the Atlantic during the Ash Wednesday Storm in 1962. The National Park Service moved the lighthouse about half a mile west in 1999. *ABC, OBHC, SANC.*

Opposite: Ultramodern sunshade structures were destroyed at Coquina Beach in the Ash Wednesday Storm of 1962. They had been erected in 1956 as part of the National Park Service's Mission 66 program. *ABC, Creef Family.*

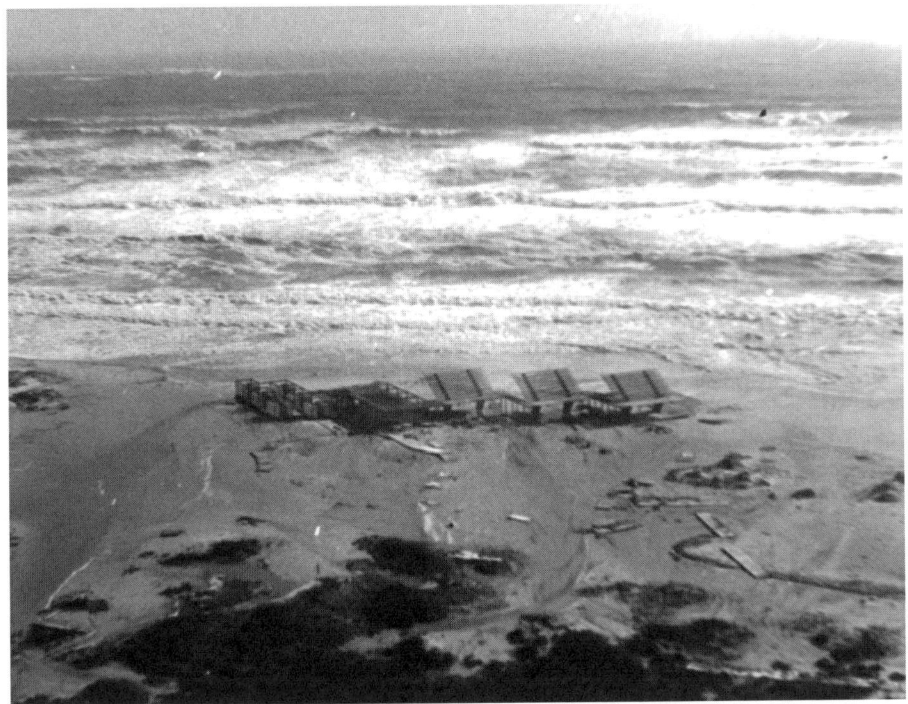

drowned and burned bodies off our coast just twenty years before. Of all the storms he'd seen in his more than thirty years on the Outer Banks, the 1962 nor'easter was the worst, with the ocean meeting the Sounds over the narrow spit of sand that divided them. Aycock met this disaster as courageously as he had the war, despite the flashbacks the storm might have sent him from that cyclone he'd experienced as a boy in central North Carolina, the one that he suspected had fired his urge to write "to…express all the terror that the cyclone spread for him and his family."

When you are out there in a late winter blow like the Ash Wednesday one, you're fighting just to stay afoot, chilled to the bone, hellish wet winds dismantling cottages and hurling timber turned deadly at you. The thump of whirling copter wings roars overhead, the pilots risking their own lives to dip down and save others. Journalists like Aycock and emergency workers run on adrenaline, never more alive than when they're facing death, straining through sanded eyes to make it to the next safe point, telling themselves they're just doing their jobs. But making it through the storm is so much more than just a job.

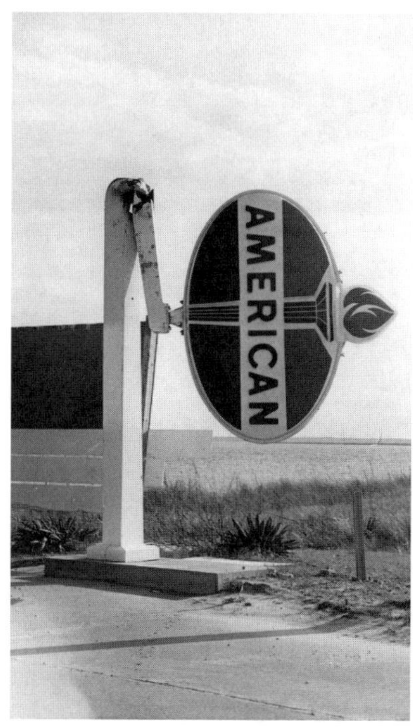

Left: A metal sign post bent like a reed was a good photograph to circulate and keep eyes on the Outer Banks in the aftermath of the Ash Wednesday Storm. The beach was devastated, but many residents of Roanoke Island, just across the Sound, initially did not know that such a severe storm had occurred. *ABC, OBHC, SANC.*

Below: At Oregon Inlet Fishing Center, the Ash Wednesday Storm generated a huge wave that swept the old store away and broke up concrete under the new restaurant. Cars went in the water, and boats went up on land. *ABC, Creef Family.*

Opposite: In true Outer Banks fashion, the people did not wait for help but got to work restoring their businesses and homes after the Ash Wednesday Storm. The Oregon Inlet Fishing Center was functional and ready for the tourist season within a few months. *ABC, Creef Family.*

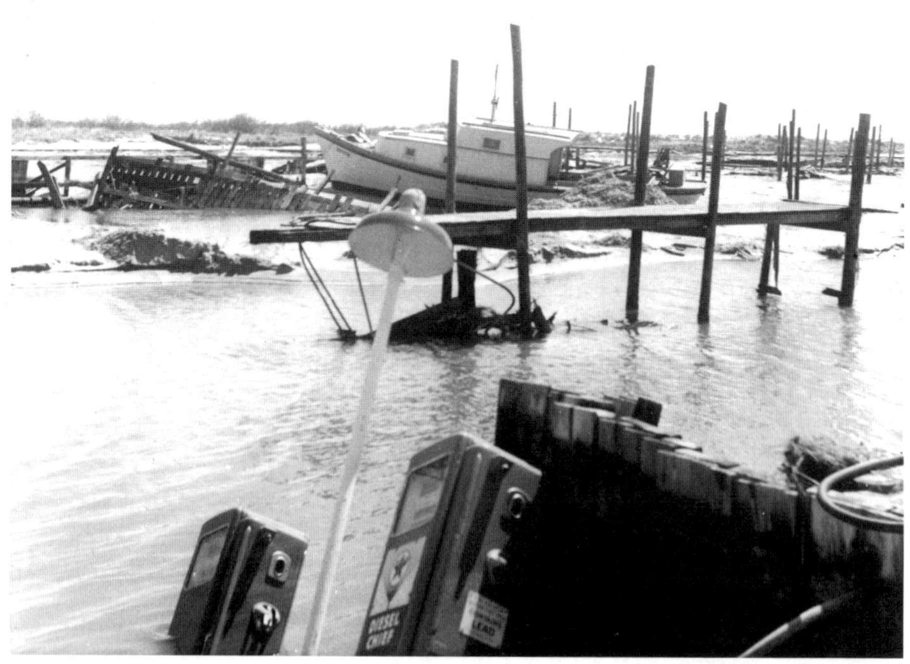

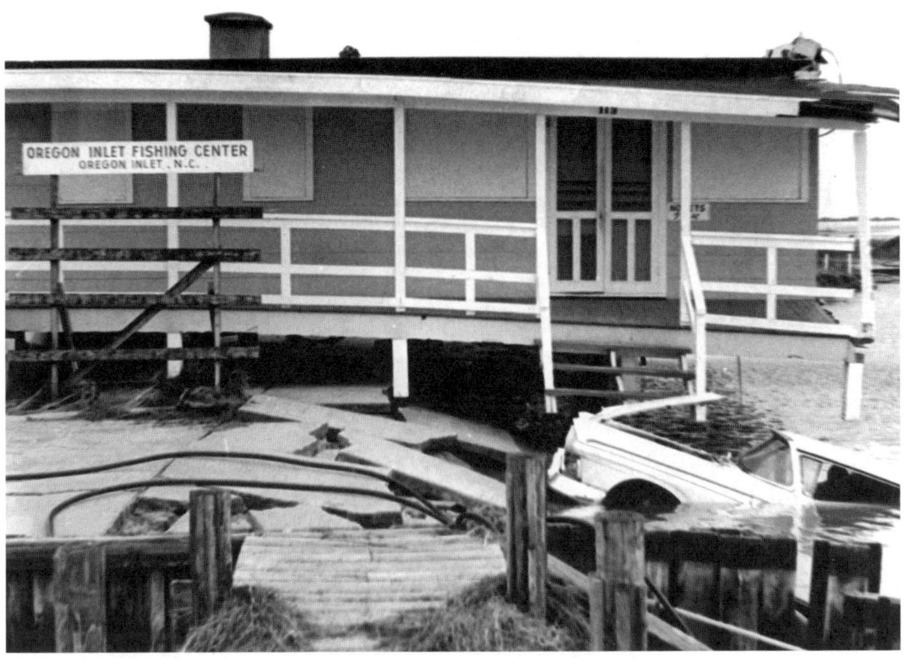

So it was for Aycock. For almost three days, with little sleep, through the banshee winds and waves, he risked his life and saved his film, rushing it back to Manteo, developing it, and sending it to his contacts nationwide to ensure that the rest of the world knew what they were going through and how badly they needed help.

David Stick later supplied the background:

> *The storm was a weatherman's dream—or nightmare. All of the elements needed to produce a "worst case" scenario for a killer storm came together at one time. There was a massive low pressure area hundreds of miles at sea; a "strong blocking high" over the Canadian Arctic with a ridge extending down the Middle Atlantic states; and a small low-pressure area forming over northeastern North Carolina and southeastern Virginia. These were the classic features needed to create what meteorologists call "an extratropical cyclone," and they came together just at the time in early 1962 when the sun, moon and earth were approximately aligned, and at the exact time of the month when lunar conditions were set to produce the highest tide—the feared Spring Tide.*

> *An extratropical cyclone, so named because it is not formed in the tropics as a hurricane, by itself poses serious potential problems of flooding and erosion along the coast; so does the traditional Spring Tide, with its expected tidal flow several feet above normal. In early March, a huge extratropical cyclone and the Spring Tide joined forces to unleash their fury on the exposed coastal areas from Canada to the Carolinas.*

On the Outer Banks, Stick wrote:

> *The storm was a late winter northeaster, a common meteorological occurrence....But this one was different. It struck almost without warning on the morning of Wednesday, March 7, with devastating results. Through five successive high tides over a period of two-and-a-half days the massive waves, fetching from far out in the Atlantic, pounded against the fragile dunes and beaches and surged against the low barrier islands.*

Aycock worked through it all. With his skinny build, he must have been especially vulnerable to the wind and cold, but he never talked about that later. He shot pictures of destroyed cottages. He knew some of the owners, and that must have been hard. What must have been harder was seeing the heavily damaged businesses and buildings of his fellow hard-workers—the Croatan Hotel and the Catholic church in Kill Devil Hills, Wink's store, Anderson's Store, and Virginia Dare Hardware in Kitty Hawk. But even in the midst of the storm, Aycock retained his eye for gimmickry, as when he shot a still-standing cash register surrounded by destroyed buildings and a smashed, overturned car at Anderson's. The register still showed the most recent charge, $2.19. Aycock knew that his shots like that had moved nationwide in happier times, and they'd go far now, too, encouraging the state and federal governments and individual Americans to send relief dollars.

But it's Aycock's eye for the suffering of his fellow Outer Bankers that really jumps out at you, as in a moving photo of storm survivors at a shelter at the Kitty Hawk School, huddled with their children around cots with their possessions stuffed into hastily packed bags. They're waiting for government passes to return to their homes and find God knows what.

Stick wrote:

> *As has been learned from the accounts of survivors, there was no set pattern in the destructive force of the storm. Madge Eggleston described it well*

when she said "the water came over the dunes in fingers, hitting one house, missing the next." It struck so unexpectedly and with such force that the only thing many people could think about during the first few minutes of awareness was whether they should stay where they were or try to leave.

Aycock waded through the devastation, snapping countless photos of residents finding shelter and the heroes who'd rescued them, local men in boats, such as storeowner Carl Nunemaker, and National Guardsmen. At times, Aycock caught a ride on rescue copters, shooting the damage from above. At Aycock's beloved Oregon Inlet, he shot the carnage, cars and boats tossed asunder. When he'd documented the devastation German subs wreaked on U.S. boats, he must have been horribly amazed by those subs blowing his paradise to hell. Now, twenty years later, he was seeing Mother Nature render its own hell on the paradise that had been rebounding.

Aycock later recalled how he tagged the name of the storm: Being a lay reader at his church, St. Andrew's Episcopal, "I just happened to know it was Ash Wednesday," he later said. "When I put that name on it in my stories and photographs, other writers and photographers picked up the name, and it stuck."

That was fortuitous. The name meant the storm would hold its own among named hurricanes in the push to secure government funding for recovery efforts.

7

PROMOTING THE LEGENDS

There in Aycock's beachscape was Ras Wescott, the owner of the hard-rocking Casino in Nags Head, and shots of his employees checking patrons' shoes at the door for barefoot dancing.

Throughout his career, Aycock shot photos of some of the best Outer Banks characters, people who were making the beach the unique success it became. His photos made them legends. There was Ras Wescott, the owner of the Casino in Nags Head.

The Casino, built in 1937, had featured Duke Ellington, Tommy Dorsey, Bill Deal and the Rhondels, and Doug Clark and the Hot Nuts. The music shook the frame building painted yellow and white and drifted out the open windows, tantalizing young teenagers not old enough to be admitted to the second-floor dancing. They'd drift inside to the first floor to bowl and try to use fake IDs to get past Delnoy Burrus and her almighty handstamp, a rite of passage to get upstairs. Up there, crew-cut bouncers with tattooed arms and big bellies stretching their T-shirts kept order, tossing out rowdies. Blood sometimes flowed. Men spat out teeth during fights. Fingers—and sometimes ears—were bitten. Aycock probably shot, but did not publish, the brawls in the 1960s outside the Casino among hippie visitors, locals, Wescott, and Nags Head Police Chief Donnie Twyne Sr.

Among Aycock's published shots were charter boat captains Sam and Omie Tillet and their namesake cozy restaurant at Whalebone Junction in

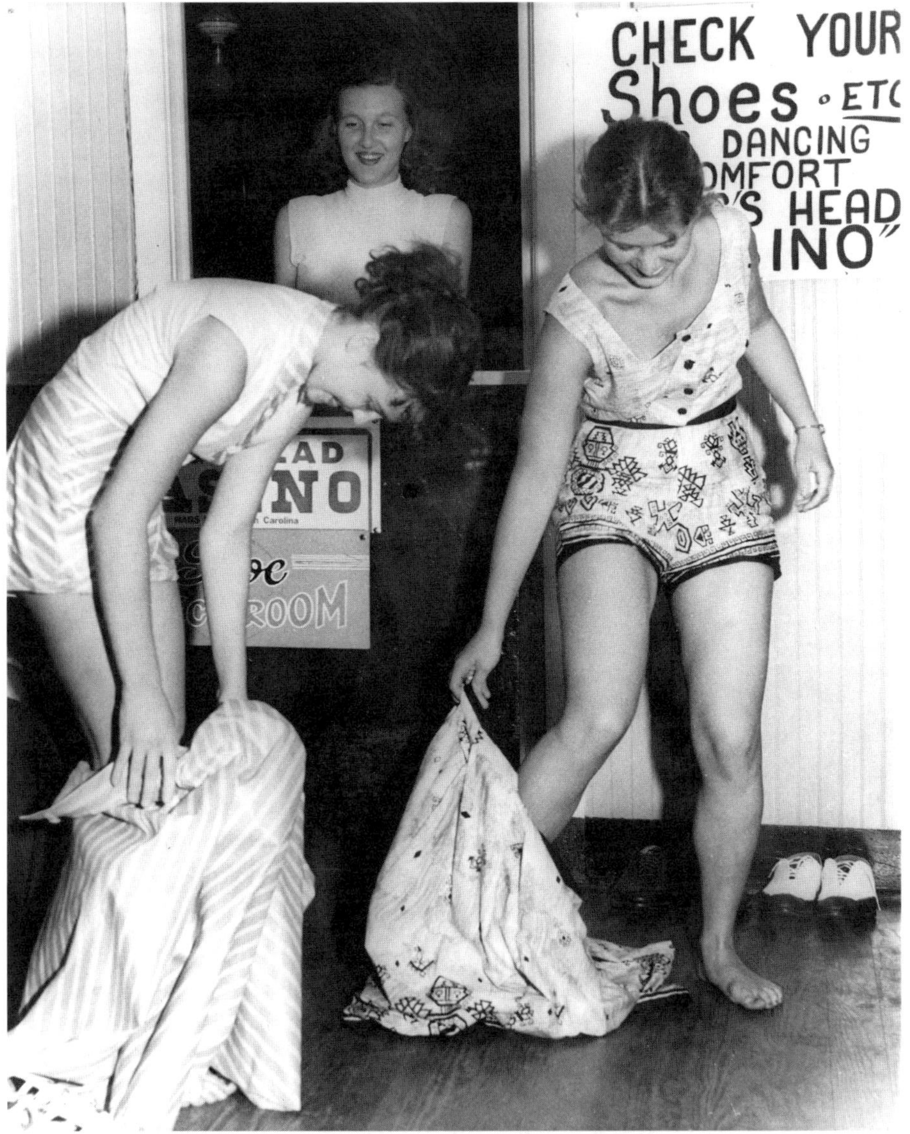

Above: Patrons of the Casino had to check their shoes before dancing barefoot to the live music of Louis Armstrong; Duke Ellington; Woody Herman; Glenn Miller; Guy Lombardo; Tommy Dorsey; the Tams; the Platters; Fats Domino; Blood, Sweat, and Tears; and other big names. *ABC, OBHC, SANC.*

Opposite: Nellie Myrtle Pridgen handles diamondback terrapins in front of her parents' store in Nags Head. In her later years, she walked the beach for miles each day, enjoying an intimate oneness with nature while fostering contentious relationships with many humans. *ABC, OBHC, SANC.*

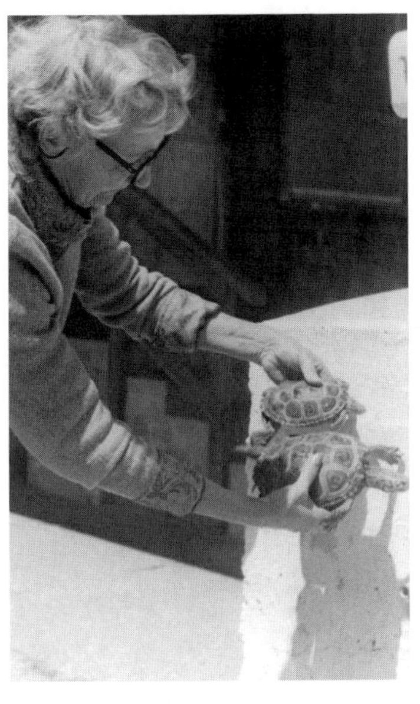

Nags Head, which survives to this day, albeit under a different, but equally beloved owner, Carole Sykes, and her fine crew.

There was the Hayman family that reigned at the Arlington hotel in Nags Head before the sea took it away in a 1973 winter storm. In true Outer Banks resiliency, the family bounced back, just across the Beach Road, with a new restaurant, The Seafare. There was Nellie Myrtle Pridgen of Nags Head, who beachcombed for decades, pounding the sand to her own drummer, assembling an amazing collection of shells and other finds. There was Carolista Baum, who almost single-handedly saved the sand mountain of Jockey's Ridge by standing in front of a bulldozer, stopping developers and leading the way for Jockey's Ridge to become a state park.

There was Jimmy Austin of the Austin Fish Company in Nags Head and Jimmy's buddy Tommy Daniels, who'd started his department store, Ben Franklin, in Manteo and eventually opened a second store at Nags Head.

One of the best characters Aycock promoted was flamboyant George Crocker of Nags Head. He'd arrived on the Outer Banks in 1953, a Navy veteran out of Norfolk with $15,000 from a good-hearted family friend who'd embezzled money from the Norfolk bank where she worked, Robin Hood style. David Stick wrote in an unpublished profile of Crocker:

> [Crocker] *paid a thousand dollars down on a strip of prime oceanfront property, built a 40-room hotel* [The Beacon] *almost entirely on credit, and in not much more than a decade emerged as a leading area entrepreneur with his widely known Galleon Esplanade and other enterprises. In a 1995 interview, he credited his success to his own stupidity. "Not knowing that something can't be done is a great asset," he explained.*

Crocker was a survivor, bravely weathering the Ash Wednesday Storm and many metaphorical storms. He soon expanded his holdings around Milepost 11 on the Beach Road to include the Cabana East hotel and then his masterpiece, the Galleon Esplanade, a perfumed boutique clothing shop for women and men unlike anything that had been seen on the Outer

Banks. Crocker had a talent for employing smart people, many of them local, and sending them to New York trade shows to bring back the best trends in clothing. He promoted the store through fashion shows, often featuring his female employees in bikinis and high heels, which Aycock

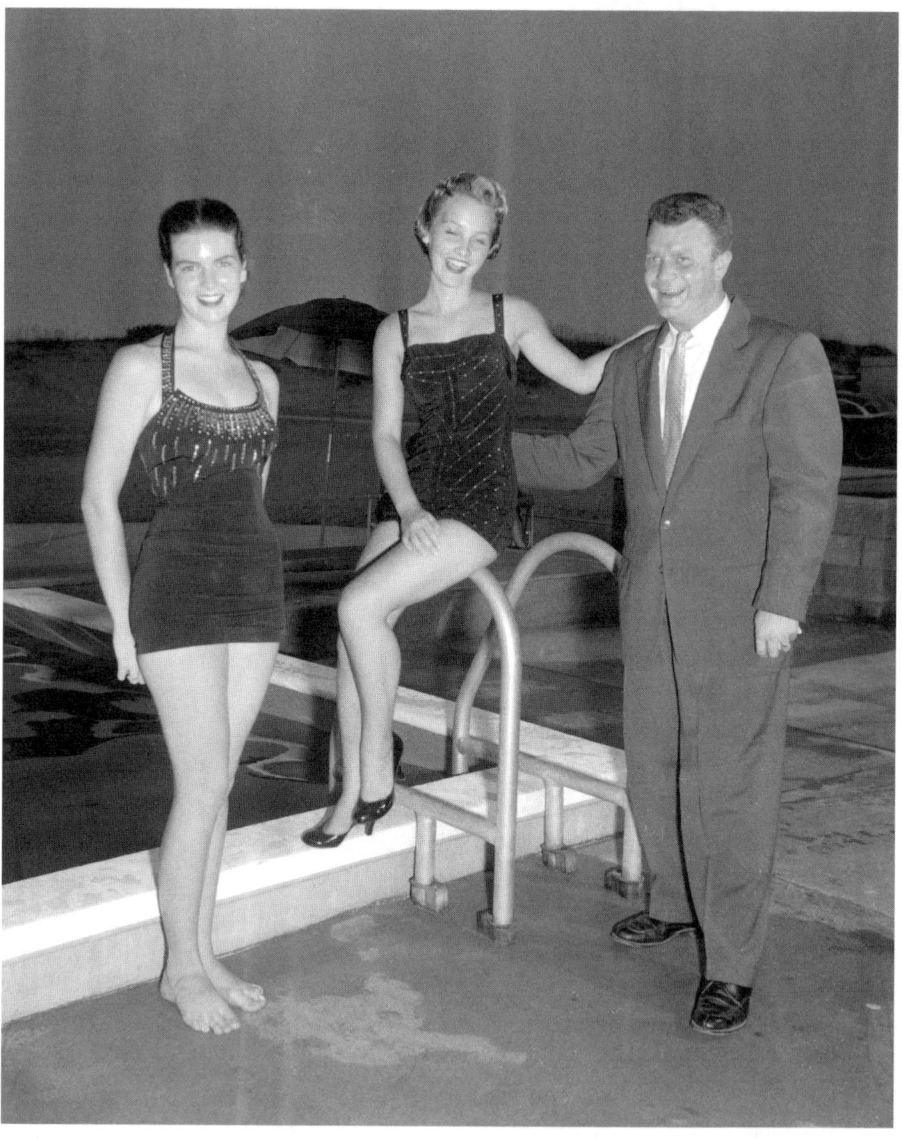

In promoting his Beacon Motor Lodge, George Crocker posed with bathing beauties by the oceanfront swimming pool in 1955. Crocker was a savvy businessman and self-promoter who lived out his rags-to-riches dream on the Outer Banks. *ABC, OBHC, SANC.*

photographed, drawing in men and women. He knew that women would check out what their peers were sporting and that men would check out the women.

Crocker enlarged the Galleon property to include A Restaurant By George, a high-scale restaurant with spiral staircases, fan-backed rattan chairs, and waiters dressed in pith helmets and safari shirts and shorts, something like British colonials meeting the Outer Banks in a stone building that evoked Rick's Café in *Casablanca*, the Humphrey Bogart classic. With Crocker's usual knack for talent, he lured Mike Kelly from the venerable Seafare to manage his restaurant. It quickly became wildly popular among locals and visitors. Meanwhile, Crocker continued to expand his retail property, spreading out from the Galleon building to include numerous shops over two stories and even another restaurant, Sinbad's, with exotic offerings. Altogether, it was a fantasyland crowned with a waterfall and ship's prow. Aycock shot it all, probably loving it because Crocker was a fellow visionary with an intriguing past who'd remade himself on the Banks.

8

BUILDING THE LEGACY

The bottom line for me is that Aycock Brown represented the gold standard in photography and was a huge influence on the development of my own career.
—Outer Banks photographer Drew Wilson

Aycock always remained keenly aware of the Outer Banks' unique place in American history. The bookends: the lost colony of 1587 and the first powered flight, by the Wright brothers, on December 17, 1903. Aycock spent thousands of hours shooting photos of the outdoor drama based on that lost colony and chronicling, through his photos, the commemoration of that first flight.

One of Aycock's most evocative photos is from the 1950s, and features Johnny Moore, who witnessed the flight as a young teenager and then ran off spreading the news, yelling, "They done it, they done it, damned if they ain't flew!" By the time Aycock shot Moore, he was late in life but still tough, jauntily wearing a weathered fedora and sporting a two- or three-day growth of beard. Aycock might have borrowed a bit of his own jaunty style from Moore, as journalists have been known to do with favorite subjects just once or twice. Moore was a respected fishing and hunting guide, a barefoot legend who would soon die at his Colington Island home, in the shadow of the memorial to the Wright brothers.

In the 1960s, Aycock shot astronaut John Glenn visiting the Wright Memorial soon after Glenn's orbit of the earth. Around the same time, Aycock, with his eye always on the everyman, or everywoman, shot a photo of two blond airline stewardesses viewing the memorial.

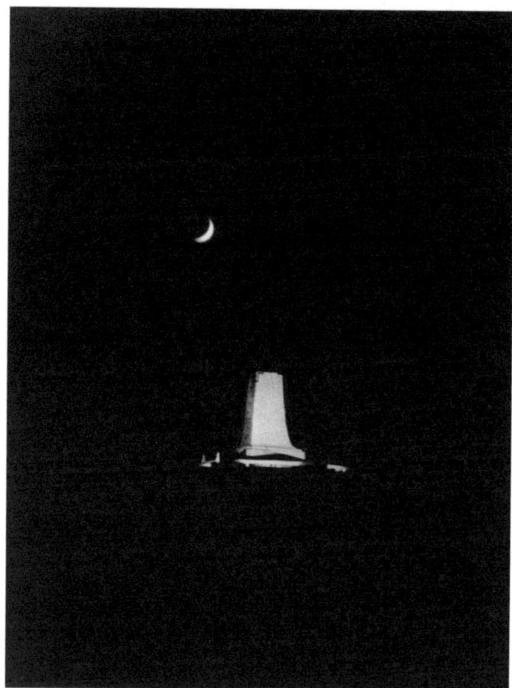

Left: Aycock's most famous photo was taken when he shot the Wright Brothers National Monument on July 21, 1969, at the exact moment astronaut Neil Armstrong set foot on the moon. Two years later, he took a similar, but unheralded, photo when Apollo 14 splashed down in the Pacific. *NPS, CHNS.*

Below: During a 1963 visit to the Wright Brothers National Monument, astronaut John Glenn touched a replica of the Wright flyer. Glenn was the first U.S. astronaut to orbit the Earth and was awarded the Presidential Medal of Freedom in 2012. *ABC, OBHC, SANC.*

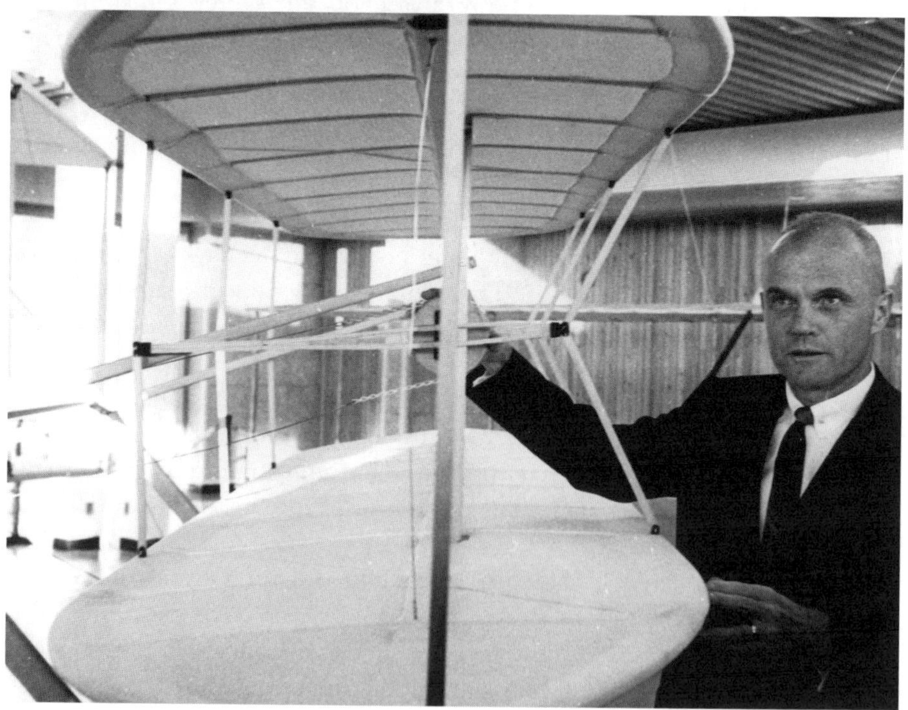

Right: Johnny Moore received a painting of the Wright Brothers Memorial at his home in Colington in 1952. Moore was a young witness to the brothers' first flight. A sculpture depicting a teenaged Moore was added to the Memorial 102 years later. *ABC, OBHC, SANC.*

Below: With cigarette in hand, Aycock photographed a ranger and guests exiting a reconstructed camp building at the Wright Brothers National Memorial. Aycock was a familiar face there, annually on December 17, the anniversary of flight. *NPS, CHNS.*

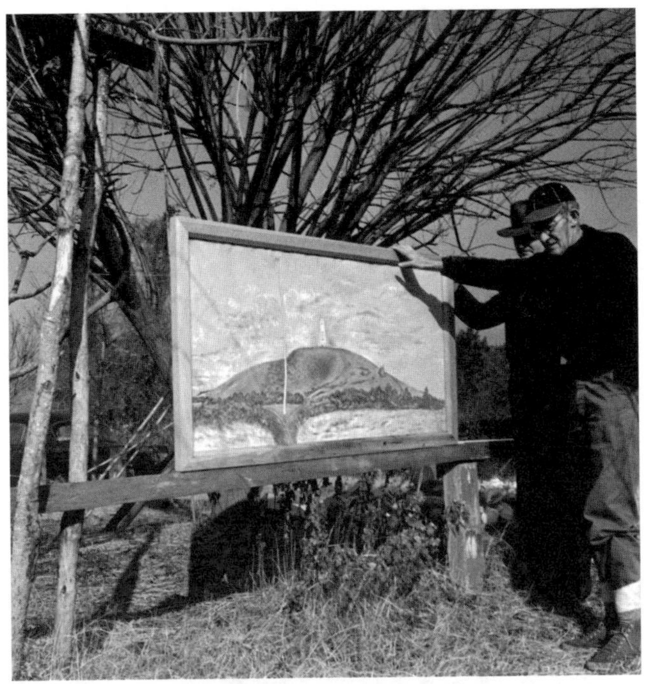

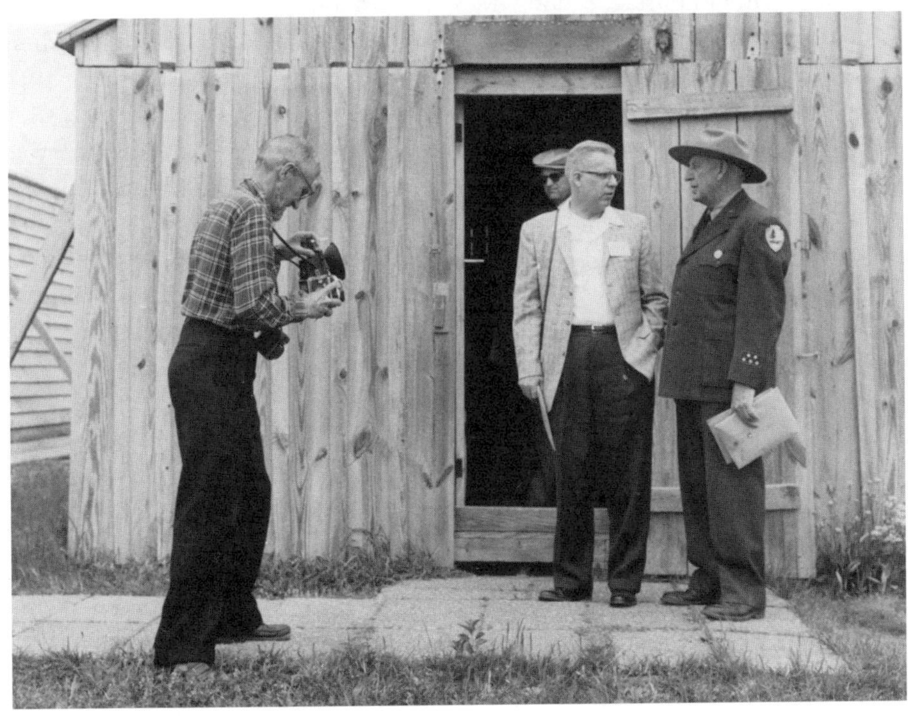

Then there is Aycock's iconic shot of the crescent moon rising above the memorial during the first moon landing in 1969. Outer Banks author R. Wayne Gray wrote: "Perhaps the most famous photograph of the estimated 100,000 that Aycock took was of the lighted Wright Memorial at night with the moon above. With a portable radio in hand, he snapped the shot at the exact moment when man first set foot on the moon."

Ira David Wood III, a director and author who was in *The Lost Colony* at the time, said in 2025 that he'd suggested the shot to Aycock. "Well, of course, he knew a good tip when he got one. He drove to Kill Devil Hills and took a photo of the monument with the moon hanging in the night sky above it at the moment Armstrong stepped onto the moon's surface," Wood wrote in an email. "My girlfriend and I had enjoyed a great dinner at the old Arlington hotel, and with two bottles of champagne in tow, had driven to Kill Devil Hills to witness the historic event on TV sets set up by the National Park Service. I caught a glimpse of a familiar figure in the assembled crowd. It was Aycock. The photo he took that night won every award there was and got reprinted everywhere. I never heard a peep from Aycock, so every time I passed his office, I'd stick my head in, glance at that now-famous photo framed and placed on his wall, and I'd call out, 'You're welcome, you old bastard!' It always gave him a big laugh."

Aycock kept working. Later in 1969, three days before Christmas, when he was sixty-five, he donned hip boots and waded out into roaring surf near Oregon Inlet to photograph the copter rescue of the fishing trawler *Oriental* in distress. Harking back to Aycock's earlier work, the *Oriental* was a German pleasure boat captured during the war and repurposed for commercial fishing. The shot won a national photography award.

On November 16, 1972, Dare County surprised Aycock with a day named for him. With a large crowd that included his family and greetings sailing in from across the country, the event took on the feel of the last minutes of the film *It's a Wonderful Life.* Aycock spoke briefly: "I really love y'all and I appreciate everything you've done for me tonight. I don't deserve it."

David Stick praised his friend's work and included one solemn note, based on some of his chats with Aycock: "What have we really wrought, and are we, in the process of publicizing and building on the Outer Banks, are we going to end up destroying the very thing that we were attracted to in the beginning?"

Kathy Spencer of Manteo remembered recently that Aycock was "a little melancholy" about development because he was worried about the infrastructure and "where to build and how to build."

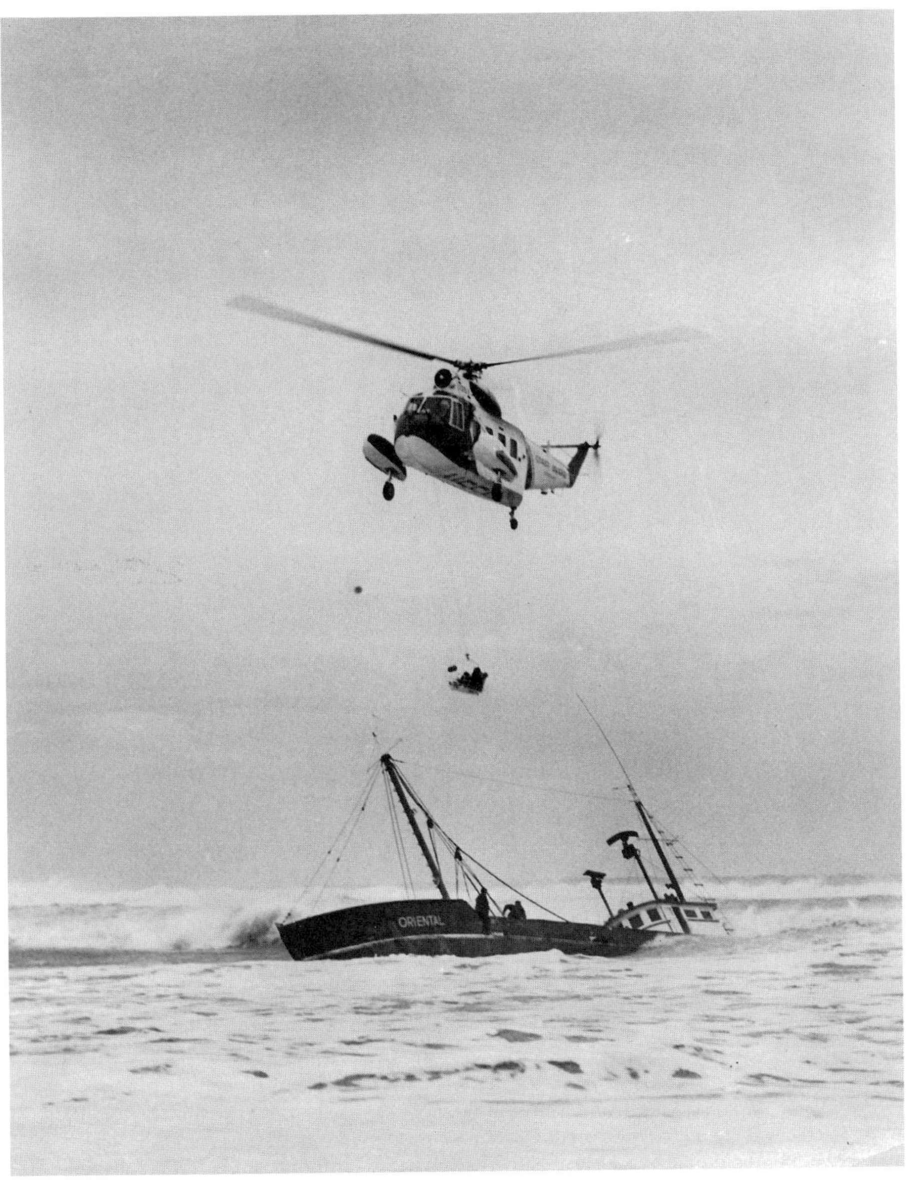

The ninety-foot *Oriental*, a World War II German luxury craft repurposed as a fishing trawler, ran aground near Oregon Inlet when the night watchman mistook the lighthouse for a sea buoy. The Coast Guard skillfully extracted a small crew from the wreck. *ABC, OBHC, SANC.*

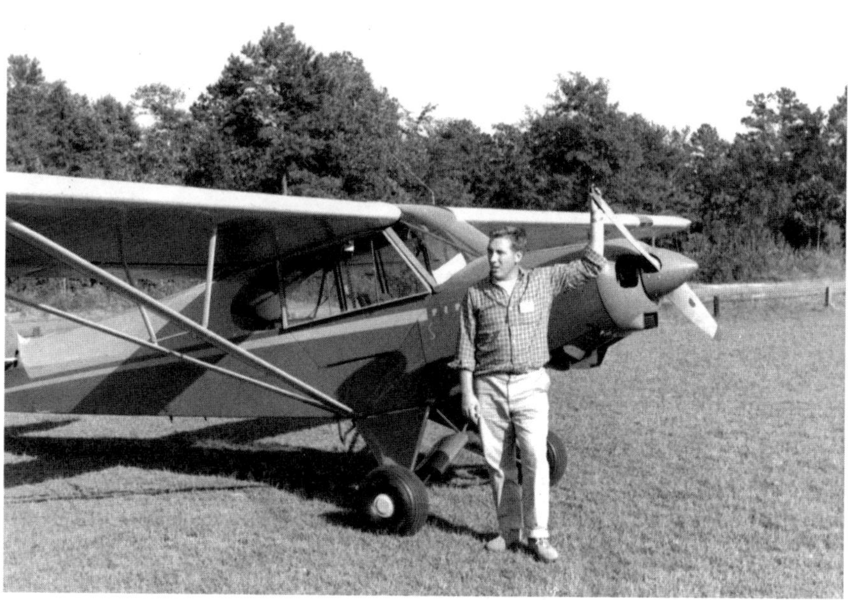

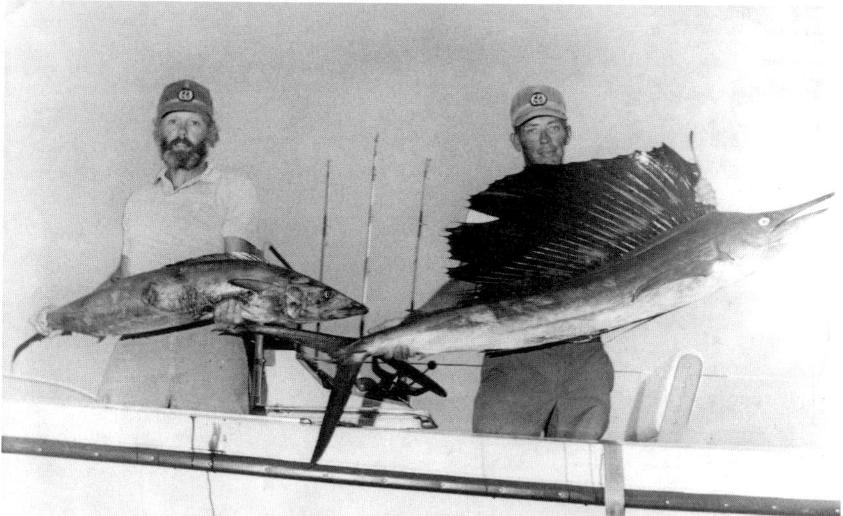

Top: Aycock's oldest son, Brantley, began flying at age sixteen. By the time of this 1957 photo, he was flying for the North Carolina Forestry Service. He eventually received his commercial pilot's license and landed a job with Piedmont Airlines. *ABC, Nettie Brown Tisch.*

Bottom: Aycock's younger son, Billy (*right*), used his experiences as an artist, hunter, charter boat captain, and Army veteran to be an entertaining history teacher for thirty years. He and fellow Manteo Middle School teacher Jeffrey Midgett shared a great day of fishing. *ABC, OBHC, SANC.*

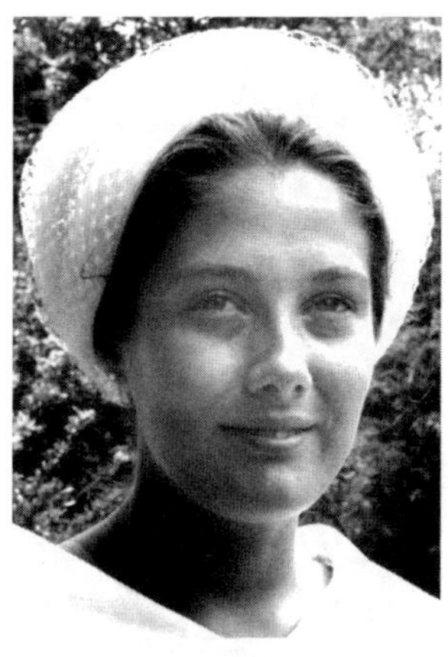

Gale Brown Ballance raised two children and taught in the Dare County school system for twenty-five years. Like her brother Billy, she made sure her students got a good dose of regional culture and history. *ABC, Patrick Byrd.*

In 1977, Aycock stepped down as the director of the Dare County Tourist Bureau to become part-time news manager of the bureau. He told a reporter for *The News & Observer*: "My favorite spot out here now is Manteo. I used to like Ocracoke, but it's kind of overrun with tourists now." He smiled wryly. "Of course, that's my fault."

His beloved wife, Esther, had died that year. Karen "Spooky" Phillips, who got to know Aycock by working in an administrative role with *The Lost Colony* and learning photography from him, said he always bragged on his wife and went into a time of mourning after her death. He and Esther had shared all from their fateful meeting on Ocracoke when they were so young and the Outer Banks had seemed young too. For a while after Esther's death, Aycock wasn't even going out to take pictures. Then one day Sarah Owens suggested to Spooky that she take Aycock with her to photograph a harrier jet on display at the tiny Manteo airport. He went along reluctantly, but it turned out to be Aycock's return to the game.

"At a recent boat commissioning in Wanchese, he was seen climbing the rigging until he was balanced precariously on top of the vessel's bridge, aiming his camera down at the notables lined up on the deck below for the ceremony," according to one story.

All along, Aycock was mentoring new Outer Banks photographers. Lisa Griggs of Point Harbor began shooting as a child, and when she needed a hand pursuing her dream vocation, she turned to Aycock. He helped her land a job at Jim's Camera House on the Beach Road in Kill Devil Hills. Jim Lee, an accomplished shooter whose cozy shop was the mecca for the best photographers on the beach, taught Lisa all, with a lot of help from Aycock. She became a star shooter and remained close to Aycock.

Vanessa Croswait Foreman, who grew up in Aycock's Manteo neighborhood, got to know him while working at the Tourist Bureau as a young adult. He kindly taught her photography, including how to set the aperture just right. He taught her to work in the darkroom, using just her sense of touch when needed. They also had a lot of fun. During an Oregon Inlet tournament, he crowned her with one of his trademark straw hats, that

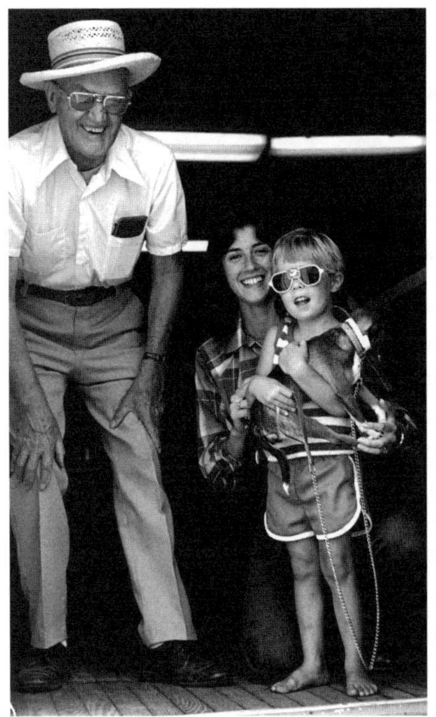

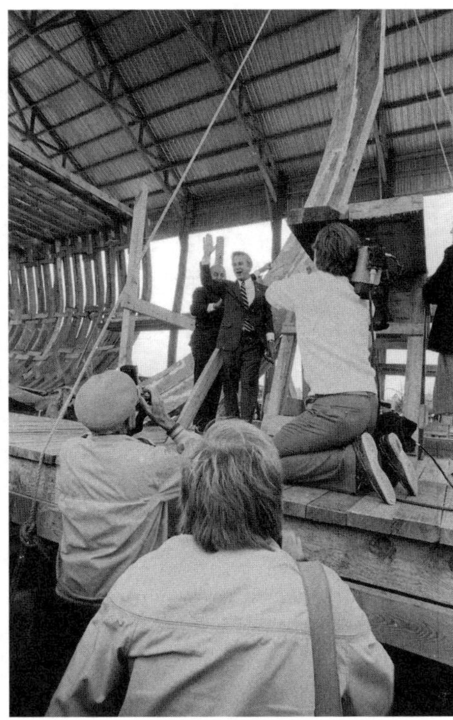

Left: Karen "Spooky" Phillips worked for *The Lost Colony* but honed her photography skills by going on shoots with Aycock. After moving away, she and son Jonathan Daniels and their Chihuahua stopped by to visit Aycock in 1978. *J. Foster Scott, Karen "Spooky" Phillips.*

Right: In a woolen cap, Aycock was front and center with his younger colleagues to get a photo of North Carolina Governor Jim Hunt in the early 1980s. Next to Hunt are the ribs of the *Elizabeth II*, a wooden ship being built to replicate the one that brought the first colonists to the New World. *Walter V. Gresham III.*

one made in Italy. She treasures it to this day, along with one of his Yashica cameras. He gave her that camera and another, which she in turn gave to one of Aycock's grandsons, Patrick Byrd.

Photographer Drew Wilson said of Aycock:

> *The bottom line for me is that Aycock Brown represented the gold standard in photography and was a huge influence on the development of my own career. His verve lived through the thousands of photographs he made throughout his career. I will forever admire him for his creativity and tenacity in recording with his camera some of the legendary events on the North Carolina coast from Beaufort to Carova Beach. He was one of a*

kind and deserves every bit of praise. He left us a photographic record of the North Carolina coast that is unparalleled by any other lensmen of the 20th Century.

Aycock was also inspiring writers. Angel Khoury was associate editor at *The Coastland Times* in the early 1980s and often saw Aycock in the newspaper office in downtown Manteo, or she'd go next door to his office in hopes of getting him interested in labeling and filing the hundreds of photos scattered about in his small office at the Tourist Bureau. They'd meet for coffee and pie seated in the bay window of the Elizabethan Inn's restaurant in Manteo or have lunch high above the docks at Fisherman's Wharf in Wanchese. One afternoon, Angel asked Aycock where seagulls sleep. Aycock asked her to take a ride with him in his landboat of a car. They stopped up and down the beach, asking locals, who shrugged. Finally, it was time to meet the boats coming in at Oregon Inlet. "Don't really know, don't much care," seemed to be the consensus. That was fine. The journey, as with all things Aycock, was what it was all about.

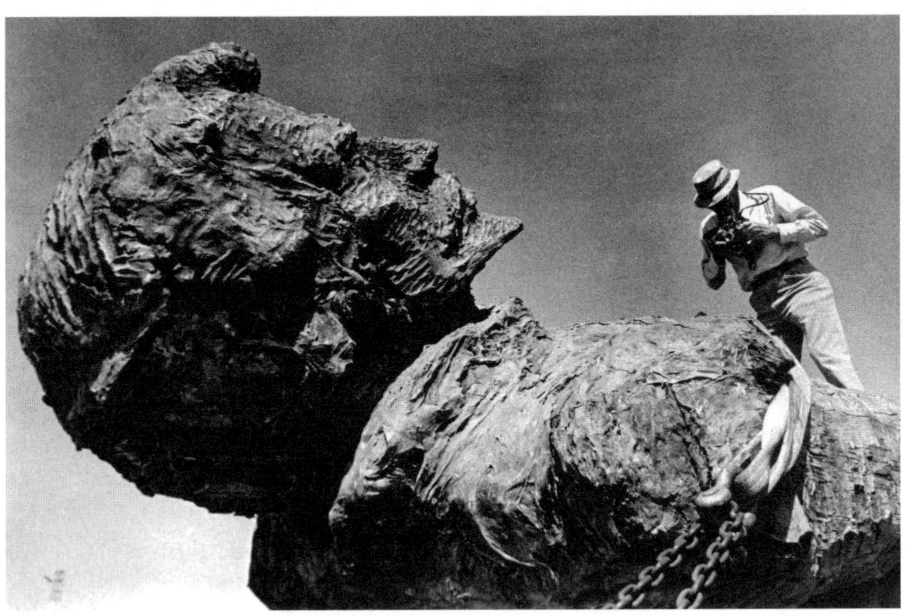

In 1976, Aycock risked life and limb to get the best shot of a twenty-four-foot cypress statue of Sir Walter Raleigh before it stood on its feet. It occupied Manteo's Bicentennial Park for fourteen years before it succumbed to termites. *Manteo Centennial Exhibit Collection, OBHC, SANC.*

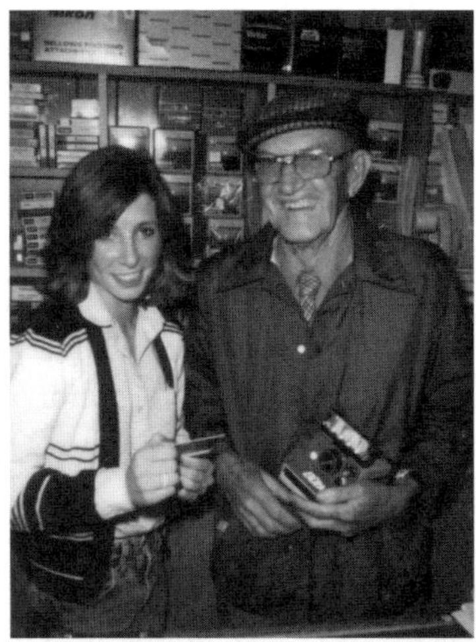

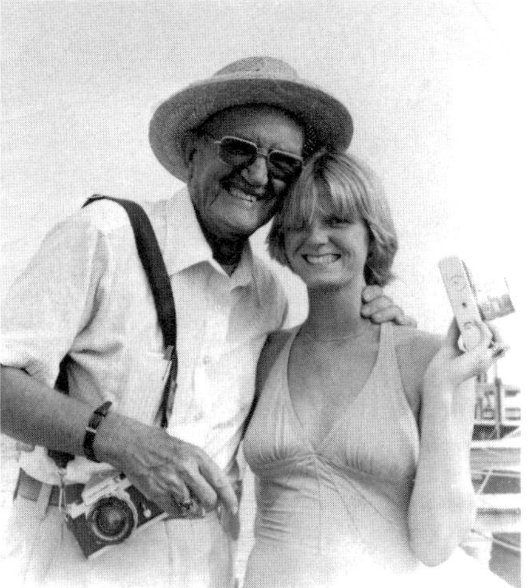

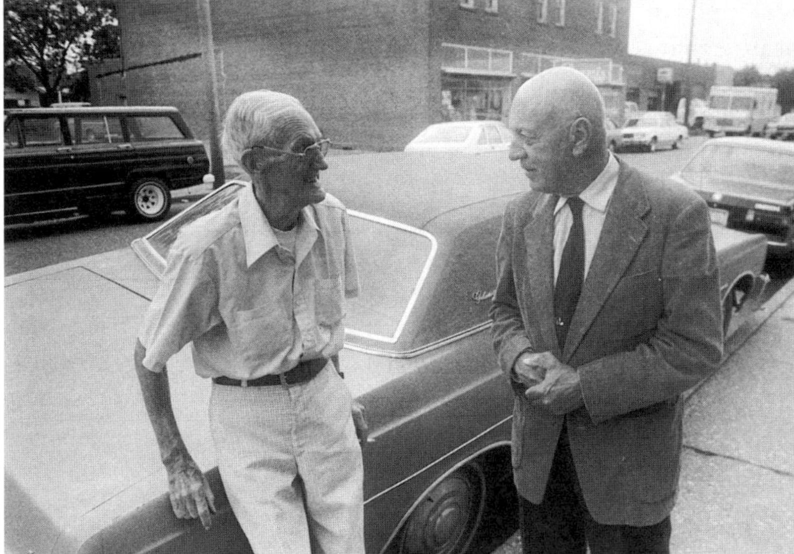

Top left: Aycock helped Lisa Griggs get a job at Jim's Camera Shop in Kill Devil Hills while she was still in high school. Later, she was able to open her own studio and camera shop, keenly aware that she was tutored by two of the best—Jim Lee and Aycock Brown. *Lisa Griggs.*

Top right: Tourist Bureau employee Vanessa Croswait Foreman learned the ropes from Aycock at Oregon Inlet Fishing Center, taking pictures of tourists with their catches. As Vanessa recounted, when her first son was born, she gave him "all the names," Charles Aycock Ivan Quidley. *Vanessa Foreman.*

Bottom: Photographer Drew Wilson caught Aycock in conversation with colleague Luis Marden outside The Coastland Times building in Manteo. Marden, a prominent photographer, worked for *National Geographic* magazine. *Drew Wilson Collection, OBHC, SANC.*

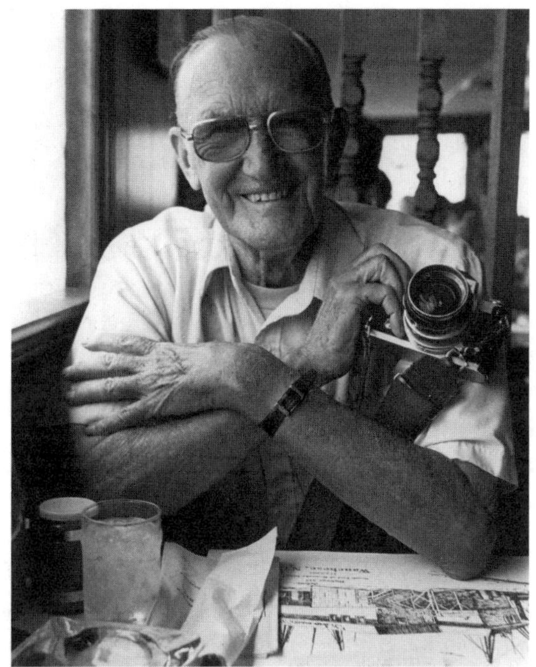

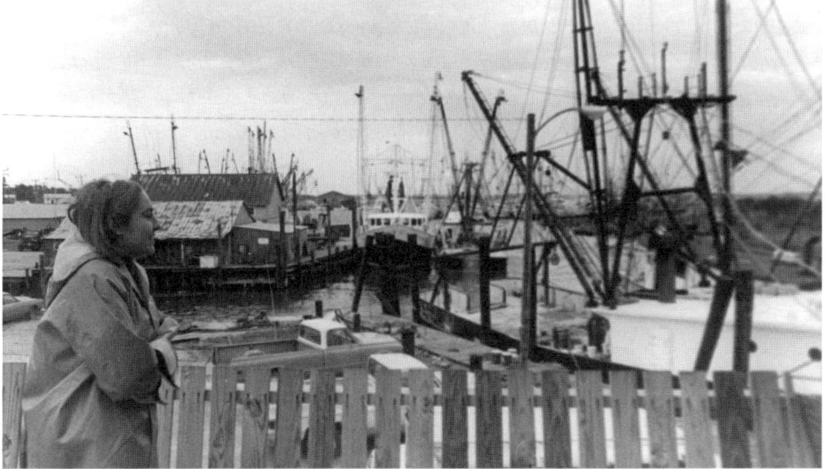

Top: Angel Ellis Khoury snapped this photo of her pal at Fishermen's Wharf Restaurant in Wanchese. He once told her, "You'd be right pretty if you wore red lipstick." The intimation was that his wife, his highest standard of beauty, wore red lipstick. *Angel Ellis Khoury.*

Bottom: Angel Ellis Khoury looks over Wanchese Harbor in the early 1980s, a lucrative time for commercial fishing. Khoury is a renowned author who got her start as an associate editor for *The Coastland Times* newspaper. Aycock was a friend and journalistic mentor to her. *ABC, Angel Ellis Khoury.*

~

Aycock never forgot his war work. On trips to Ocracoke, he might have stopped by the Methodist church, where a piece of wood that bore the nameplate of Jim Baum Gaskill's torpedoed freighter had been used to craft a cross. And Aycock never forgot Thomas Cunningham, the British sailor he'd met in World War II who, along with several shipmates, was killed by a German submarine, the bodies he'd identified as part of his war work. Year after year, he'd ferry over to Ocracoke for memorial events, recording them with his camera. He corresponded with their survivors, a living link and tribute to the war days that must have haunted him.

The remembrances continue, as Kevin P. Duffus wrote in his 2007 book, *Shipwrecks of the Outer Banks*:

> *Throughout the years, tens of thousands of people have visited the British Cemetery on Ocracoke, a foreign field from England. But the Cunningham family had been unable to visit—whether for emotional reasons, travel difficulties, or schedules. That changed in May 2005, when retired Royal Navy Commander Thomas Cunningham Jr. traveled to Ocracoke for the first time—the son whose impending birth had brought Tom Cunningham so much joy. In a private moment amidst the fragrant smells of cedar, Live Oak and oleander, Tom Jr. spent a quiet moment with his hero, the father he never knew.*

9

LAST ACTS

Beyond his meager salary as the tourism director, Aycock had never profited off the Outer Banks, even though he sure could have from real estate.

In 1976, David Stick published a book tribute, *Aycock Brown's Outer Banks*, composed of salutes to Aycock from many of his media sources along with hundreds of his photos. Stick and Aycock were the yin and yang of Outer Banks chronicling, with Stick on the curmudgeonly, pipe-smoking writerly side and Aycock on the cigarette-smoking, photo-snapping, backslapping end. With Sarah Owens and others, they had put the Outer Banks on the map. The purpose of the book was to honor Aycock and, through its proceeds, help him with retirement money. Beyond his meager salary as the tourism director, Aycock had never profited off the Outer Banks, even though he sure could have from real estate.

The book has the feel of a TV celebrity roast, which were big in the mid-1970s. The book is well-meaning, and there are some insightful passages, but many of the descriptions of Aycock are repetitive and one, though meant to be light-hearted, contains unnecessarily cruel words, calling Aycock a "con man" in his efforts to sell the Outer Banks. He was no con man. Con men push nonexistent or worthless products. Aycock's unlimited horizons were right there and boundless in value.

At events celebrating the book's publication, including one at George Crocker's Galleon, Aycock met friends with his trademark candor. Talking to a reporter, he flipped through pages of the book:

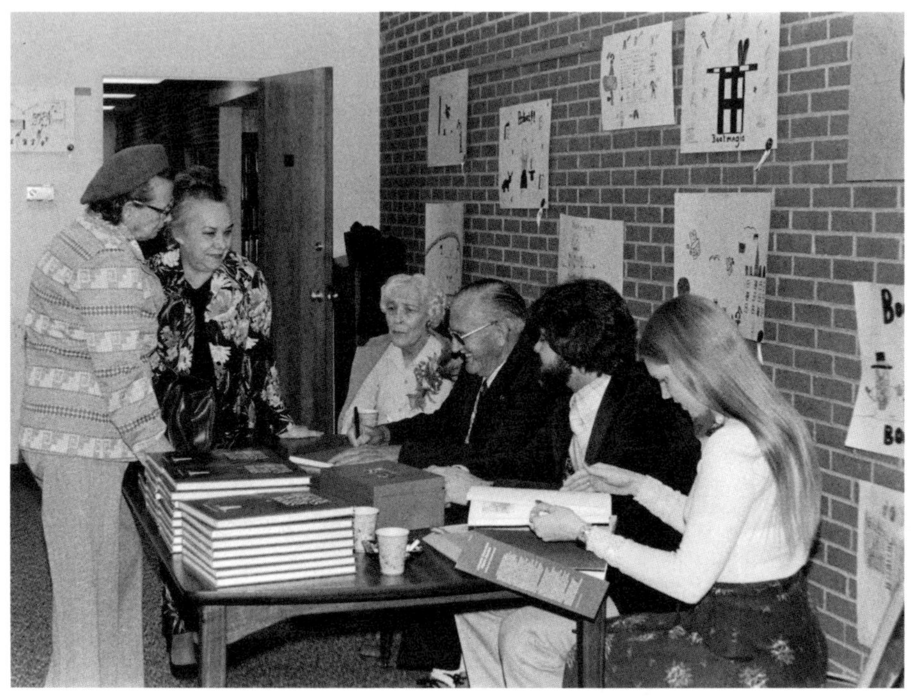

> *"See here," he said, pointing to a picture of a pretty girl on the beach, seashell held to her ear. "Now that's what everybody can relate to: a beach—girls, seashells, sand. They immediately get the feel of the warm sun and the water. Makes them want to head to the Outer Banks!" he laughs in his staccato fashion.*

Art Latham, a reporter for *The Virginian-Pilot*, tackled, light-heartedly, Aycock's appeal through his buxom models in a changing world:

> *The weeklies* [newspapers], *the dailies loved him, the wire service loved him, and they all still do, because cagey Aycock Brown had discovered two of the truths of life in the newsroom. First, ERA* [the Equal Rights Amendment] *notwithstanding, the great majority of writers and editors are hairy-knuckled men. Second, as far as the great majority of writers and editors are concerned, flesh sells. The way they reason it, those great patriarchs of the newsrooms of the country, goes like this: A man will look at a picture of a scantily clad woman out of prurient interest, and that sells papers; a woman will look at a picture of a scantily clad woman to see what the competition is up to, and that sells*

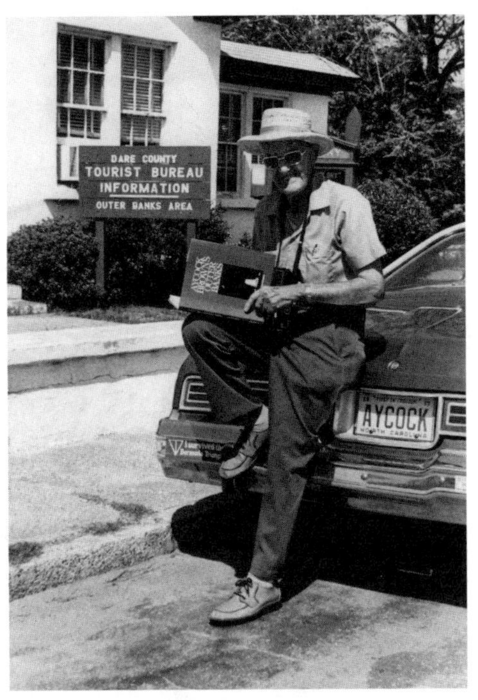

Opposite: In 1976, Aycock cheerfully signs copies of *Aycock Brown's Outer Banks* at the Dare County Library in Manteo. His wife, Esther, and the Tourist Bureau's manager John Blizzard are on either side of him. *Karen Dankin, Dare County Tourist Bureau Collection, OBHC, SANC.*

Right: When asked for a good Aycock story, many of his acquaintances could not come up with a specific recollection. That phenomenon speaks to the way he did his job. He did not take center stage but was present as an observer and a recorder of his world. *Dare County Tourist Bureau Collection, OBHC, SANC.*

> *papers; and then there's that fish to look at, for those who don't care about the other two reasons.*
>
> *Brown isn't noted solely for his cheesecake shots, however. Any photo in any textbook about North Carolina printed in the last 30 years that deals with the Outer Banks will have a photo of the Cape Hatteras Lighthouse or the Wright Brothers Memorial or the isolated beaches of the Outer Banks with the credit reading "Photo by Aycock Brown."*

In fairness to Aycock, "he was a strong supporter of women's rights and [was] always willing to help a woman get ahead in a male-dominated world," Shawna Hubbard wrote in her COA paper. "In the late 1930s, Brown used his relationship with a U.S. Congressman to try and obtain employment in Washington, D.C. for two young women....In 1979, the Equal Rights Amendment was gaining steam in Washington. There was a press to get the final ratifications needed by holdout states to pass and enact the amendment. Brown joined forces with local icons Mollie Fearing and Cora Mae Basnight to advertise and gain support for the amendment, which would give women equal rights with men in all capacities. The Equal Rights Amendment was never [fully] ratified and continues to be brought before Congress."

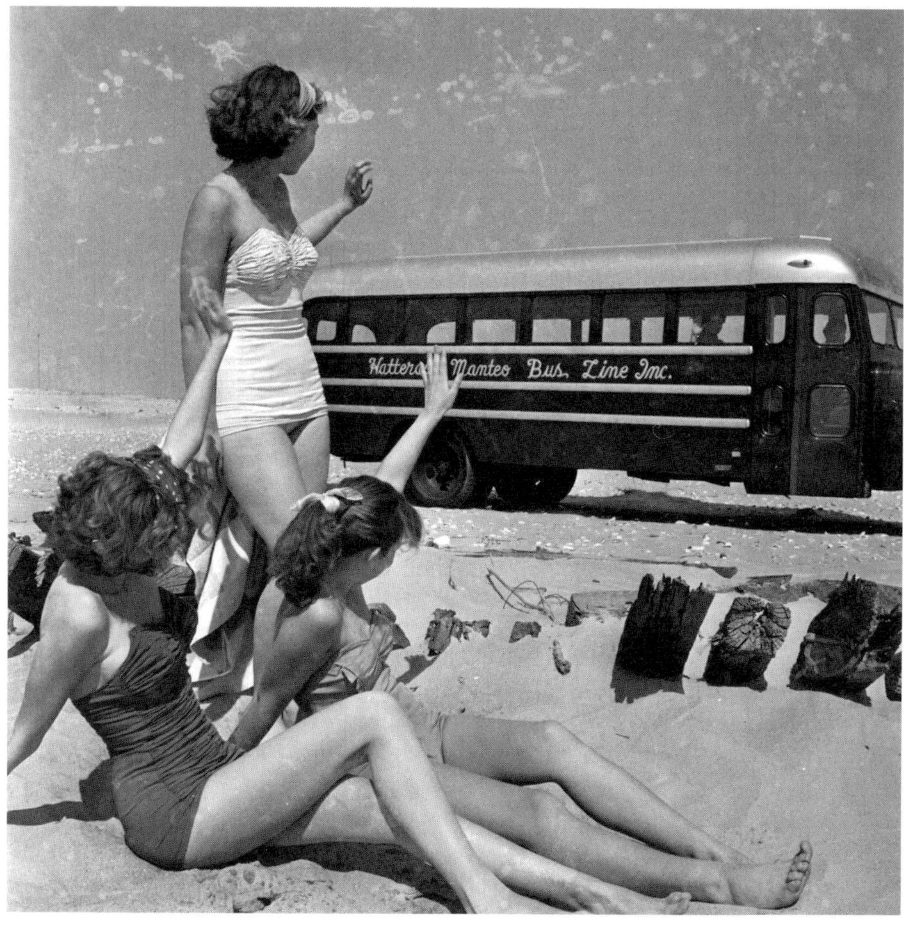

Above: Pretty girls, sand, a shipwreck, and a unique way of life were Aycock's tried-and-true elements to get a picture printed. Sally and Sarah Alford and Lydia King (*right*) wave at the sand-going bus that met the ferry at Oregon Inlet each day. *ABC, OBHC, SANC.*

Opposite: Old friends and Manteo residents Mollie Fearing, Aycock, and Cora Mae Basnight share a moment of genuine affection in the early 1980s. At one time, they all worked together to promote *The Lost Colony* outdoor drama. *J. Foster Scott Collection, OBHC, SANC.*

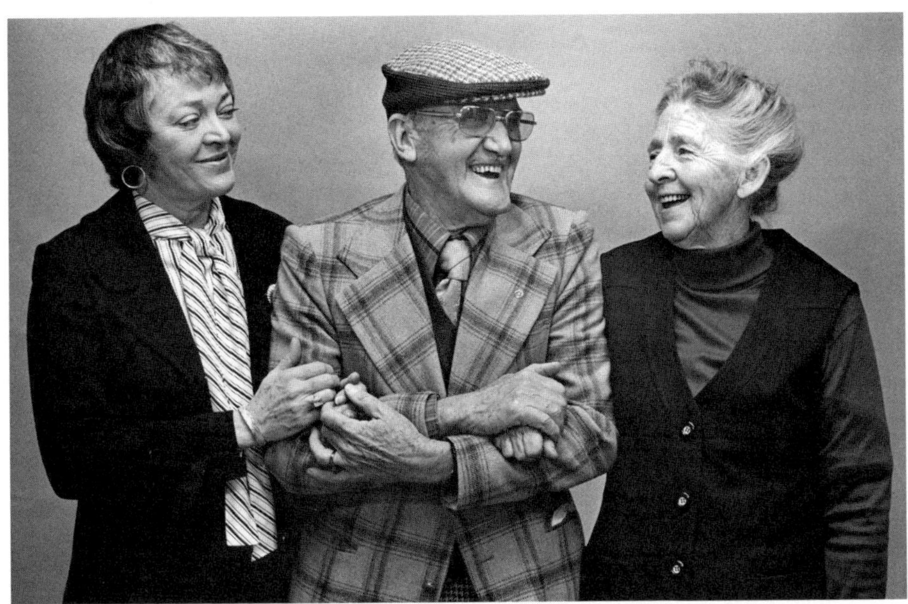

That was Aycock, happy to tilt at the occasional windmill and open-minded in his own way from the time he left the mainland behind through his brief venture in New York City to his arrival on the Outer Banks in his twenties, "coming home to a place he'd never been before," as John Denver sang in "Rocky Mountain High."

Aycock's wife, Esther, had died in 1977. He was lost without her, putting fresh-cut flowers by her picture in their home every day.

He kept working on his rapidly changing Outer Banks. The rumrunners and moonshiners he had seen almost fifty years before had been replaced by maritime drug smugglers, some of them local, hauling in loads of marijuana from overseas to unload on trucks pulled up in secret spots by the Sounds or the thousands of canals leading into the Sounds. Smugglers coming in off the ocean, facing federal boats coming for them, routinely dumped their bales of pot into the sea. A popular T-shirt of the 1980s had a painting of a couple of bales with "Save the Bales" underneath the picture, a takeoff on the environmentalists' slogan of "Save the Whales."

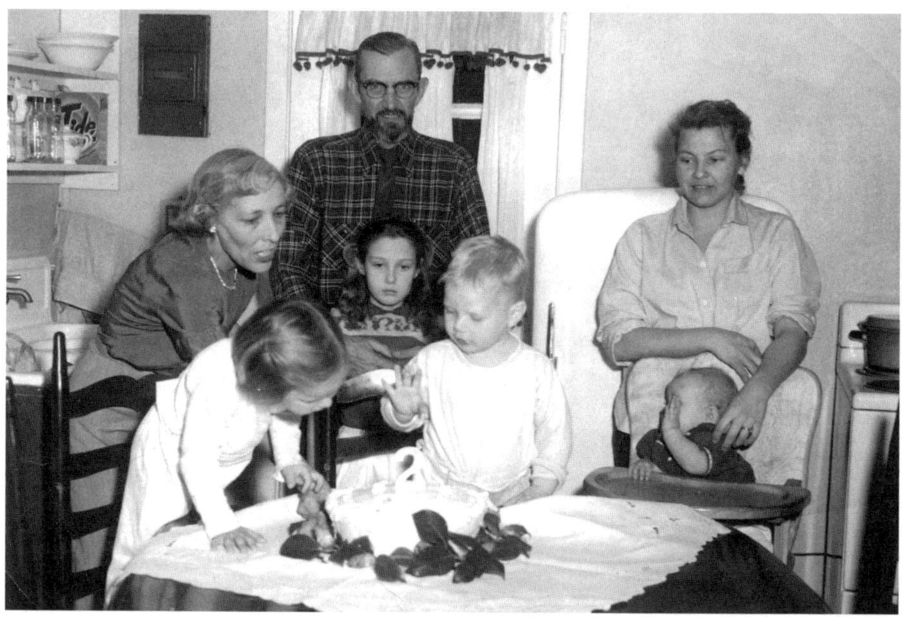

A local charter captain who'd been dealing with the costs of fixing a blown boat engine snagged one of the bales. He got on his maritime radio, telling his fellow cappies that his financial troubles were over because he'd snagged a bale. The cappie's mate stored the bale in his attic. The feds quickly found it, thanks to the cappie's radio traffic. Fortunately, the captain and his mate somehow got off without charges.

Aycock probably heard this story, characteristically keeping his lips sealed, as he always did with friends. He kept his confidences and talked little of himself, but he was not feeling good.

"Aycock lived for several years following the death of his beloved Esther, but he was a different Aycock," David Stick wrote. "The cameras and the typewriters were still at hand, but the will and drive were gone. Often, he spoke to close friends of the void left by Esther's passing."

Aycock retired. Sarah Owens worked on for a few more years.

Aycock fell into poor health. Maybe he thought back over his journey, the roaring torpedoes of World War II, the hellish winds and waves of that storm he'd named, and the booming tourism that followed. In his last days, he talked with Stick regarding his promotion of the Banks and all the tourism it had rendered, saying he "worried about what he had done," Lorraine Eaton reported in *The Virginian-Pilot*:

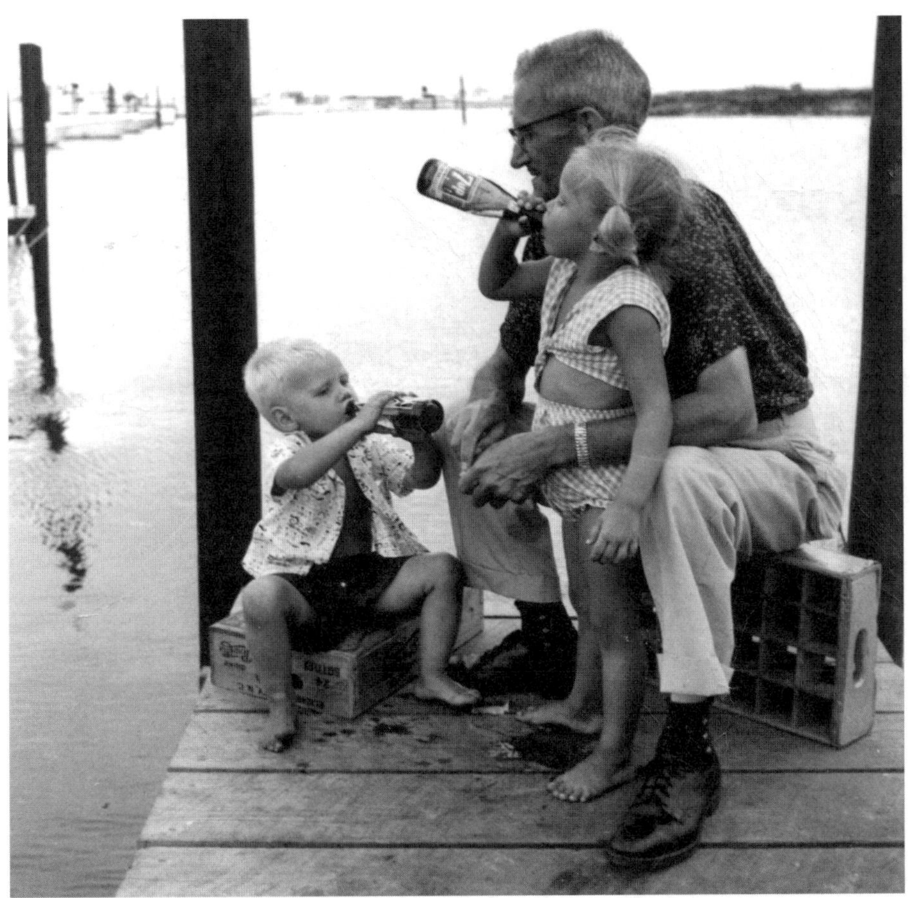

Opposite: The Brown grandchildren called Aycock "GanGan" and Esther "Ma Brown." Celebrating Charlie Brown's second birthday in the late 1950s are *(from left)* Esther, granddaughter Nettie, Aycock, daughter Gale, grandson Charlie, daughter-in-law Millie, and grandbaby Margaret. *Brantley A. Brown, Nettie Brown Tisch.*

Above: Grandchildren Charlie and Nettie enjoy a treat on the dock of Oregon Inlet with GanGan. His grandchildren often reminisce about visiting Aycock's house and being allowed to help him in the darkroom. *Nettie Brown Tisch.*

In the 1950s, [Outer Banks] *tourism was measured in the tens of thousands. When Aycock fully retired in 1982, millions of people each year* [visited the Outer Banks]. *Along the way, owners of small grocery stores, restaurants, motels and tackle shops had been squeezed out by new owners who built bigger places with lower prices. Neighborhoods were springing up with little attention to the environment. Schools were packed. Roads were crowded.*

"It had gone so much further than he [Aycock] *ever anticipated," Stick said.*

Larry Maddry, another *Virginian-Pilot* journalist, wrote of Aycock: "The last time I saw him he knew his days were numbered, a husk of a man lying on white bedsheets":

Even then he lightened my heart by reminding me of the good times. "Did anyone ever have such a loving family?" he asked as his relatives gathered around the bedside.

No one expected Aycock to go simply. He was too much the showman to make an exit without a statement. Mark Twain said he would go out with Halley's Comet, and did. I expected something like that from Aycock, a man with an exquisite sense of timing. He had, after all, named the Ash Wednesday Storm of 1962. He had taken that famous photograph of the Wright Brothers monument at the moment of the first manned landing on the moon.

Aycock died on April 13, 1984, at the age of seventy-nine in his Manteo house on Sir Walter Raleigh Street. In those pre-digital days, reporters scrambled through the heavy clip files labeled "Aycock Brown." The sharpest of them caught contradictions in the way Aycock had told his life story. It was almost like Aycock was winking at them. "Hell, you'll never be able to make anything of my life," he'd once told Maddry. "It's been a perfect muddle."

Like Sir Walter Raleigh and many of the Banks people Aycock had covered, he had helped create his own legend. Maddry wrote from Norfolk:

When the message of his death reached me by phone, I put down the receiver as if in a trance. My eye fell to the desk calendar. It was Friday the 13th. There was a lively thunderstorm the night of his death. Through the bedroom window I could see electrical flashes behind the dark clouds.

I imagined that Aycock was up there, bouncing across heaven with his camera, the bursts of lightning merely his flash attachment winking away as he photographed the Wright Brothers standing in front of hang-gliding angels. That's Aycock for you.... He had a rare quality of irresistibility, a blend of charm, wit, laughter and a carefree graciousness that made others feel better about themselves.

Other writers, including those at Maddry's paper, confirmed Aycock's magic. "Brown was a legendary figure on the Outer Banks of North Carolina, and his photographs and stories about the state's northeastern coast helped to spur the phenomenal growth of the Nags Head-Kitty Hawk region as one of the nation's leading resort areas," *The Virginian-Pilot* reported.

Aycock went to his grave having strictly honored countless confidences. He could have written a tell-all bestseller, *Real (Human) Wildlife of the Outer Banks*, anticipating today's reality TV shows, but that was not in his honorable nature.

Meanwhile, his Banks were rapidly changing. "The Outer Banks of North Carolina used to be a vacation traveler's secret, perhaps in the same way Sanibel Island, Florida was before everybody learned of its shelling grounds," *The Insider's Guide to the Outer Banks of North Carolina* reported in the early 1980s. "Many Tarheels and Virginians knew of its getaway, restorative pleasures, but invitations to Nags Head cottages were reserved only for special friends and family." The guide noted that "the pace and character of the barrier islands remain in contrast to the accustomed places of most people," but the Banks "attract over a million visitors each year." That number would multiply in the ensuing decades.

EPILOGUE

Over the next few years, Aycock's legend continued to grow. In 1987, a photographer who had learned much from Aycock and become a fine Outer Banks shooter in his own right, Walter V. "Walt" Gresham III, teamed up with David Stick to produce *The Ash Wednesday Storm*, a moving book on the storm. Andy Griffith supplied the foreword, praising Stick's writing and adding, "The dramatic photographs of Aycock Brown, a fine friend to all of us, bring a second dimension to the drama of the storm."

Stick supplied the text, based on his previous work and many new interviews with survivors. Walt matched Aycock's 1962 photos of the storm with his own fine scenes of the storm sites in 1986. The juxtaposition shows both the resilience of the beach communities and the overdevelopment that was beginning to overtake them.

The most major move to memorialize Aycock had come in November 1984 when the welcome center in Kitty Hawk at the northern entrance to Outer Banks was named for him. At the dedication for the center, David Stick said that if Aycock were present, he'd probably be on the roof of the center:

> *And he'd take a photograph that would make it appear that there were thousands here instead of hundreds. He was simply the most pleasant, unaffected man I have ever been associated with.*

On a prominent wall at the Aycock Brown Visitors Center are these lines, written by Bud Cannon, then of the Dare County Tourist Bureau:

A mountaineer by birth raised in the piney-woods hills of Carolina, Aycock Brown wound his way to the Tarheel coast more than half a century ago. His love of the ocean, the beaches, and the colorful characters who populated the villages and fished the waters was immediate, and contagious. For two decades, he worked his press agentry magic in the Morehead City area and on Ocracoke Island. In 1948, Brown brought his work as publicist to "The Lost Colony." Here, he found his niche, made his home, and never left. The Dare County Tourist Bureau was created in 1952 as a vehicle through which Brown could use his unique talents to get publicity for the area. And, as a result of those talents, the Dare Coast–Outer Banks would emerge from its somewhat remote and sleepily isolated character at mid-century to become the bustling vacation spot it is today.

The subjects of Brown's articles and news releases distributed far and wide to the media encompassed literally everything under the sun. But, if a picture is indeed worth a thousand words, it was Brown's photos that put the Outer Banks on the map. From bathing beauties frolicking on the beach at Cape Hatteras Lighthouse to 800-pound blue marlin

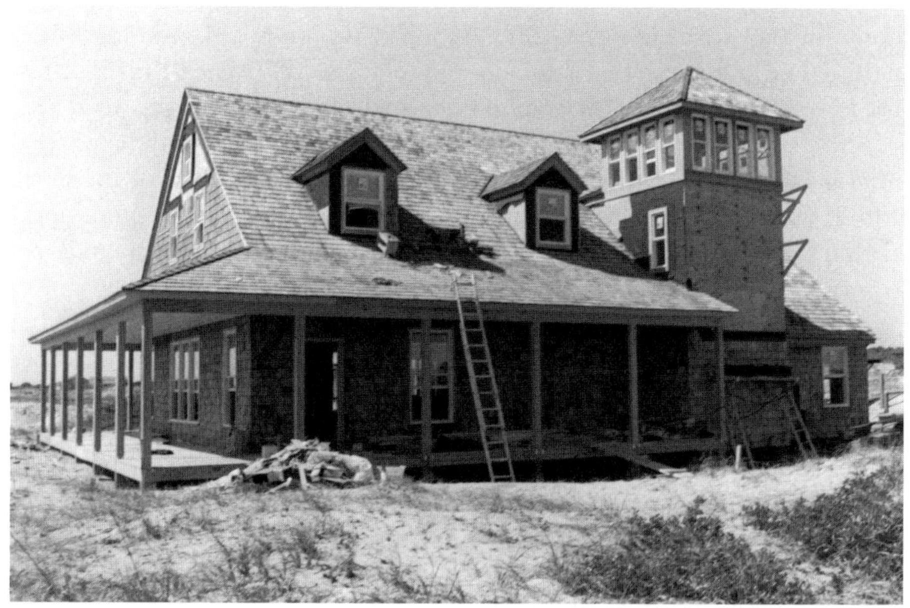

There was a dedication of the Aycock Brown Welcome Center in Kitty Hawk on November 17, 1984, seven months after his April death. The invitation read, "What better tribute to Aycock's vision than this center, built to greet those who have come to see the land his camera made famous." *ABC, OBHC, SANC.*

taken just offshore, the dignitaries visiting the Elizabethan Gardens to a photojournalist's view of the destruction left behind by hurricanes and "Ash Wednesday" type storms, from wildfowl "touring" Pea Island Wildlife Refuge to babies making their first discoveries of sand and surf, Aycock Brown covered the waterfront like no one ever had.

Called by his contemporaries of the media everything from the "Boone of the dunes" to "multifaceted" to "con artist, par excellence," Aycock Brown, sporting his pixie-like grin and colorful bow tie and carrying his ever-present camera, was exactly the kind of character a younger Aycock Brown would have loved. However else his contemporaries might have described him, they all knew him as one of a kind, a legend—"Mr. Outer Banks."

Mary Beauchamp, an Aycock friend, added these lines:

A Sonnet and Then Some for Aycock

His restless fingers caught our times and captured
Not only ancient history but living,
Not only shipwrecks but our smiles, enraptured
Bermuda shorts and teenaged giggles, giving
Us memories in color, black and white,
Among the weatherbeaten boats are faces
Of relatives and babies, second sight
Of forty years recording coastal places.
But giving is his game—in steady flowing
As regular as tidal flow on beaches
His gifts flow outward, unassuming, glowing
With grinning care for all the friends he reaches
A cap, a book, but always, yes—a picture—
An offhand offering to the one it features.
He has become a patron saint, a fixture
And to himself unknown, one of our teachers—
Not through his words, which tumble,
Stop and start,
But through his skill, expanded by heart.

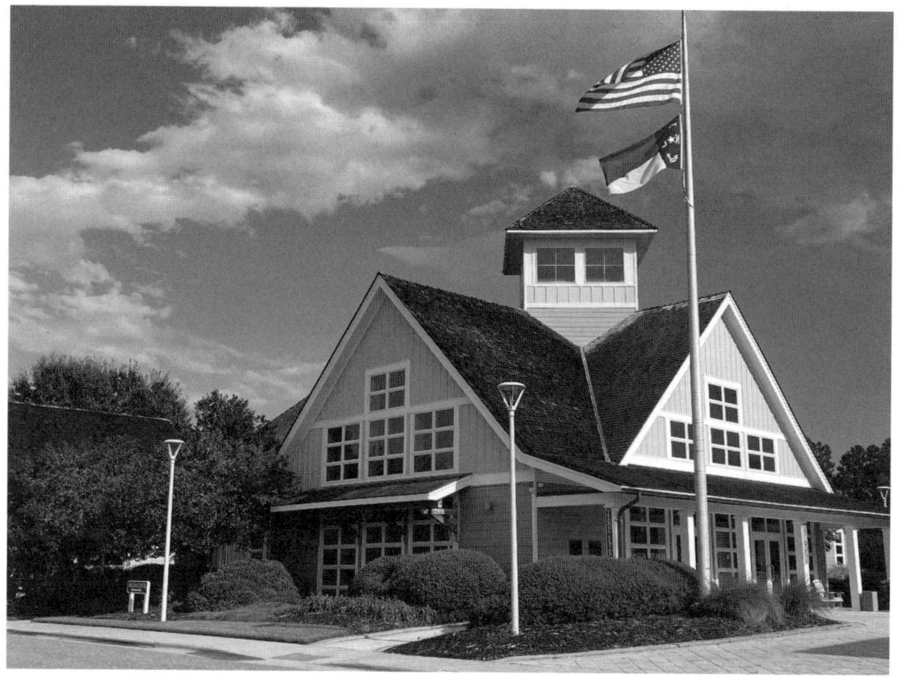

Located at the base of the Virginia Dare Memorial Bridge on Roanoke Island, the Sarah Owens Welcome Center can be a first stop for eastbound vacationers. Opened in 2002, the complex also is home to the Outer Banks Visitors Bureau with a staff large enough to astound Sarah Owens. *Nancy Beach Gray.*

Outer Banks author R. Wayne Gray would later write:

> *Fittingly, Dare County named the welcome center in Kitty Hawk after the man who worked so hard to put the Outer Banks on the map....Largely as a result of his efforts, the mid-century history of the Outer Banks is recorded in black and white 8 X 10 prints.*

In September 2002, a new visitors' center near the highway entrance to the Southern Outer Banks, in Manteo, was justly named for Sarah Owens. She died in 2015, just over thirty years after Aycock.

Aycock's family flourished, including through three teachers beloved in the local school system: Esther "Stormy Gale" and her daughter, Esther, and Billy.

In the early 1980s, there was hoopla in the Outer Banks real estate world when the first oceanfront cottage, offered by Joe Lamb Jr. & Associates, broke the $1,000-a-week rental mark for the summer. Now, that cottage rents for almost $11,000 on its biggest week. One of the Banks's top weekly rentals, in Kill Devil Hills, gets $65,000 a week in prime summer season. Many Outer Bankers, longtime residents and seasonal ones, curse the overdevelopment, even while being happy with their chunk of sand and with some of them selling more of it to newcomers at constantly rising prices.

Toward the end of his life, Aycock half-joked that the overdevelopment was his fault. But he'd done it all for his fellow Outer Bankers.

Today, most tourists have no idea who Aycock Brown was, much less Sarah Owens. The visitor's center named for Sarah says little about her. Much more could be said. Aycock's center has a bit more, just his photo and some words of applause. But the vast majority of the center is devoted to the Outer Banks, as at Sarah's center, with colorful exhibits and tons of pamphlets about Outer Banks attractions. Sarah and Aycock might have approved of their scant mention *and* that the staff are warm and welcoming.

Overdevelopment rages up and down the Outer Banks. Affordable housing for everyone from restaurant staff to teachers to doctors is a huge problem. Dare County's permanent population of about 37,000 residents swells to about 225,000 to 300,000 from June through August. Old-timers and newcomers curse the traffic jams and growing stream of visitors and new residents, as if they could somehow put the genie that Aycock unleashed back in the bottle, the magic that had drawn them to the Outer Banks and continues to draw so many others. Nostalgia rages for "the good old days," with that nostalgia, depending on whom you talk to, surfing a sliding scale from the 1950s to the 1980s.

That magic can never be recouped. But much of it remains, in the sands by the ocean and the Sounds, the dolphins playing just offshore and the families frolicking in the sand. These scenes and many others are timeless. They are classic, set in drifting sand by Aycock, who might have known that constants would remain in the dreamscape he introduced to the world. In Kill Devil Hills, there is a road named for Aycock. It leads from the Beach Road and doglegs across the bypass to Kitty Hawk Bay, past new cottages and old, a microcosm of the Banks culture Aycock knew so well.

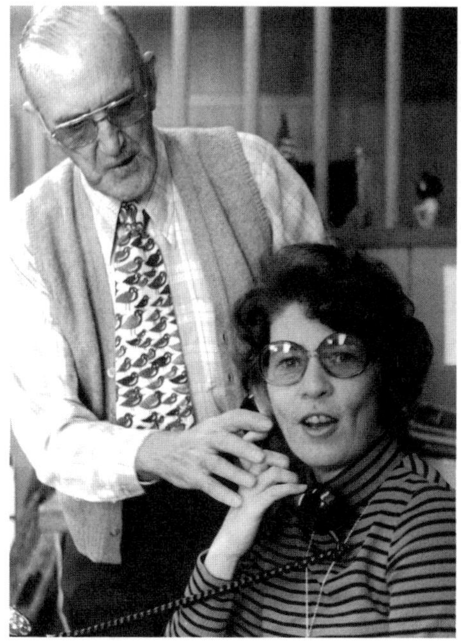

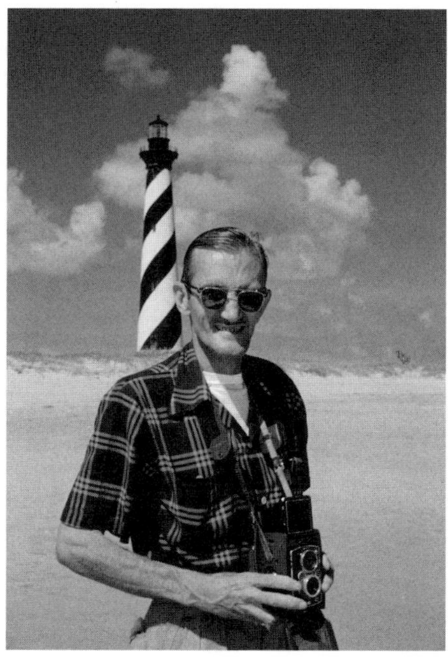

Left: Complementary personalities enabled Aycock and Sarah Owens to work well together at the Dare County Tourist Bureau. They both liked greeting the public, but Sarah was more reserved than her counterpart. Each one had a desire to make the Outer Banks well known. *Dare County Tourist Bureau, RV Owens.*

Right: The invitation to the dedication of the welcome center bearing his name reads, "Thanks to Aycock, Dare County has a solid economic future. That is Aycock's gift to us. What we do with his legacy is our gift to Aycock." *Hugh M. Morton, Wilson Special Collections Library, UNC–Chapel Hill.*

Lorraine Eaton said it well in writing about Aycock and the visitor's center named for him.

> *Aycock's portrait greets guests at the entrance. He looks like he always did, a* [straw] *boater on his head, Hawaiian shirt on his back and cameras slung round his bony neck, now bearing silent witness to the streams of visitors who are his living legacy.*

He was an Outer Banker, one of the best. You're here because of him.

ACKNOWLEDGEMENTS

John Railey

Aycock Brown's photos have been the dreamscape for my Outer Banks books. One of his granddaughters, Nettie Tisch, is a good friend. In her Wanchese home a few years ago, she graciously let me hold one of Aycock's cameras, a mystic touch.

When I was in my first year of college, my brief time at the University of Virginia, I was lost and lonely, a native swampbilly uncomfortable with the mountains that closed in around me. For my nineteenth birthday, my sister Mimi, as usual sensing my unease, sent me David Stick's tribute to Aycock, *Aycock Brown's Outer Banks*, with an inscription about our shared fun on the Outer Banks. Night after night, I would read that 1976 book, Aycock's photos taking me back to my beloved Banks until I fell into dreamland with them, often sleeping too late to make early classes, not caring because I was on Banks time.

So many friends have helped me with this book, including the fine Outer Banks photographers Drew Wilson and Walt Gresham; Nags Header Buster Nunemaker; director and author Ira David Wood III; businesswoman and former Lost Colony actor Susan Guthrie Lowrance; Bill and Cindy of 102.5 The Shark on the Outer Banks; Dare County Public Information Officer Dorothy Hester; Molly Trivelpiece of the Graveyard of the Atlantic Museum on Hatteras; Pat Hardy of Joe Lamb

Jr. & Associates; Shelley Tolbert of Twiddy and Company; and Outer Bankers Ken Mann, Kathy Spencer, Juanita Wescott, Elaine Gregory, Claudia Harrington, and Pam Merritt. Angel Khoury of Manteo, a brilliant author, supplied superb editing. Cam Choiniere generously helped with some last-minute formatting.

Inga and Rick Francis once again provided me with a second home in Kitty Hawk for my work. The owners and staff at Sam and Omie's restaurant and tavern at Nags Head and Lagerheads bar at Wrightsville Beach, as always, gave me strong encouragement.

We both thank our associates at Arcadia: Chad Rhoad, Abigail Fleming, and Jonny Foster; and the Outer Banks History Center on Roanoke Island. Several years ago, Aycock's family generously donated the bulk of his surviving work, thousands of photos and negatives, to the center. That donation will help Aycock's work live for generations to come. Thanks to Tammy Woodward, Katherine Daugherty, and Emily Dingler of the center, which is supported by state funds and donations.

And most of all, thanks to my wife, Kathleen, and my coauthor, Nancy. They are the best.

Nancy Gray

I would like to thank John Railey for approaching me about collaborating on a book about Aycock Brown. I didn't think I was capable of working with an author other than my late husband, but our easy working relationship has produced a better result than either one could have done on our own.

Aycock's children are no longer living, but his grandchildren Nettie Tisch, Esther Doxey, and Patrick Byrd went out of their ways to help us. Aycock's protégés Spooky Phillips and Vanessa Foreman provided insights that no other sources could have.

Julie and RV Owens were so generous with their time and family photographs. They helped us understand the major role that Sarah Owens played in promoting the Outer Banks and keeping Aycock on track.

John Havel, whose interest lies in the Cape Hatteras Lighthouse, knew he had some photos of Aycock and by Aycock that would be valuable to us. He also shared the promotional postcard that Aycock helped design.

I appreciate the stories that Pam Jones related, and the guidance that Angel Khoury gave. Jamie Lanier of the National Park Service is always accessible and well-informed. As always, my friend Francesca Marie came to my rescue with her technical and photographic knowledge.

I join with John in thanking the staff at the Outer Banks History Center who are such an asset to our community. I also thank our associates and editors at Arcadia Publishing and The History Press.

BIBLIOGRAPHY

We drew from numerous interviews with those who knew Aycock, hundreds of articles in *The Coastland Times*, *The Virginian-Pilot*, *Outer Banks Magazine*, *The News & Observer* of Raleigh, *The State* magazine, *The Saturday Evening Post*, R. Wayne Gray's writing, the papers and photos of Aycock and David Stick at the Outer Banks History Center, and these books:

Balance, Alton. *Ocracokers.* The University of North Carolina Press, 1989.

Bradsher, Bethany, and Charles Perry. *Big Fish, Better Boats: The History of Sportfishing and Boatbuilding on the Outer Banks.* Charles Perry, 2023.

Duffus, Kevin P. *Shipwrecks of the Outer Banks*: *An Illustrated Guide.* Looking Glass Productions, 2007.

Gray, R. Wayne, and Nancy Beach. *Legendary Locals of the Northern Outer Banks*. Arcadia Publishing, 2015.

———. *Sport Fishing on the Outer Banks.* Arcadia Publishing, 2023.

Hickam, Homer H., Jr. *Torpedo Junction: U-Boat War off America's East Coast, 1942.* Naval Institute Press, 1989.

Khoury, Angel Ellis. *Manteo: A Roanoke Island Town.* The Donning Company Publishers, 1999. 2nd ed, 2024.

Parker, LeVern Davis. *Manteo During World War II & Manteo Boat Building Company.* One Boat, Inc., Publisher, 2024.

Railey, John. *Andy Griffith's Manteo: His Real Mayberry.* The History Press, 2022.

Stick, David. *The Ash Wednesday Storm*. Gresham Publications, 1987.

———. *Aycock Brown's Outer Banks*. Donning Company/Publishers, 1976.

———. *Graveyard of the Atlantic.* University of North Carolina Press, 1952.

———, ed. *Outer Banks Reader*. University of North Carolina Press, 1998. (This collection contains "I Wore a Dead Man's Hands.")

Whedbee, Charles Harry. *Legends of the Outer Banks and Tar Heel Tidewater*. John F. Blair, Publisher, 1966.

ABOUT THE AUTHORS

John Railey has spent much of his life on the Outer Banks. His previous books from The History Press, *The Carolinian Murder at Nags Head: The Janet Siclari Story* (2025), *Murder in Manteo: Seeking Justice for Stacey Stanton* (2024), *Andy Griffith's Manteo: His Real Mayberry* (2022), and *The Lost Colony Murder on the Outer Banks: Seeking Justice for Brenda Joyce Holland* (2021), have been top sellers on the Outer Banks. A graduate of the University of North Carolina at Chapel Hill, he is a former editorial page editor of the *Winston-Salem Journal*. He is working on a novel about a fictional murder on the Outer Banks in the 1970s.

Nancy Beach Gray and her family owned and operated Queen Anne's Revenge Restaurant in Wanchese for almost three decades. After the restaurant closed, she and her husband, R. Wayne Gray, sought to capture much of the history of the Outer Banks in their books *Legendary Locals of the Northern Outer Banks* (2015), *Roanoke Island's Boating Heritage* (2017), *Lost Buffalo City* (2018), *Commercial Fishing on the Outer Banks* (2019), *Manteo* (2020), *Corolla and the Currituck Outer Banks* (2021), and *Sport Fishing on the Outer Banks* (2023). She recently published a collection of her late husband's poetry, *A Place of Peace* (2025).